Appeal to Popular Opinion

APPEAL TO POPULAR OPINION

Douglas Walton

THE PENNSYLVANIA STATE UNIVERSITY PRESS
UNIVERSITY PARK, PENNSYLVANIA

Library of Congress Cataloging-in-Publication Data

Walton, Douglas, 1942–
    Appeal to popular opinion / Douglas Walton.
      p.   cm.
    Includes bibliographical references and index.
    ISBN 0-271-01818-6 (cloth : alk. paper)
    ISBN 0-271-03017-8 (pbk. : alk. paper)
    1. Appeal to popular opinion (Logical fallacy)   I. Title.
BC175.W322   1999
168—dc21   98-31384
                                                                                           CIP

Copyright © 1999 The Pennsylvania State University
All rights reserved
Printed in the United States of America
Published by The Pennsylvania State University Press,
University Park, PA 16802-1003

It is the policy of The Pennsylvania State University Press to use
acid-free paper for the first printing of all clothbound books.
Publications on uncoated stock satisfy the minimum
requirements of American National Standard for Information
Sciences-Permanence of Paper for Printed Library Materials,
ANSI Z39.48-1992.

For Karen, with Love

CONTENTS

ACKNOWLEDGMENTS   XI

Chapter One
   PUBLIC AND POPULAR OPINION   1

1. Public Opinion Polls   2
2. Why Do Public Opinion Polls Look Accurate?   6
3. Push Polling   8
4. The Tyranny of the Majority in American Democracy   11
5. Worries of the Logic Textbooks   13
6. Public Perceptions as Premises   16
7. The Meaning of "Public Opinion"   19
8. The Meaning of "Popular Opinion"   22
9. The Difference Between Public and Popular Opinion   24
10. The Problem with Arguments Based on Popular Opinion   27

Chapter Two
   INFERENCES AND FALLACIES   33

1. The Gore Vidal Case   34
2. The Jury Deliberation Case   36
3. The Golden Rule Case   37

4. The Democratic Civilization Case — 41
  5. The Falling Objects Case — 43
  6. The Inquisition Case — 45
  7. The Mark Antony Case — 48
  8. Inflammatory Language — 51
  9. How the *Ad Populum* Is Used to Manipulate Opinions — 54
 10. Appeal to Expert Opinion — 56

Chapter Three
THE STANDARD TREATMENT — 61

  1. Origins of the *Ad Populum* — 62
  2. Early Modern Textbooks — 65
  3. The Middle Period: 1935–1959 — 68
  4. Multiplicity of Types: 1961–1968 — 72
  5. Cracks in the Surface — 77
  6. Broadening the *Ad Populum* — 80
  7. The Dual Approach — 85
  8. Multipliers — 88
  9. The Unifying Form — 91
 10. Summary of Developments — 94

Chapter Four
PRESUMPTIONS, COMMON STARTING POINTS, AND PUBLIC JUDGMENT — 97

  1. Bandwagon and Mob-Appeal Arguments — 98
  2. Are *Ad Populum* Arguments Fallacious? — 100
  3. Premise Adequacy of Dialectical Arguments — 103
  4. Conflicts with Expert Opinion — 106
  5. Common Starting Points — 109
  6. The Status of Presumptions — 112
  7. Presumptive Reasoning in Dialectical Arguments — 116
  8. Popular Opinion and Common Knowledge — 119
  9. Mass Opinion and Public Judgment — 124
 10. The Two Faces of the *Ad Populum* — 126

Chapter Five
    THE OLD DIALECTIC   129

1. Platonic Dialectic   130
2. Aristotelian Dialectic   133
3. Endoxic Premises   138
4. Seneca on *Ad Populum* Arguments   144
5. Eikotic Arguments   148
6. The Medieval Period   152
7. The Shift Away from Dialectic   155
8. *Consensus Gentium* Arguments   158
9. The Antiskeptical Dilemma and Pascal's Wager   161
10. Toward a New Dialectic   166

Chapter Six
    THE NEW DIALECTIC   169

1. Types of Dialogue   169
2. Persuasion Dialogue   171
3. The Inquiry   175
4. Negotiations and Quarrels   178
5. Information-Seeking Dialogue   182
6. Deliberation   184
7. Dialectical Relevance   186
8. Relevance of *Ad Populum* Arguments   188
9. Persuasion Dialogue and Public Policy   191
10. The New Perspective on Evaluation   193

Chapter Seven
    AD POPULUM SUBTYPES   195

1. The Mob-Appeal Subtype   196
2. The Pop Scheme   199
3. Position to Know   201
4. Informed Deliberation   205
5. Moral Justification   207
6. Popular Sentiments   209

7.	Common Folks, Snobbery, and Vanity	212
8.	The Rhetoric of Belonging	217
9.	Structure of the Mob-Appeal Subtype	220
10.	Summary of Subtypes	223

Chapter Eight
A NEW BASIS FOR EVALUATION — 229

1. Evaluation as Contextual — 230
2. Evaluation as Dependent on Identification — 232
3. Bolstering and Critical Questions — 234
4. Seeking a Basis for Acceptance in Persuasion Dialogue — 236
5. The Maxim of Nondisputativeness — 238
6. Dialectical Bias in Argumentation — 241
7. Mob Rhetoric and Mass Enthusiasm — 243
8. Appeal to Snobbery and Vanity — 247
9. Identification and Analysis — 249
10. The Four Steps of an Evaluation — 250

Chapter Nine
WHEN IS IT A FALLACY? — 253

1. The Inquisition Case — 253
2. Public Opinion Polls and Fallacies — 257
3. *Ad Populum* Appeals in Commercial Ads — 261
4. Common-Folks Appeals and Relevance — 263
5. Two Explanations of the Fallacy — 265
6. Hastily Jumping to a Conclusion — 267
7. Evaluating the Golden Rule Case — 269
8. Divisive Rhetoric in Mob-Appeal Arguments — 271
9. Three Types of *Ad Populum* Fallacy — 273
10. Evaluation for Fallaciousness — 274

BIBLIOGRAPHY — 277
INDEX — 283

ACKNOWLEDGMENTS

My thanks are due the Social Sciences and Humanities Research Council of Canada for a research grant that made the work on this project possible. For discussions that have helped to shape the ideas in the book, I would like to thank Erik Krabbe, whose collaboration with me over the past several years on a related research project has been a valuable source of insight on modeling dialogue structures. For help with translating some Greek terms, I would like to thank Craig Cooper. For helpful discussions of various topics at one time or another, I would like to thank Frans van Eemeren, Rob Grootendorst, David Hitchcock, Ralph Johnson, Christopher Tindale, Tony Blair, Bob Pinto, Hans Hansen, Alan Brinton, Mike Wreen, Jonathan Adler, and Harvey Siegel.

My thanks are also due to the University of Winnipeg for granting me study leave, the Department of Philosophy of the University of Western Australia for support while I was a research associate there in 1996–97, and the Oregon Humanities Center for inviting me as a Distinguished Visiting Research Fellow in 1997, and for providing facilities that made this work possible.

For word-processing the first draft, I would like to thank Louise Lepine, and for the subsequent and final drafts, I thank Amy Merrett. For help with the proofreading, I would like to thank Harry Simpson; for preparing the index, I thank Rita Campbell.

Chapter One

PUBLIC AND POPULAR OPINION

The goal of this book is to provide a method of evaluating appeals to popular opinion, appeals of a kind that are commonly used to support or refute arguments on matters that are often extremely important to us. The problem is that while this type of argument, traditionally called the *argumentum ad populum* (argument to the people) in logic, has been recognized as important by logic textbooks, and is typically introduced as a form of argument to introductory students of logic, no serious attempt has ever been made to study it at any advanced level. The purpose of this book is to fill that gap.

There are two questions about popular opinion that we as human beings are concerned with in our daily lives and personal decisions on how to act and what to accept as true. One is to know what popular opinion is. The other is to know what conclusion to draw from popular opinion, once we know, or think we know, what it is. The first question is taken up in Chapter 1, and the second question will then be addressed in Chapter 2, leading on to a more detailed examination of the *argumentum ad populum* in subsequent chapters.

1. Public Opinion Polls

In North America, the public opinion poll is the accepted scientific way of finding out what popular opinion is, on any particular question. Such polls are everywhere: in the media, in business, and especially in politics. And people take what the polls say quite seriously, judging from the attention they pay to them, even on questions where it would appear to be quite plausible that the respondents in the polls are lying, or deceiving themselves, or where the outcome of the poll could be biased by loaded questions that put a particular spin on an issue that supports the interests of whoever paid for the poll. Should we trust the polls as much as we evidently do, and be guided by them as much as we evidently are? The analysis of appeal-to-popular-opinion arguments presented in this book will support criticisms of those (still in a minority, but a growing minority) who are saying, "Definitely not."

The premise of an *ad populum* argument, to the effect that everybody accepts or believes the proposition in question, can be stated in several ways. One way is to state as an absolute generalization that *every* person, without exception, believes that this proposition is true. However, the more usual way to express this premise is as a numerical or probability statement to the effect that *most* people, or the majority of people, believe that this proposition is true. In fact, the accepted way of measuring public opinion in Western democracies is the public opinion poll. The statistical techniques used by the pollsters have become very sophisticated in recent years as they have gotten more and more practice in conducting polls and testing them out, and as statistical methods for the polls have been developed.

There are two principal weaknesses in arguments based on the use of such statistical polling techniques. It is often said that a public opinion poll is like a snapshot that measures public opinion in an instant of time, but the problem is that public opinion in many instances changes very rapidly and can quickly contradict what it appeared to be just a short time before (Yankelovich 1991). The other weakness is that these polls inevitably have to be based on questions that are asked of the respondents, and the questions have to be expressed in natural language, the language of the respondents. The problem is that terms in natural language are vague and ambiguous and have connotations that are very difficult, perhaps even impossible, for statisticians to measure or control in any quantified or exact way. Polls often give a misleading impression of scientific accuracy, however, by stating that they are accurate according to some numerical figures, like ninety-nine times out of one hundred. Thus, although pollsters take careful steps to attempt to minimize or eliminate the effects of language used in questions, unexpected mistakes can happen (Campbell 1974).

According to Sharon Begley, Howard Fineman, and Vernon Church, some organizations identify the candidates in a political opinion poll by name only. Others give party affiliation in the wording of the question used to take the poll. But the problem is that if a candidate is identified as belonging to a particular party—being a Democrat, for example—then he will do better in a poll in certain cities and worse in other cities. Another problem is order of arrangement of the questions. In a poll cited by Begley, Fineman, and Church, respondents were asked only to choose between George Bush, Bill Clinton, and Ross Perot (1992, 39). Another poll asked Bush or Clinton first, and then, only later, added Perot. According to a representative of the Gallup organization, when the three-way question was asked after the two-way question, the results were significantly different. This pollster remarked that these effects are subtle, but since voters are so fickle in their affections, such small differences in the wording of a question can significantly affect the outcome of a public opinion poll.

It is a little-understood aspect of polling, and of the collection of statistical data generally, that statistical conclusions can be heavily influenced by how terms are defined or understood.

Case 1.1: In 1992, arson offenses in Canada were reported as taking "a flaming leap" of over 12,000 cases, according to a report by Statistics Canada (Canadian Press 1992). However, analysts commented that the increase was largely due to a change made to the definition of "arson" in the criminal code. The statistical increase was a 20 percent jump from the figure of 10,371 fires reported in 1990. This increase represented the largest increase in any given year since arson data were first collected in 1974. In previous years, figures for arson had always been relatively stable. However, in July 1990, the Criminal Code of Canada was amended to include more kinds of incidents under the category of arson. New categories included mischief fires. The previous definition had been restricted to willful setting of fires to specific types of properties.

In this particular case, it is known that the radical increase in arson offenses was mainly due to changing the legal definition. However, the case illustrates how statistical figures can be influenced by changing definitions or changing conventions concerning the meaning of a key term in natural language. This kind of case, then, illustrates how the subtle factors of meaning and connotation in natural language can be an underlying influence in any kind of statistical collection of data or argumentation based on polling.

An experimental method of testing for "question-wording effects," has been developed by social scientists. It involves posing the same question to two comparable groups of respondents, except that one word in the question is changed to an apparently equivalent word when asked of the second group, and then the difference between the two responses is measured. According to David Moore, in an experiment conducted in 1940, two groups of respondents were asked two questions using terminology that appeared to be logically equivalent (1992, 334). One group of respondents was asked if the United States should forbid public speeches against democracy, and 46 percent said "No." Another group was asked whether the United States should allow public speeches against democracy, but only 25 percent said "Yes" to this question, though presumably to "forbid" something is the same as (logically equivalent to) "not allowing it." Why then was there a 21 percent difference in the outcomes of these two polls? The difference was in the wording of the question.

Howard Schuman and Stanley Presser duplicated this experiment, and the results are reprinted as Case 1.2 (1981, table, 281).

Case 1.2   Forbid-allow speeches in favor of communism

Forbid form		Allow form	
Do you think the United States should forbid public speeches in favor of communism?		*Do you think the United States should allow public speeches in favor of communism?*	
Yes (forbid)	39.3%	No (not allow)	56.3%
No (not forbid)	60.1	Yes (allow)	43.8
Total	100 %	Total	100 %

In Schuman and Presser's experiment the difference between the response to the "forbid" form of the question and the "not allow" response was 17 percent.

Another kind of response effect of the wording of a question found by Schuman and Presser had to do with the structure of the question. In the pair of questions cited below, one question was put in an "agree-disagree" form, while the apparently equivalent question left the respondent an alternative (346).

Case 1.3   Voting is the only way that people   Do you think voting is the only
           like me can have any say about   way that people like you can
           how the government runs things.   have any say about how the
                                                 government runs things, or that
                                                 there are other ways that you
                                                 can have a say?

           Percentage agree   51.4   Percentage voting
                                                 is the only way   40.8

The difference in the responses to these two questions is one of 10.6 percent.

Another pair of questions of this type studied by Schuman and Presser concerned housing (347).

Case 1.4   The federal government should   Some people feel the federal
           see to it that all people have   government should see to it that all
           adequate housing   people have adequate housing,
                                                while others feel each person should
                                                provide for his own housing. Which
                                                comes closest to how you feel about
                                                this?

           Percentage agree   59.8   Percentage government
                                                see to it   37.1

In this case, the response effect due to the structure of the question was 22.7 percent. The interesting aspect of the question on the left in Case 1.4 is that it is easy to see how the results obtained from it could be used to support an argument for government-funded housing.

Some question-wording effects are produced by the use of words that have familiar positive or negative connotations in everyday speech, of a kind that may not be too obvious at first, and would be hard to predict in advance. Moore cites one interesting experiment that revealed the effect of this kind of wording difference (1992, 343–44).

Case 1.5   One example of question-wording with important implications for public policy was found in an experiment showing differences between the public's perception of "welfare" and "assistance to the poor." It is poor people, of course, who receive welfare, and at first glance one might expect public support for welfare to be interchangeable with support for programs that assist the poor. But such interchangeability is not in the mind of the public. In 1985, for example, one national survey showed that only 19 percent of the people said too little money was being spent on welfare, but 63 percent said too little was being spent on assistance *to the poor*, a difference of 44 points. The researcher surmised that the term "welfare" conjures up images of fraud, while the phrase "assistance to the poor" may be "a more valid measure" of people's support for programs to "equalize conditions and provide for care of the people." Still, for political leaders who pay attention to public opinion in this area, very minor differences in wording would give them radically different pictures of what the public wants.

This experiment was particularly revealing, because it showed how such a large variance could be created by the negative connotations that apparently existed for respondents with respect to the term "welfare."

2. Why Do Public Opinion Polls Look Accurate?

On the surface, it seems highly implausible that a public opinion poll could determine the "public pulse," or what the public "really thinks" about an issue, and yet people seem to have a high degree of confidence that public opinion polls represent accurate data or real evidence on public opinions. Why do we have such confidence in these polls? One factor is that the polls are presented as being the outcome of scientific research; attached to the finding of each poll there is even a numerical figure given, said to represent the margin of error. It seems hard to challenge this scientific methodology. Marvin Field expresses this attitude very clearly.

> There is . . . an aura of infallibility associated with any kind of poll data. As a society which puts an inordinate value on impeccable arithmetic, we always feel comfortable about something which adds up to 100 percent. Although the 100 percent total will occur with answers to even the most cockeyed questions, the impression of certainty conveyed unfortunately inhibits close scrutiny of question wording and sampling methodology. (1990, 389–90)

Most people do not realize that the margin-of-error figure presented with a poll finding does not represent the probability that the result of the poll is wrong or biased. It is only a technical measure of how the respondent group has been sampled in the poll method.

Another reason that people think that public opinion polls can be relied on to produce very accurate results is that such polls are always used in the final stages of presidential election campaigns, and they have always (at least in recent years) proven to be quite an accurate indicator of the vote. Seymour M. Lipset has cited this reason for public confidence in the polls.

> Public confidence in the polls rests largely on the fact the pre-election surveys have a good track record for their particularly elaborate efforts to anticipate the reactions of the electorate presented with a choice between two men, or occasionally three, in a Presidential contest. Fortunately for the image of election polls, no one has bothered to check up on their record in forecasting results in primaries, referenda, or mayoralty or state-wide contests. (1990, 291)

As Lipset puts it, the polls have a public "image" of being provably scientifically accurate, and they are widely accepted as such because they are proven, time and time again, as producing exactly the figures that later match up with how the public actually votes. At least that is the perception. As Lipset notes, however, the reality might be quite different if election polls other than the high-profile ones, publicized in presidential elections, were taken into account.

Cynthia Crossen comments that polling looks scientific because of all the statistical jargon, like cross-tabulations, margins of error, and statistical significance used to describe the finding. But then, she adds, much of the polling, and especially the asking and answering of questions "is a soft science built on the shifting sands of human language and psychology." Hence, according to Crossen, the problem is that public opinion, because it is so constantly changing, makes the replication of the finding of any public opinion poll questionable. The polls "can never be exactly duplicated" so that "there is no way to judge" the accuracy of a public opinion poll (1994, 104).

According to Daniel Yankelovich, the weaknesses of public opinion polls are not due to inadequate sampling methods but to the kinds of questions asked in a poll. Yankelovich suggests that, since sound methods of probability sampling became standard in public opinion polls, the inaccuracies of the poll findings are not due to "sloppy sampling." Instead, "the primary sources of poor-quality poll findings are: dumb questions, obtuse questions, single questions that focus on limited aspects of complex issues, questions without proper context or framework, questions that elicit people's opinions on subjects to which they have not given a moment's thought, and so forth" (1991, 41). Hence, even Yankelovich, himself a leading pollster, admits that there can be poor-quality polls, and that even good-quality polls that are based on sound methods of probability sampling can lead to mistaken or misleading outcomes in some cases.

3. Push Polling

Apparently insignificant differences in wording in polls that had been used were not recognized at first. One example cited by Moore is the long-standing practice by pollsters of asking people questions about business, labor, and government, while there were subtle differences in the wordings used to refer to these agencies (1992, 344). Some pollsters, for example, would use the term "big business" while others would simply use the term "business" in their questions.

Case 1.6   The differences in results reported by various polling outfits led some analysts to suspect that these minor differences in wording were strongly affecting people's evaluations in surveys. And a couple of polls by Louis Harris confirmed these suspicions. When people were asked whether the federal government should regulate "big business" rather than "business," support for regulation jumped by as much as 19 points. Support for "increased" regulation jumped by an even greater margin of 22 points. Similar effects seemed evident with the use of "big labor," rather than just "labor." The word "big" conjured up more negative pictures of these institutions, and more public willingness to exert government control over them.

In such a case, a seemingly insignificant, minor difference in wording can have a significant effect on the outcome of a poll because a particular word, or combination of words, can have highly negative connotations for a group of respondents, which may be hard to anticipate.

In many cases, people may not know the answer to a question and may be reluctant to admit their ignorance. So, if the question is put in a yes-no form, with only two alternatives offered, they may just pick one alternative at random in order to get on with the poll and save time. But it is the pollsters themselves who tend to put questions in a yes-no form, presumably to get more interesting results. Michael Wheeler cites an example of this kind of poll (1990, 196–97).

Case 1.7   Pollsters are instinctively hostile to the idea of people without opinions. They go to great lengths to get people off the fence, both in the interviewing process, by forcing people to state a preference even if they have not really made up their minds, and in reporting the results, when people who are undecided are sometimes thrown out of the sample.

During the 1972 presidential campaign, for example, George Gallup reported, "The Democratic Party currently holds a marginal lead over the GOP, 53 to 47, as the party voters believe can better handle the problem they consider to be most important." In a year when there was great disenchantment with the candidates in particular and politics in general, it was preposterous to think that everybody preferred one party or the other.

Indeed, that was not what people had told Gallup's interviewers. Only 34 percent had thought the Democrats were more competent, compared to 28 percent who favored the Republicans. The largest group, 38 percent, either said that there was no difference between the two parties or did not express any opinion. That figure may well have reflected the alienation and apathy in the country. Gallup, however, simply discarded it, arbitrarily allocating half of the group to the Democrats and half to the Republicans!

There is a natural tendency inherent in the polling of public opinion to try to make the outcome appear more dramatic by forcing a choice in the question or by not reporting "don't know" responses.

Suspicions that advocacy groups use statistics based on friendly definitions and biased questions in polling in order to influence public policy to support the interests of their own advocacy group have been a source of considerable commentary in recent years. The advocacy groups who have been engaged in such questionable practices, and criticized for them, have a feeling that the end justifies the means. Such advocacy groups tend to consider questions about their polling techniques and methods of collection of data as being attacks on their goals—even suggesting that such attacks have harmful consequences—and that, therefore, anyone raising questions about their methodology should not be listened to. The idea seems to be that bending statistics is OK because it helps save lives or contributes to human rights. Unfortunately, this suspect use of argumentation from consequences contributes to a growing public distrust about the use of polling techniques giving reliable findings about public opinion. So, it seems that at the present there is a climate of suspicion to the effect that statistical polls are too often used as a convenient political tool for promoting the interests of advocacy groups, and even for lying and deceiving people.

In order to illustrate the importance of the structuring of a question used in a public opinion poll, one case, noted by Michael Kesterton, may be sufficient (1995, A24). To illustrate what he calls the telephone tactic of "push polling" in surveys of the opinion of voters, Kesterton cites the following question asked in a poll of people in Colorado in 1994:

Case 1.8   Please tell me if you would be more likely or less likely to vote for Roy Romer if you knew that governor Romer appoints a parole board which has granted early release to an average of four convicted felons per day every day since Romer took office.

The problem with this kind of question is that it is stacked toward one side so that one particular outcome is virtually guaranteed. However, what is less obvious in many other cases of public opinion polling is that the poll can be subtly influenced to a certain degree toward one side or the other by the connotations of the terms used in posing the question in order to solicit the response. The problem is that it is difficult, and perhaps even impossible, to quantify the margin of error related to this verbal factor. Hence, it is wise to take public opinion polls with a grain of salt.

According to the *Christian Science Monitor*, the latest development is that phone calls are made to a mass group of respondents by callers purporting to be conducting a survey, but the real purpose of the call is to plant negative suggestions about a candidate by using loaded questions that pose a personal attack on the candidate. For example, "a caller might ask how the voter's views might be affected if candidate 'X' were known to be a pervert" (Monitor, 1996, 20). Professional associations of pollsters have condemned this practice. Evidently, they see that it is yet another step in the erosion of the public's faith in the polling process—a process that has already led to a decrease in the willingness of the public to participate in polling. Polling rests on public trust, and public confidence in the worth of polling as an institution. But, according to the *Monitor* report, "many Americans are jaded about the whole idea of polling, feeling that measures of public opinion play too big a role in politics and policy making." It seems then that the abuse of public opinion polling by those politicians who use push polling techniques has shaken the public trust in a method that they were initially mistrustful of but were gradually brought to accept because of its perceived scientific accuracy. It remains to be seen which way public opinion will go in the next few years.

4. The Tyranny of the Majority in American Democracy

The French writer Alexis de Tocqueville, who published the first two volumes of his *Democracy in America* in 1835, saw some dangers in the power of the appeal to popular opinion in a democratic system of government. According to Tocqueville, "the absolute sovereignty of the will of the majority is the essence of democratic government," and, therefore, this "omnipotence of the majority," (Tocqueville 1966, 227) as he called it, despite its value, could have certain negative effects. Tocqueville, who used the term "tyranny of the majority" to describe the problem (231), argued that the omnipotence of the majority has the effect of increasing "the legislative and administrative instability natural to democracies" (229). This instability is the result of the fast changes in popular opinion. "All of the projects [of the majority] are taken up with great ardor; but as soon as its attention is turned elsewhere, all these efforts cease" (230).

Tocqueville was an astute observer of the American scene, and his comments on the coercive power of popular opinion in America were remarkably insightful for their time, describing with perfect accuracy the illusion of political freedom and the sharp boundaries of so-called freedom of speech that are characteristic of "political correctness" constraints on the university campus at present. Tocqueville states flatly, "I know of no country in which, speaking generally, there is less independence of mind and true freedom of discussion than in America" (235). Tocqueville perceived quite accurately that while there is apparent freedom of opinion in America, there are sharp penalties just outside a well-defined boundary for anyone who firmly states any opinion that contravenes the popular opinion of what is the right or "correct" viewpoint at any particular time. Loss of job or having to attend "re-education" therapy sessions is the current penalty. Tocqueville explained clearly and concisely how this process works.

> In America, the majority has enclosed thought within a formidable fence. A writer is free inside that area, but woe to the man who goes beyond it. Not that he stands in fear of an *auto-da-fé*, but he must face all kinds of unpleasantness and everyday persecution. A career in politics is closed to him, for he has offended the only power that holds the keys. He is denied everything, including renown. Before he goes into print, he believes he has supporters; but he feels that he has them no more once he stands revealed to all, for those who condemn him express their views loudly, while those who think as he does, but without his courage, retreat into silence as if ashamed of having told the truth. (235)

Since the majority opinion is what is important in a democratic system of government, once a proposition appears to be lodged into place as representing that majority opinion, then there is a great push, a "great ardor" as Tocqueville puts it, to please that majority opinion. At the same time, this majority opinion seems to have an apparent moral force or standing, so that anyone who visibly goes against it or ventures an opposed opinion is seen as someone who needs to be "re-educated" or silenced, so that they are shown that they are not allowed to give public expression to such an offensive viewpoint. Anyone who speaks out on anything that really matters to the advocates of the position temporarily regarded as the popular opinion, at any given time, will quickly find that he is presumed to be in the wrong, and that the penalties brought against him are presumed to be "correct" without any argument necessary to give support to them. But such presumptions can also change very quickly with the advent of some new development or change in political alignments.

But how does this dominant popular opinion really work, and what is objectionable about it? Why does Tocqueville take such a negative attitude toward it when he admits himself that government by the majority is a "natural strength" of a democracy (227). His objection seems to be that in the American system of democracy, majority opinion has become "omnipotent," but the problem is that majority opinion at any particular time is highly fallible and changeable, just as any individual person's opinion on matters of controversy and public issues is fallible and subject to changes, retractions, corrections and qualifications. In fact, Tocqueville goes so far as to put forward the hypothesis that popular opinion can be viewed as a kind of individual opinion. "What is a majority, in its collective capacity, if not an individual with opinions, and usually with interests, contrary to those of another individual, called the minority?"

(231). This comment was an astute and revealing remark because it indicates how appeal to popular opinion can be viewed dialectically as a distinctive type of argument. Tocqueville suggests that you need to see the majority opinion as representing the opinion or the commitment of one party, in a dialogue, who is putting forward a particular argument or point of view.

But that point of view needs to be seen in the light of an opposed point of view. In other words, the majority opinion should not be seen as infallible or "correct," and that is where the problem of "omnipotence" comes in. It needs to be seen as representing the commitment of a group of advocates whose position is the popular opinion of the moment, but whose proponents are likely to have interests at stake. So, to assume that this position does not represent a particular point of view supporting the interests of a particular group, a point of view that should be regarded as beyond criticism or open to doubt, is a species of logical error or a misunderstanding about the logic of the appeal to popular opinion as a type of argument. It is wrongly treating something as infallible or beyond criticism that is inherently fallible, and against which there is an opposing point of view.

The textbook treatments of appeal to popular opinion as a type of argument would appear to have sided with Tocqueville's view, that is, in seeing it as a type of argument that is both powerful and powerfully deceptive—something to be cautious about. But, as indicated briefly in the next section (and more fully in Chapter 3), their worries stem from a different kind of concern.

5. Worries of the Logic Textbooks

In the past, logic as a field has been highly suspicious about appeal to popular opinion. This tradition continues right through to even the most recent logic textbooks, where *argumentum ad populum* is treated as a worrisome kind of argument that can easily be used by dictators and mob leaders to whip up the masses. Monroe Beardsley, for example, treats appeal to popular opinion under the heading of "emotional appeal," as a species of fallacy called identification with audience (1950, 132).

Case 1.9   I. *Identification with audience.* "You and I are just plain folks . . . we understand each other . . . we ain't gonna let them fool us . . . ." By such phrases as these, a speaker seeks to make us identify ourselves with him, to feel friendly toward him, and to trust what he says. What he *suggests* is that he has our true interests at heart; but

> the only evidence he gives is that he dresses like his audience, uses colloquial grammar and diction, and speaks in a hearty and confidential manner. He suggest that he is "one of the boys," a "man of the people," a "great Commoner," and so on through many variations. The speaker uses identification as an *emotional appeal*, instead of giving *reasons* (say, by quoting from his record in Congress) for believing that he has the interests of his audience at heart.

The appeal to popular opinion described here is more than just identification with an audience. It is an appeal that whips up the audience emotionally, which certainly sounds like the speech is manipulating the audience in a way that is contrary to the aims of logic and critical thinking. Appeal to popular opinion, under this description, sounds like an instrument of propaganda.

In another textbook, John Eric Nolt describes appeal to popular opinion as an argument having two forms, where p is a proposition and x an action (1984, 249).

Factual Version	Prescriptive Version
Believing that p is popular	Doing x is popular
$\therefore p$	$\therefore x$ is permissible (or should be done)

Both forms are described as "generally fallacious" on the grounds that "logic does not support" the "feeling that large numbers of people doing or believing the same thing are unlikely to be wrong." This feeling, or powerful belief, is described by Nolt as "insidious," and even as tied in to "modern propaganda" of a worrisome sort.

> Instances of widespread false belief abound. Great portions of the earth's population have at one time or another affirmed that the earth is flat, that tomatoes are fatally poisonous, that heavy objects fall faster than light ones, that there is nothing wrong with slavery, that the stars are little bits of fire, that certain charms bring good luck, that there are innumerable anthropomorphic gods, that the sky is a solid inverted dome, that consciousness is located in the heart, that plants have souls . . . the list goes on and on. Science and civilization have managed to disabuse us of many of these false beliefs, but widespread falsehood remains. In fact, in some ways it has become more insidious.

The effects of modern propaganda are a case in point. Hitler managed to delude much of the German nation into thinking that they were a superior race. We know the result of that. Simultaneously, Japan waged a war motivated in part by the preposterous proposition that its emperor was a god. (249)

The reader of this textbook gets the idea that appeal to popular opinion is not only a fallacy but it also represents a kind of thinking that is scary and potentially explosive, leading nations stimulated by this kind of propaganda into mass delusions and even marching off to war.

Some logic textbooks have gone so far as to treat the *argumentum ad populum* as inherently fallacious, by even defining it as a type of argument that involves a failure of relevance. Francis W. Dauer defines the *argumentum ad populum* as the following kind of argument:

> *We are led to accept a claim C just because so many people accept C, a reason that isn't decisively relevant to the truth or correctness of C.* (1989, 80)

The examples cited by Dauer suggest that the *argumentum ad populum* is inherently illogical.

> Iron ships were relatively late innovations, which suggests that many people committed the Fallacy of the *Argumentum ad Populum* in accepting "A ship can't be built of iron." The prevalent belief in witchcraft in the old days of Salem, Massachusetts, might again be partially attributable to the people having committed the Fallacy of *Argumentum ad Populum*. Nor should we think that we are immune from this fallacy today. Often winning a string of primaries creates a bandwagon effect for a presidential candidate [leading] a number of people to commit the fallacy [of arguing from the premise "Many people accept that X is the best candidate" to the conclusion, "X is the one for whom one should vote"]. (81)

These examples suggest that, as a type of argument, appeal to popular opinion is fallacious. But, by connecting it with belief in witchcraft and the "bandwagon effect" in politics, they also suggest that this type of argument is deeply worrisome and is a kind of mass lapse of logical reasoning that could have the bad outcome of being responsible for superstition and mass hysteria (in the case of the witchcraft tribunals).

In Chapter 3, I shall show in detail how the treatment of appeal to popular opinion in logic textbooks has moderated its tendency to define this type of argument as fallacious and link it with frightening outcomes like propaganda and mass hysteria. But even so, what comes out very clearly is that the general tendency in logic is to be highly suspicious about the *argumentum ad populum* and see it as linked with manipulative practices of mass rhetoric that are not only illogical but also highly dangerous. The general idea is that appeal to popular opinion is potentially a raging beast of an argument that needs to be kept on a short chain.

6. Public Perceptions as Premises

The textbook treatments of *ad populum* seem to have lost sight of the old dialectical idea (see Chapter 5) that if you are trying to reasonably convince someone to accept a proposition as the conclusion of an argument you need to use as premises propositions that this person accepts or is willing to accept. Many of the textbook treatments of the *ad populum* (surveyed more extensively in Chapter 3) assume that, where a speaker attempts to convince an audience by using premises that reflect that audience's underlying values and commitments, the speaker is engaging in an inherently fallacious type of argumentation. In fact, many of the textbooks describe this kind of situation as catering to the prejudices of the audience. But should the practice of basing your arguments on premises that are commitments of your particular audience be considered fallacious?

According to Michael Billig, all the classical textbooks in rhetoric emphasize that "the successful orator should understand how an audience thinks, and, before addressing an audience, the orator should be well aware of its opinions" (1987, 194). Billig cites both Quintilian and Aristotle as vouching for the proposition that a successful speech delivered by an orator depends on the beliefs of the audience and also on generally received opinion. Billig cites Aristotle (*Rhetoric*, 1367b), who wrote that "one must represent, in one's speeches, that which is honored by each set of people one is addressing." In other words, Aristotle was saying that, in a successful rhetorical speech, the speaker has to be able to identify the particular values or commitments of a particular audience and base his arguments on those propositions in order for his speech to be successful in persuading that audience.

Although logic in the past has frequently been suspicious about rhetoric—and appears to have forgotten altogether about dialectic—room should be made within logic for the idea that persuading an audience to come to accept a proposition is a legitimate and common use of argument. Simply because an argument is used rhetorically to persuade a mass audience, that argument should not be condemned in a blanket fashion as fallacious.

The point needing clarification here is the distinction between evaluating the premise of an argument as true or false (acceptable or not acceptable) and evaluating the inference or transition of the argument from the premise to the conclusion. It is one thing to base your argument on a premise accepted by an audience, but it is quite another to bring the argument from that premise to a designated conclusion as a strong or weak (correct or fallacious) inference.

Another important point is that rhetorical advice given to an arguer, by advising that she ought to base her argument on a premise accepted by an audience—if she wants to be successful in persuading that audience to accept her conclusion—could, in some cases, be perfectly good advice.

In the following case, Larry Grossman, a former leader of the Ontario Conservative party, argued that universities get little public sympathy when they complain that budget cuts are making things difficult for them. The reason, according to Grossman's assessment, is that workers in all walks of life are beset by layoffs, plant closings, wage cuts, and bankruptcies, and it is the prevalence of these conditions generally at the present time that forms the basis of public perceptions.

Case 1.10   No matter how good a case the universities can make to the politicians about their importance to society, they must also reach the public with their message. "The public has to be on our side."

Mr. Grossman, who was not speaking on behalf of Ontario's current Conservative government, said political experience has taught him that "public perception need not have been fair or accurate to have been important in setting the public agenda."

He acknowledged the anger in the university community about generalizations that university professors have short work years, short work weeks, few classroom responsibilities, cushy jobs, tenure, "all of that."

But, whether the public perception is fair or not, universities must be aware of the climate in which they are fighting budget cuts. Universities have not been singled out for harsh treatment by "anti-intellectual" governments, Mr. Grossman said (Galt 1996, A6).

Grossman's advice to universities is for them to redirect their line of argument, if they want to be successful in persuading the public to continue supporting them. What they must do is to base their arguments on current public perceptions, on how the public generally sees things, instead of simply trying to make a positive case that what universities do is important to society. Instead of complaining about the hardships created by cutbacks, according to Grossman's advice, universities should stress how they can deal creatively with them by reducing inefficiencies and redundancies, and introducing measures that will cut costs.

Grossman's advice, in this case, is rhetorical in nature, and he is suggesting to the universities that they base their arguments on a premise that the public has a particular perception of the situation at the present. His advice, although it could be described as advising the use of an *ad populum* argument, should not be described as fallacious or as advocating the use of deceptive or logically defective rhetoric. It should be taken for what it is worth. And in principle, it is possible that it could be very good advice for the universities to follow in crafting their arguments to influence public opinion in favor of their aims.

The universities may see public perception as unfair or false, but Grossman points out that, given the general situation in the economy at the present time, it could be very hard to change it. He advises, therefore, instead of trying to refute the premise, try to work with it, base your argument on it, and use it to try to get from there to the conclusion you want. From a practical point of view, this rhetorical advice could be sound and prudent as a basis for the public relations campaigns of the universities in responding to their budget problems. Then again it might not. But however it is evaluated, it would be leaping to a hasty conclusion to condemn it as an *ad populum* appeal that fallaciously caters to the prejudices of the audience. Institutions such as universities that depend on public support and government funding and are engaged in the political system in a democratic country, whether they like it or not, are well advised to take a careful assessment of public opinion and sympathy into account. They would be badly advised to ignore or disdain such considerations altogether in trying to defend the thesis that their mission is worth support.

At this point, then, we have reached a contradiction in popular opinion about popular opinion. On the one side are those who say that in business—

say, marketing a product—or in politics—say, in deciding whether to support a particular policy or party—popular opinion is extremely important, and it would be naive and impractical to ignore the realities imposed by popular opinion. To do so would not be intelligent thinking and would lead to bad decisions about what to do. Indeed, popular opinion is so important, even decisive, in a democratic system of government, that it often seems to be almost the only thing that really matters in determining government policies. On the other side are those who, like Tocqueville, warn about the danger of popular opinion being too powerful. There are also those who feel that following popular opinion is "conformism" of the most superficial kind. They say that a critical thinker—or perhaps a deep thinker—will always go by the evidence of whether something is true and not just unthinkingly follow popular opinion. Since popular opinion could never be relevant evidence that a proposition is really true (or false), accepting that a proposition is true (or false) merely on the basis of popular opinion is a fallacy. These kinds of worries were expressed emphatically by the views of the logic textbooks covered in section 5. Before going on to point in a direction that can lead us out of this impasse (in section 10, below), we need to clarify what is meant by the terms "public opinion" and "popular opinion." Although these terms are often used interchangeably, they appear to be used by different groups (or disciplines) for different purposes. Some clarification of both terms is needed before the kind of argument we seek to analyze can be clearly identified and defined.

7. The Meaning of "Public Opinion"

It is interesting to reflect on the meaning of the two expressions "public opinion" and "popular opinion," as terms already in use by different groups of language users. The term "public opinion" is used by social scientists, as well as by social theorists and by those involved in or commentating on politics (Oskamp 1991). "Popular opinion" is a more specialized expression used in logic to represent a certain kind of argumentation, or perhaps to represent the premise of a kind of inference usually evaluated in logic textbooks under the heading of informal fallacies (Hamblin 1970). The expression "public opinion" sounds more dignified and suggests some sort of important consideration that needs to be taken account of in democratic politics or other matters of state. "Popular opinion" sounds slightly derogatory, as though something that is "popular" may be somehow superficial or possibly even misleading. Both expressions seem clear enough, initially, but both are highly ambiguous. And it is very important, before coming to understand how reasoning based on public (or popular) opinion works, to grasp the ambiguity in both terms.

According to Susan Herbst, the phrase "public opinion" as commonly used by social theorists and social science researchers is ambiguous, but the various meanings of it can be sorted into four categories.

1. *Aggregation of opinion* is the outcome produced by the collection of anonymously expressed opinions in an opinion poll (Herbst 1993, 44).
2. *Majoritarian opinion* assumes "that the opinions of most consequences are those expressed by the largest number of citizens" (45).
3. *Societal consensus opinions* represent generally accepted opinions or social norms that bind people together through their understanding of acceptable bounds of behavior, so that anyone who flouts them is labeled an outcast (43–44).
4. *Legitimating artifact public opinion* is a kind used as a projection of media or elite opinion, manipulated by parties "to legitimate their positions or actions" (46).

Herbst states that she avoids choosing one of these meanings as the correct one because it is important to recognize that "public opinion" has meant different things during different periods and is a word that is used "in polemical fashion" by politicians.

The problem with the first meaning, *aggregation of opinion*, is that it is simply not true (in many instances, as is shown below) that the outcome expressed by "anonymously expressed opinions in an opinion poll" is a representative reporting or "aggregation" of the opinions of the group polled. The group polled always has a lot of different opinions, which very often conflict with each other, and the outcome of the poll almost always represents a distillation and coloration, a kind of slant or viewpoint on the supposed opinion of the group. So, to use the term "aggregation" to represent this type of public opinion is misleading. But still, the outcome of a standard opinion poll is one meaning of the term "public opinion" that is in common usage—it could, perhaps, better be called "poll-determined public opinion." But behind poll-determined public opinion there is the idea of "the public mind," or what the public is really thinking about some particular issue at any given time. The poll is supposed to be a measure or indicator of this target concept of what the public is really thinking. But there is always a gap between the two things because the poll questions contain wording that always, or almost always, puts a certain "spin" on the poll results.

The distinction between Herbst's meanings (1) and (3) is also very significant. Poll results representing public opinion in sense (1) seem to be value-neutral, in that they are just an objective measure of how people respond, for or against, to some matter where opinions are divided. But, in fact, once the results of such a poll indicate strong public support for some policy, rule, ethical principle or point of view on some moral issue or issue of public controversy such as abortion or euthanasia, it sets in place a presumption to the effect that this is the way we are going now, and that everyone who wants to be "with it" ought to go along and accept this new idea. Thus public opinion may appear to be value-neutral and objective but, in many cases, it is not at all, and it definitely has the effect on respondents of exerting a moral pressure to adopt new commitments and drop old ones—to accept social policy as moving in a certain direction. For, in Western democratic countries, social values and public opinions about social values are always changing and moving in a particular direction (which can change, or even reverse itself, very suddenly).

What is important to be aware of, in this connection, is that interest groups are constantly trying to accelerate or decrease this process of change and move it in a direction that supports their own interests, as well as the views they advocate. They are using public opinion of type (1) that is associated with poll outcome in order to get a mass audience to accept the idea that things are inevitably moving in a certain direction, apparently reflecting a growing public consensus on values or ways of doing things, so that a public opinion of type (3) reflects a social and moral consensus on how one should "correctly" behave, in line with new values. In other words, the technique of imposing meaning (3) of public opinion onto meaning (1) represents a strategy of argumentation that is commonly and successfully used to influence mass opinion and behavior.

The tricky part of this ambiguity is that public opinion in the poll-determined sense (1) is an empirical concept of the social and behavioral sciences. It represents how social scientists determine (supposedly) what people really think about an issue—what their beliefs are. Of course, mass beliefs of a disparate collection of individuals are hard to measure or determine, so we all accept that public opinion in this sense is a kind of artifact or hypothesis. But we think of it as something objective and factual, and are encouraged to do so by the margin-of-error figures and other trappings of numerical accuracy utilized by the pollsters.

But whenever the results of such a poll on some controversial issue of values, ethical conduct, or public policy are reported, there is inevitably an ethical spin on how the finding is taken, and what inferences are suggested by it at level (3), where movement toward norms of conduct is implied.

8. The Meaning of "Popular Opinion"

In logic textbooks, "appeal to popular opinion" is used as the name for a certain kind of argument or form of inference that is used to justify or support a conclusion as being based on evidence in the form of a premise. The premise has the form of a statement to the effect that everybody (or everybody in a designated group) accepts some proposition as true. The expression "popular opinion" is being used in a normative way, in this kind of usage, as opposed to the empirical way the expression "public opinion" is used in the social sciences. By "normative" it is meant that the inference based on popular opinion is being used to justify or support a particular conclusion as being based on good reasons or good evidence. In this book, the meaning of "normative" will also be taken in a dialectical way—as meaning that a proponent of the conclusion, in a dialogue exchange with a respondent, is trying to get the respondent to accept the conclusion put forward by the proponent on the basis of reasons being offered by the proponent.

Actually, there are three parties involved in the communicative situation for the use of argumentation from popular opinion. As well as the *proponent* and the *respondent* of the proposition being put forward as acceptable, there is also the *mass of citizens*, or respondents in a poll, whose collective opinion is being put forward as the reason for the acceptance of the thesis or claim at issue. What is presupposed, in other words, is a dialogue exchange between the proponent, or her representative, a pollster, who has put a certain question, or series of questions to a mass group of respondents, and who has tabulated and interpreted the results so that some particular proposition is represented as the outcome or "popular opinion."

According to the dialectical analysis of the appeal to popular opinion presented in this book (see Chapter 6, especially), this form of argument should be evaluated as having some standing (or weight of presumption as an argument based on good reasons) to the extent that the proponent has engaged in a conversation (dialogue) with the mass group of respondents (who could be "everyone," or "everyone in a particular society," or "the majority," or a selected group of typical respondents, and so on), and the group of respondents has a set of commitments that have been revealed and refined in the dialogue. This idea of a dialogue exchange with a mass group of respondents is a hard one to grasp at first. But it will be shown, through the analysis of the case studies in this book, how it makes sense as a normative model of the appeal to popular opinion type of argument, and how it is required to properly evaluate this kind of argument in the kinds of cases where it has typically been used.

This dialectical method of evaluating *ad populum* argumentation has already been used by Yankelovich in his criticism of the shortcomings of public opinion polls as a way of attempting to judge what the public is really thinking about a particular issue at any given time. According to Yankelovich, the poll is only a one-dimensional "snapshot" that does not take into account the context of how a particular opinion at any particular time fits into a larger dynamic of public deliberation on an issue. In his view, most public opinion polls are misleading because they fail to distinguish between people's merely offhand views and their thoughtful, considered judgments on an issue. Public judgment is "a genuine form of knowledge" (1991, xii), because it represents the movement and refinement of public opinion through various stages of deliberation on an issue.

In the dialectical framework for the evaluation of *ad populum* arguments that I shall develop in this book, deliberation is a type of dialogue or conversation that is a context of use of arguments that appeal to popular opinion (see Chapter 6, section 6). In a deliberation, as the participants discuss an issue or problem to be resolved, they consider various alternatives and bring forward arguments to the effect that such-and-such a proposed course of action would be a good idea or not. As the dialogue proceeds, the commitments the participants began with are clarified and articulated through the course of the argumentation, and as the arguments of the opponent test out these commitments and pose objections to their weak points.

Most of us these days—in North America, say—read the same stories in the newspapers and other media sources, and are affected by the same kinds of problems. So the "public mind," or our ways of thinking about these problems or issues at any particular time, can often be crystallized into a well-defined, typical position or argument. The problem is: How do you figure out what it is? This problem is faced by pollsters and social scientists who try to figure out public opinion.

The problem confronted by this book, however, is how to evaluate an appeal to popular opinion used in an argument in a given case. The solution to the problem that is developed in the book is dialectical. The answer given is that you can only judge how popular opinion has been appealed to in a given case by articulating the appeal in a dialogue. The process of engaging a dialogue articulates commitment so that the deep commitments in popular thinking can be clarified and articulated in such a way that they can be seen to have a kind of standing or weight of presumption behind them (even if it is only a weak and fragile weight of presumption that is open to challenge and critical questioning).

It may be difficult for the reader to grasp this abstract idea of a dialectical framework of use of an argument at first. It is an ancient idea, but it is scarcely known in the twentieth century, and at first appears unfamiliar, or even alien, to those who are not familiar with quite recent developments in argumentation theory. However, the examples of *ad populum* arguments featured in the case studies in this book will bring out the usefulness of this dialectical approach.

9. The Difference Between Public and Popular Opinion

The question of what the difference is between public opinion and popular opinion is not easy to answer. "Public opinion," as we have seen, is a vague and ambiguous expression that is already widely used by social scientists. Herbst (1993), as indicated above, cited four key meanings of the expression "public opinion." But Stuart Oskamp (1991, 17), citing work of H. L. Childs (1965, 15–24), who reviewed debates among social scientists on how to define "public opinion," cites an even wider variety of nine different definitions, each of which emphasizes specific aspects indicated below.

1. RATIONALLY FORMED—*Public opinion is the social judgment of a self-conscious community on a question of general import after rational public discussion.* (Young 1923, 577–78)
2. WELL-INFORMED (ELITE GROUP)—*Public opinion may be said to be that sentiment on any given subject which is entertained by the best informed, most intelligent, and most moral persons in the community.* (MacKinnon 1828, 15)
3. HELD BY SECONDARY GROUP—*When the group involved is a public or secondary group, rather than a primary, face-to-face group, we have public opinion.* (Folsom 1931, 446) *What the members of any indirect contact group or public think or feel about anything and everything.* (Bernard 1926; quoted in Childs 1965, 21)
4. IMPORTANT TOPIC—*The attitudes, feelings, or ideas of the large body of the people about important public issues.* (Minar 1960, 33)

5. EXTENT OF AGREEMENT—*A majority is not enough, and unanimity is not required, but the opinion must be such that while the majority may not share it, they feel bound, by conviction, not by fear, to accept it.* (Lowell 1913, 15–16)
6. INTENSITY—*Public opinion is more than a matter of numbers. The intensity of the opinions is quite as important. Public opinion is a composite of numbers and intensity.* (Munro 1931, 222)
7. MODE OF RESPONSE—*Public opinion consists of people's reactions to definitely worded statements and questions under interview conditions.* (Warner 1939, 377)
8. EFFECTIVE INFLUENCE—*Public opinion in this discussion may simply be taken to mean those opinions held by private persons which governments find it prudent to heed.* (Key 1961, 14)
9. GENERAL DEFINITION—*The study of public opinion is, therefore, the study of collections of individual opinions wherever they may be found.*

The sources of these nine different ways of defining "public opinion" can be found in Childs (1965). One thing that Oskamp emphasizes is that (in his opinion) the term "opinion" in "public opinion" should mean "belief." "The viewpoint that we prefer is that opinions are equivalent to beliefs" (1991, 12).

The root idea of public opinion seems to be that people in a state or country have access to a lot of common information presented daily by the media. And given the way people normally think about things, one can expect that they will draw certain inferences, in a somewhat predictable way, from any new information that is released and spread widely for public consumption.

Tocqueville captured this idea when he compared public opinion to the opinion of one person. What we do when we speak of public opinion is to construct an artificial way of speaking so that "the public" is seen as thinking like one person, or as a small group of persons, who has ways of thinking about things that are habitual enough to be somewhat predictable, though by no means always. The idea of public opinion presupposes a democratic kind of political system in which people are free, within boundaries, to say what they really think without penalty, and it presupposes wide access to media so that controversial stories of wide interest are generally known to a lot of people who take the trouble to follow media reports. So it can be generally assumed that people will draw more or less expected conclusions from these widely reported events. Public opinion can be divided, but it can also be expected to exhibit quite a bit of consistency in some cases, so that knowledge about it could be useful for economic and political purposes.

The idea of public opinion seems to be a political idea, or at least an idea that is closely tied in to politics and to a democratic political system in particular—though it does not need to be restricted completely to democratic countries or systems of government. But public opinion seems to be much more important in a democratic system and, as Tocqueville observed, it is so important in the American system that it seems to drive everything else, and often seems to be the only opinion that is of any real political importance. Naturally, then, since public opinion is such an important factor in a democratic political system, social scientists would devise empirical tests and procedures for measuring it. And once these procedures were found useful, and became part of an accepted practice or cultural institution called the public opinion poll, this widely accepted and understood practice would itself help to define the idea of "public opinion" as something that is familiar to anyone.

As good a definition of "public opinion" as we might hope to have is the one given by Herbst (1993), outlined above, which emphasizes the multiple nature of the concept and indicates that "public opinion" has an ethical aspect as well as a numerical one. The numerical aspect is what Herbst calls *majoritarian opinion*, referring to the opinion expressed by the largest number of persons. The ethical aspect has to do with the legitimation or use of generally accepted social norms. If we distill out the ethical aspect and concentrate on the numerical aspect, we get popular opinion.

Popular opinion seems to be a simpler idea that can be expressed much more exactly. The basic idea of popular opinion is that of everybody in a certain group, or the majority, or a preponderance of the individuals in the group, having a particular opinion. What it means is that this group accepts a particular proposition in such a fashion that it can be said to be, or to represent, their opinion. Here, there are two problems to be investigated further. First, what is an opinion? And, second, why are there three degrees of popular opinion, in the account expressed above?

An opinion can be defined as a proposition that is accepted by some person, some participant in argumentation in a context where differences of opinion are possible. So, an opinion is a proposition that someone accepts or holds as true. In short, an opinion can be said to be a proposition that a participant in argumentative discourse is committed to.

As expressed above, there are three degrees of popular opinion that can be attached to a proposition A.

1. Everybody accepts *A* as true.
2. The majority accept *A* as true.
3. A preponderance of people (not necessarily quantified as over fifty percent) accept *A* as true.

Each of these three degrees can represent a way that a particular proposition may be said to be a "popular" opinion.

The difference, then, between popular opinion and public opinion is that the latter is a more complex notion that takes into account accepted values and norms of conduct, whereas popular opinion abstracts from this ethical aspect and only generalizes about widely accepted opinions. Public opinion is a matter of public beliefs, values, and norms of conduct. Popular opinion is a matter of how many people accept a particular proposition as true.

What is called the *ad populum* or appeal to popular opinion type of argument, then, seems to be based on a premise of the form, "Everybody (or the majority, or a preponderance of people) accept proposition *A* as true." This premise is then used in an inference to draw a conclusion to the effect that there is some reason to accept *A* as true. So conceived, then, appeal to popular opinion as a type of argument could sometimes rest on a supposed finding about public opinion, but it does not need to.

The best terminological assumption to go ahead with, then, is that public opinion is a complex and ambiguous idea that is widely used by social scientists but has not been unanimously or clearly defined by them. Appeal to popular opinion, as a type of argument, can be defined in a simpler way that is useful for purposes of logic. But we must be careful to remember that appeal to popular opinion is not always (or necessarily) the same thing as appealing to public opinion.

10. The Problem with Arguments Based on Popular Opinion

Ever since Plato denounced rhetoricians who can inflame a crowd and sophists who can plausibly argue for a proposition, and then again plausibly argue for the opposite proposition, there has been a distrust of arguments based on popular opinion. Our distrust of arguments designed to manipulate public opinion, or to gain acceptance for actions and policies by appealing to popular opinion, is probably even greater today. Manipulating public opinion to support a cause has become big business. Public relations firms, marketing organizations, so-called spin doctors, specialists in guiding public persuasion and mass opinion, are paid billions annually by advertisers, politicians, corporations and governments, all big spenders on this form of argument. Despite the justified suspicions about arguments based on appeal to popular opinion all these activities have generated, a democratic system of government must ultimately be based on the presumption that this type of argument is reasonable.

This reliance on public opinion, while at the same time distrusting it, produces a marked ambivalence in Western democratic countries on how appeal to popular opinion is a treated form of argument. On the one hand, our system of democratic government is based on this form of argument; so we have to see it, at least in principle, as a reasonable form of argument. On the other hand, there is the worry that this form of argument is routinely exploited by politicians who have gotten so used to basing all their policies on public opinion polls that any kind of intelligent planning or leadership based on long-term decision making seems to have been left behind. Even more worrisome are the indications that democracy may be going along the road toward strangling itself on the pressures of advocacy groups and special interests, all laying claim to setting in place the "correct" view for everyone. The worry is that the increasing fragmentation and deterioration of public discourse—promoted by the energetic determination of these groups to shut out any and all they deem as adversaries from the arena of free public discussion—will lead to a loss of credibility in politicians, or anyone who purports to represent intelligent deliberation on public issues not tied to the advocacy of interests of special groups who have a financial stake in the outcome of an issue.

The ultimate danger may seem to be the emergence of a man or woman of the people who exploits the feelings of the people to draw everyone (or enough of a majority) together under a philosophy (or it could be called a religion) such as fascism or communism, that makes possible a deliverance from democracy. Such philosophies or political viewpoints—whatever one might call them, perhaps ideology or religion are better words—relieve the citizen from the need to struggle any longer with the difficult process of intelligent and informed deliberation and the weighing of the estimated prudence of possible courses of action. Instead, simple surrender to the popular passion—giving the individual the swelling of self-esteem that he or she can now feel by belonging to this powerful group—is all that is required. But the more subtle worry pointed about by Tocqueville is not the disappearance of democracy but its slavish adherence to the all-powerful dictates of the tyranny of the majority.

Hence, our ambivalence about appeal to popular opinion as a type of argument has an important place in the conduct of everyday deliberations, especially in matters of politics. On the one hand, our system of democratic government is based on the principle of resolving important issues of the day by majority vote. But the extent to which such a system is successful in directing policy in a constructive and productive direction depends on a kind of assumption about the quality of argumentation in the system. It assumes that the voters have at least some capacity for arriving at a thoughtful decision on the basis of informed deliberation on an issue, taking the (conflicting) needs and demands of the whole group into account. So appeal to popular opinion must be (at least generally) a reasonable form of argument for the democratic system to function with at least some degree of success.

On the other hand, we know of situations in the past—the advent of the fascist dictatorships of Hitler and Mussolini are the leading cases in point—where appeal to popular opinion has been the instrument of destruction of the democratic system. It is precisely the popular rhetoric of the crowd agitator who appeals to popular passions so successfully that is ultimately the greatest threat to democracy.

At a more mundane level, even apart from this ultimate threat, the worry is that politicians have become so expert at pandering to trendy, superficial popular opinions and feelings, in ways that chip away at intelligent and reasoned, long-term deliberation on matters of public policy. Mass opinion is frequently uninformed, emotional, short-term, and thoughtless. But politicians know that they ignore it, or go against it, at the possible cost of their jobs (often an important consideration, not only for financial reasons, but if you do not hold power, you cease to exercise so much influence). Hence, there is a powerful incentive for politicians to agree as much as possible with what they perceive to be the prevalent popular opinion of the moment.

Tocqueville's warning about the omnipotence of popular opinion in American democracy is more worrisome than the possibility of a Big Brother (or Big Sister) who exploits mass rhetoric to effect a dictatorial takeover of democracy, because there is plenty of evidence that the situation Tocqueville warned about is the reality of American democracy today.

This ambivalence about public opinion in American democracy today is based on the underlying contradiction in appeal to popular opinion as a type of argument. It seems that to resolve the apparent contradiction between the advocates and the detractors of popular opinion, some kind of accommodation needs to be made. It seems that public opinion is one factor to take into account in deciding what to accept or how to proceed in making decisions in areas like politics and business, but it needs to be balanced off against other factors that also need to be taken into account. But what kind of formula or system can we use to make such a balance as a basis for drawing the right conclusion in an argument in which popular opinion is one factor? No one seems to have answered this question or even raised it. We still seem to be stuck in the dilemma posed by the opposition between the advocates and the detractors of popular opinion.

Evidently, the detractors of popular opinion fear the most common mistake of drawing the wrong inference from a premise of popular opinion, that of uncritically leaping to accept the conclusion because of the pleasures and pressures of conformity. And to be sure, that is a danger and a common misfire of inference. But we need to get beyond the point of a blanket condemnation of following popular opinion and address the real problem, as stated above, of finding out how to reason on the basis of it in a balanced way. Here, then, is the central problem confronted by this book: How can one reasonably, intelligently, and critically evaluate arguments from popular opinion?

How could one hope to solve such a difficult problem, and one that has so many practical ramifications as this one does? Ultimately, the solution will be scientific in nature, in the form of a logical calculus for the evaluation of this kind of argument. But before that stage can be reached, the problem can only be solved by an ancient method, called "dialectic" by Aristotle, a method that takes a conflict of opinions on some controversial issue of importance to many and probes into the issue by examining the strongest arguments on both sides. Ironically, even paradoxically, this method of dialectical reasoning was characterized by Aristotle as being based on premises that represent the accepted views of the majority or the wise (see Chapter 5, section 2). So what we will have to do is use the dialectical method to solve the problem of how to evaluate the kind of argumentation that is itself most central to and characteristic of the dialectical method. This makes the problem sound quite hard, and even perhaps circular or reflexive, in a way that makes it seem that it feeds on itself. But once we begin to see how the problem is solved, it won't seem so difficult or so convoluted.

What has been accomplished in this chapter, and will continue in subsequent chapters, is the identification of the generally received views about reasoning from popular opinion, and then the formulation and articulation of these views in a way that makes clear what they are really claiming. To do this, I have examined things such as the conventional treatments of appeal to popular opinion in the various textbooks on logic and critical thinking and case studies of common examples of arguments that are used to appeal to popular opinion to try to get a respondent to accept a conclusion. We have already looked at public opinion polling, the most widely used method for determining public opinion. From these sources, we can examine various views and attitudes about the use of appeal to popular opinion as a type of argument. Then we need to determine how these views clash with each other, and find out what their precise points of opposition are, and to study the strongest arguments that can be used to support both sides. Finally, these data must be studied in a dialectical framework developed in recent advances in argumentation theory that sets out different contexts in which an argument can be used for some purpose.

In Chapter 1, I have examined how the premise of an appeal-to-popular-opinion argument is usually supported by the use of a public opinion poll. There are other methods, such as critically listening to what people say or using focus groups to judge what people think by how they react in a group discussion. However, the polling method seems to command the most respect politically because it is the institution that is accepted as scientific and trusted by the public as being based on objective evidence.

The general problem posed then is that if some *ad populum* arguments can be reasonable, what distinguishes between the reasonable ones and the ones that are fallacious, or at least those that have been misused somehow, so that they fall below the standards of what should be considered a good argument of this type? To study this question, I shall now go on to study a number of cases, or examples of *ad populum* arguments. We shall see that the main faults identified as fallacies pertain to how the conclusion is drawn by inference in an *ad populum* argument from a premise that states or claims what popular opinion is on a given issue.

The general lesson learned so far in evaluating arguments that appeal to popular opinion is that one must begin by examining the premise of the argument. The first way to critically question an *ad populum* argument is to ask what evidence the premise is based on. If it is based on a public opinion poll, then key questions about the actual wording of the question(s) used in the poll should be a significant part of the evaluation of the argument.

Chapter Two

INFERENCES AND FALLACIES

Chapter 3 will present a survey of the textbook treatments of the *argumentum ad populum*. But before getting to that point, it may be helpful to the reader to get a basic grasp of what the *argumentum ad populum* is generally supposed to be, by looking at some of the classic cases that define this type of argument or indicate how it is generally conceived in logic.

As indicated in Chapter 1, section 5, the *ad populum* is a type of argument that is seen as worrisome by logic textbooks. It is generally seen as a fallacy rather than as an argument that is reasonable or legitimate. Given the dialectical nature of the problem posed in Chapter 1, Chapter 2 is important because it is necessary to try to get a grasp of what the *ad populum* is taken to be by the popular, or generally accepted, opinion of it typically found in the logic textbook accounts of it. In Chapter 3, I go into more specific details of how this generally accepted view has changed and evolved over the years.

I shall now turn to a number of cases of arguments that would traditionally be considered instances of the "appeal to the people" or *ad populum* fallacy. In these cases, the problem is not (primarily) with the truth or acceptability of the premise of the appeal to popular opinion.

1. The Gore Vidal Case

Some of the cases of *ad populum* fallacies cited in the textbooks seem to be instances of a type of argument that could be called leaping to a conclusion prematurely on the basis of hasty reasoning (Walton 1992a, 64–80). An example of this sort is the case cited by T. Edward Damer (1987).

Case 2.1   I'm going to buy a copy of Gore Vidal's new book. It must be a good one: it's been at the top of the bestseller list for ten weeks.

In this case, the premise that Vidal's book has been at the top of the bestseller list for ten weeks would be relevant as a premise to the conclusion that it might be a good book to consider buying. However, if that premise were taken as a sufficient justification for going ahead with the action of buying a copy of this book, it would be open to criticism as being too slender a basis of argument. As Damer points out, the book could be a piece of "literary trash that nevertheless appeals to the nation's large number of unsophisticated readers" (124). What should be added here is that the book may have been at the top of the bestseller lists for ten weeks but still, given your special tastes in books, you may not find it an enjoyable book to read, nor might it be a book that you should buy because you would enjoy reading it. Your tastes may not agree with those people who buy the book and make it a bestseller.

However, it should be said that, if the book has been at the top of the bestseller list for ten weeks, a lot of people are finding the book very interesting, which might therefore suggest that the book probably is quite interesting to most readers or to the general reader. And if you fit into this category of being a general reader, then it is quite likely that you might enjoy this book, or you might at least find its success among other readers a sign or indication that it might be worthwhile for you to buy it. So it seems, then, that the argument does have some merit and the premise is relevant. But it could be considered to be a fallacious argument on the grounds that, by running out and buying a copy immediately, exclusively on the basis of the popularity of this book, the person in the example could be acting prematurely or attaching too much weight to this particular premise as a conclusive reason for buying the book.

Damer's classification of the argument as an instance of the *ad populum* fallacy is somewhat harsh. "The point is that nothing about the book's quality can be inferred from the fact that large numbers of people buy or even read it"

(124). It may be true that very little or nothing about the book's intrinsic literary quality can be inferred from its popularity, that is, from the fact that large numbers of people buy it. Nevertheless, if it is popular and large numbers of people are buying it, that could be a consideration that would reasonably suggest to this particular buyer, depending upon what his interests are, that it might be a good buy for him. He may not be so much interested in literary merit. He may just be interested in reading books that he finds enjoyable or that he can read on the plane during his next business trip.

If this is the case, the premise of the argument would be relevant and should carry some plausible weight as a reason for buying the book. But by itself, of course, this premise would not be absolutely conclusive as a reason for dictating the conclusion that the person should immediately run out and buy this book. So the *ad populum* fallacy, if there is one here, is that the premise is one factor, or perhaps a slender basis, that should be taken along with other considerations in weighing the practical wisdom of buying the book. If, as suggested in the example, the person simply takes this one premise of the popularity of the book and then immediately leaps to the conclusion that he should immediately run out and buy a copy of this book, the argument simply seems to be a case of a hasty conclusion based on premature deliberation.

So what we see in this case is not a fallacy of relevance (Walton 1995, chap. 6). The premise is at least weakly relevant to the conclusion in the sense that it could be some part of the reasonable deliberations that would properly lead toward suggesting that that conclusion could be reasonable. That premise, by itself, is only a weak and incomplete basis for directing an arguer toward the conclusion indicated. So the *ad populum* fallacy, if it should be called a fallacy, is the inflation of this weak premise to make it appear stronger than it is or to appear to lead to a conclusion that is not really warranted by such a weak premise by itself without taking other factors into account. The failure here, then, seems to be a pragmatic one in that the practical conclusion, the action indicated of buying the book, has not been based on a proper sequence of deliberation, where the buyer's or the book reader's goals and interests have properly been taken into account. The alternatives have not been looked at or considered in relation to a proper base of information that would be sufficient to enable this person to reach a reasonable decision on which book to buy or, indeed, whether to buy any book at all for the purposes that he requires. The fallacy seems to be one of a conclusion reached prematurely on the basis of an inadequate sequence of practical reasoning properly carried out with adequate information in a context of deliberation.

The fallacy in Case 2.1 could be called an error of reasoning fallacy, according to the classification of types of fallacies given in Walton (1995). The error is a hasty leap or erroneous inference to a conclusion that is not warranted by the premises given. The other type of fallacy is the sophistical tactic (or sophism type, for short), where an arguer uses a tactic of trying to unfairly or deceptively get the best of a speech partner. The fault in this type of fallacy is not just a faulty or erroneous inference but a pattern of bringing undue pressure to bear against a partner in a dialogue exchange.

2. The Jury Deliberation Case

Another type of *ad populum* argument is based on the assumption that, as a member of a group, you have deliberated on or discussed a certain issue and decided that a particular proposition is true, based on the group's deliberations. The argument then presents the suggestion that if you disagree with the outcome of the dialogue and arrive at a different conclusion on the issue then you had better reconsider. The reason is that the group you disagree with has intelligently discussed that issue as a group, and therefore the outcome of this group argumentation process has a certain standing or weight of plausibility behind it as a reasoned conclusion. Therefore, since your conclusion is opposed to the group conclusion, it is sharply open to question.

An excellent example of this type of *ad populum* cited as a fallacy is the kind of case presented by Bruce Waller of one person on a jury who is pressed to go along with the majority decision (1988, 132).

Case 2.2 Suppose that after long deliberation ten or eleven members of the jury favor one verdict, and one or two members favor another. At that point, the majority will almost certainly appeal to the weight of its numbers in an effort to persuade the dissenters to agree with them. The one or two in the minority will probably be subjected to such arguments as: "Look, everyone else on the jury agrees that the defendant is guilty; you are the only one who doubts it. Since there are so many more of us who have come to the guilty conclusion, doesn't that show you that your own conclusion must be mistaken? Be reasonable, and accept the view of the overwhelming majority. After all, eleven heads are better than one."

What is appealed to in this *ad populum* argument is not only the premise that all the other jury members agree, and are in a majority, but that their majority opinion has (presumably) been arrived at on the basis of an intelligent deliberation, a reasoned group discussion based on a knowledge of the evidence presented in the trial.

Waller calls the appeal to authority used in this case a fallacious instance of the appeal-to-popularity argument. And he gives good reasons to back up this assessment, citing the case of a judge's charge to a hung jury that puts pressure on the lone dissenter to consider whether it is reasonable to hold the opinion that is not agreed to by the majority. As Waller points out, the purpose of the jury system is to allow an individual to stand by his conscience, even against an overwhelming public sentiment for the opposed view (133).

Perhaps, then, it might be the most balanced approach to the dialogue-based type of *ad populum* argument, illustrated by Case 2.2, to say that such an argument can carry a certain legitimate weight of presumption in a balance of considerations in a case, but it can also be pressed ahead too strongly in some cases. Where pressed ahead too strongly by one party against the other party in a dialogue exchange, the *ad populum* argument is used as a sophistical tactic to make it difficult for the one party to make up his mind on the basis of the evidence. The fallacy resides in the *ad populum* pressure brought to bear by the one side in the dialogue exchange.

3. The Golden Rule Case

The following case is cited by Michael Wreen as an example of an argument that is an appeal to widespread belief in a group of people, and is used as an example of a fallacious *ad populum* argument (1993, 64). This example is taken from Irving Copi's logic textbook (1986, 50).

Case 2.3   The Golden Rule is basic to every system of ethics ever devised, and everyone accepts it in some form or other. It is, therefore, an undeniably sound moral principle.

According to Wreen, the argument in this case is an *ad populum* type because its premise claims that everyone accepts the principle in question. This premise may be true, but what is questionable is the inference from it to the conclusion. In the form presented by Copi, the argument in this particular case is reasonably classified as an instance of *ad populum* fallacy, or as an error of reasoning, because of the particular way the conclusion is expressed. The conclusion of the argument states that the principle cited, namely the Golden Rule principle, is "an undeniably sound moral principle." The word "undeniably" suggests, in this case, an element of dogmatism, that is, an element of unwillingness to countenance critical questions that makes plausible Copi's classification of the argument as fallacious. At any rate, the word makes the conclusion hard to prove. It is highly dubious whether it could be proved at all on the basis only of a premise that is an appeal to popular acceptance.

Suppose, however, that the conclusion were put in a less dogmatic form. What if the conclusion said that, therefore, the Golden Rule is a moral principle that should have some claim on our acceptance? Then the *ad populum* argument would not seem so plausibly fallacious. And, indeed, considered as a nonconclusive (defeasible) argument, it could be evaluated as a reasonable (or at any rate, nonfallacious) instance of the *argumentum ad populum*.

The *ad populum* argument, in this case, is interesting because it goes beyond the kind of case where a moral principle—say, against stealing—is cited as a common popular value, and then this premise is used to argue that stealing is morally wrong. In Case 2.3, it is claimed that the Golden Rule is not just a popular value in our system of ethics or in a particular population, but it is said that this rule is basic to *every* system of ethics. In other words, what is claimed is that in every culture that has devised a system of ethics, the Golden Rule is basic to that system.

The first thing that should be considered in evaluating this case is that it may be questionable whether the premise is true or not. This question is really an empirical matter. We have to look at the different systems of ethics that have been devised and see if we can find one where the Golden Rule is not basic. But, operating on the presumption that the premise could be true, and that it is an empirical premise that could be verified or falsified, then we have to ask the structural question of whether the *ad populum* argument—from that premise to the conclusion that the Golden Rule is a moral principle that has some claim to acceptance—is a reasonable argument. Clearly, in this case, the basis of the argument is more than just the claim that everybody in a particular population accepts the Golden Rule as a moral principle. Instead, the premise states that the Golden Rule is basic to every system of ethics ever devised. Then, as a secondary premise, or an inference perhaps derived from this more general premise, the statement is made that everyone accepts the Golden Rule in some form or other.

What is implicit in this argument is the claim that a system of ethics represents the outcome of some kind of intelligent deliberation in a culture or population that has devised this system of ethics, so that if that population accepts the moral principle of the Golden Rule, it is presumably because this rule has found to be a valuable policy in their system of ethics. In their deliberations, people who accepted it have found this type of rule useful or acceptable and have found that it has value in their ethical deliberations. The inference is that if such a rule has been basic to every system of ethics ever devised, then this universal acceptance would suggest that it does have a certain justification based on the deliberations that have gone into those various systems of ethics. Moreover, there is also an implicit justification that systems of ethics may differ and vary depending on different cultural values and goals that are emphasized in a different population, but that, if this one particular principle has been found to be basic to every system of ethics that was ever devised then that remarkable unanimity would be a considerable ground for confirming or verifying its truth or at least its acceptability as a moral principle, generally.

This particular case is an interesting one because it is neither just a straightforward appeal to popular opinion, although it certainly does involve an appeal to popular opinion as an important part of the argument, nor is it a knowledge-based type of argument. It is not (apparently) based on any claim to expert opinion or scientific knowledge (see section 10, below). What it seems to be based on is a justification related to deliberation about ethical goals and values as codified in different systems of ethics. In this respect, it is somewhat similar to the justification behind the kind of argumentation we could classify as argument from a legal precedent. A conclusion arrived at and adopted by a court in our legal system functions as a precedent on the grounds that the judge or jury has deliberated about this case and has reached a conclusion on the basis of the court proceedings. Once such a conclusion has been reached, therefore, it has a certain presumptive status and can therefore function as a precedent in another case. It is not that it cannot be overturned. It is defeasible, as a precedent, applied to a new case.[1]

It may carry a certain weight in subsequent deliberations in another court, however. Especially if that court is a lower court, the precedent could be binding on that lower court more so than if the second case were in a higher court. But in our legal system, a conclusion arrived at in one court does have some weight as a precedent and, therefore, generally speaking, the kind of argument involved in this transferring kind of reasoning from one case to another could be called an argument from precedent (Walton 1996b, 94).

---

1. Meaning that it can be overturned in a new case.

The argument in this case has a similar structure, in that it is said that the Golden Rule has been an outcome of the deliberations and the practices and life experiences that went into every system of ethics that has been devised. Given that some kind of intelligent deliberation and popular values went into devising these systems, a proposition that is basic to them or has been a conclusion of the deliberations that went into them has a certain standing. It does not mean that, in our system of ethics, we have to accept this proposition just because it has been accepted in other systems, but it does mean that it is a proposition that we should pay attention to and that we should only reject if we have a strong enough argument against it. It is, in other words, a proposition that we should give weighty consideration to because it does have a *prima facie* claim to acceptance, even though, in the end, after we devise our own system of ethics, it may be a proposition that we may have some grounds for rejecting. We could see the argument in this case as a rather refined type of argument built on the presumption that an established code of ethics would be likely to have at least some backing, as based on reasonable deliberations.

But what should be added in this case is that the premise that the Golden Rule is basic to every system of ethics, while it is relevant to the conclusion that the Golden Rule is a sound moral principle or has some claim to being such, nevertheless, gives only a weight of support in this argument that should be judged as a fairly weak one. If someone wants to argue that the Golden Rule should be basic to their system of ethics or to show that this rule is a sound moral principle, then they would presumably have to fulfill the proper burden of proof to support this conclusion by giving the kind of ethical reasoning that would be appropriate to support such a proposition in a dispute about ethics. Even if the Golden Rule has been basic to another system of ethics or even to every other system of ethics, then, it cannot claim further consideration.

But that premise would not establish the conclusion in an ethical discussion of the Golden Rule as a sound moral principle, at least by itself. Such an argument from an is-statement to an ought-statement would be highly questionable as an attempt to found a basis for an ethical principle. So, although we are not given much context in this particular case, we have to fill in the context with a presumption that the two participants are having a difference of opinion about systems of ethics, with the one participant trying to argue on behalf of some particular system of ethics. We could judge, at least provisionally, that the premise is relevant to the conclusion. In the framework of such a discussion, to say that the Golden Rule has been basic to other systems of ethics would not be an irrelevant or altogether worthless premise but, certainly, it would not be by itself sufficient to prove the claim that the Golden Rule is a sound moral principle.

What we would conclude with respect to this case, then, is that, while Copi is justified as treating the argument as an instance of the *ad populum* fallacy because of the way he has phrased the conclusion, nevertheless it would be easy to rephrase the conclusion in a less dogmatic way, thus presenting the much more difficult problem of whether this revised version of the argument is fallacious or not. According to the analysis that would be appropriate for the context of dialogue sketched above, such a revised argument could be a reasonable—that is, a nonfallacious *argumentum ad populum*—on the grounds that the premise could give at least some weight in a discussion toward the acceptance of the conclusion. It could be said, therefore, that the premise is relevant to the conclusion in the context indicated. However, it would also be appropriate to point out that the premise would not be sufficient to establish the conclusion in such a context and, therefore, it would be justified to classify the argument as being weak—that is, as being insufficient to meet the requirements of the burden of proof that would seem to be appropriate for the context of the dialogue.

4. The Democratic Civilization Case

My attempt to evaluate the Golden Rule case may leave a lingering aura of puzzlement and unsettledness. Although the argument seems shifty and questionable, it is hard to diagnose the precise fault in the inference, and harder still to suppress the feeling that it could be a reasonable, if weak and inconclusive, argument but not so bad an argument that it is fallacious on some interpretations.

An interesting specimen of the *argumentum ad populum* is found in the following case, one that is even more problematic, cited in Walton (1989, 91–92).

Case 2.4 If we vote to return the death penalty in Canada, we, along with a few states, will be the only jurisdictions in the Western world with a death penalty. Not one country in Europe has a death penalty. New Zealand doesn't have it. Australia doesn't have it. It is on the books in Belgium, but there hasn't been an execution in that country since 1945. It is abolished in all other Western countries. We will be joining countries like Africa and Turkey that are not models of democratic civilization or human rights.

The strategy used in this case is to argue that from the premise that all civilized countries have banned capital punishment, to the conclusion that we should ban capital punishment as well, on the assumption that we purport to be a civilized country. Then the additional argument is advanced that if we do not ban capital punishment, we are joining Africa and Turkey, which "are not models of democratic civilization or human rights." The argument starts out with a positive *ad populum* appeal, and then backs it up with a negative argument that categorizes the respondents as uncivilized and undemocratic if they fail to comply with the line of action recommended.

The *ad populum* argument in this case is partly an ethical appeal to practices described as models of democratic civilization and human rights; therefore, it is partly a moral argument. But it is also partly based on a supplementary background inference that makes it seem to have some plausibility or reasonableness as an argument. This inference is to the effect that these other countries, which have decided not to have the death penalty because they are described as civilized democracies, must have deliberated on the issue and their decision to discontinue the death penalty should, therefore, be followed precisely because it was based on prior intelligent deliberations. The point of view of these democratic countries is being advocated as enlightened and thoughtful, it is not necessarily being advocated as being based on expert opinions or knowledge-based reasoning, in the sense of scientific knowledge. It is being advocated as a thought-out democratic view that has supposedly been based on intelligent and enlightened deliberation. But it is also being advocated as an ethical view, i.e., one based on cultivated moral values, and a respect for human rights.

The *ad populum* argument in this case, then, combines a moral basis with another kind of basis that is similar to that of the argument in the Golden Rule case. We can dismiss this case as a fallacious *ad populum* argument on grounds similar to our evaluation of the Golden Rule case, but in this case there is an added dimension, namely, the negative aspect of the argument denying that Africa and Turkey are "models of democratic civilization or human rights." This part of the argument rests on a premise that is open to questioning. But even if the premise is true, it seems to put pressure on anyone who disagrees with it in a way that seems questionable.

Perhaps the objection most of us would have to the argument, however, is that if we are to vote on the return of the death penalty in Canada, we should evaluate the question on its merits instead of being too much influenced by what other countries are doing. As one small factor in the larger picture, the *ad populum* argument in this case could be worth taking into account. But to suggest, as the argument in Case 2.4 seems to imply, that we should go ahead and definitely vote against returning capital punishment, on a basis of what these other countries are doing, is a hasty leap of logic, similar to the fallacies found in Cases 2.1 and 2.2.

5. The Falling Objects Case

The categorization of the *argumentum ad populum* as a fallacy of relevance by Dauer has already been described in Chapter 1, section 5. But one particular case, used by Dauer to illustrate this fallacy in his textbook, is particularly interesting (1989, 80–81).

Case 2.5   The Fallacy of *Argumentum ad Populum* has been committed far more often than we might think. For years it was conventional wisdom that heavier objects fall faster to the ground. It took Galileo's famous but simple experiment of dropping objects of unequal weight from the Leaning Tower of Pisa to convince people that differences in weight do not affect how fast an object falls to the ground. At least in many instances the pre-Galilean people can be taken to have committed the following fallacy:

Argumentum ad Populum: So many people accept that heavier things fall faster to the ground [therefore it is plausible that] heavier things fall faster to the ground.

At first, the fallacy in this case looks like it might be more of appeal to authority (appeal to expert opinion) than one of appeal to popular opinion. It was supposedly for the reason that Aristotle said that it was the "conventional wisdom" that heavier objects fall faster to the ground. But to head off this possible interpretation of the case, Dauer adds a footnote.

It is true that Aristotle was the leading authority for most of the two thousand years preceding Galileo, and it was certainly Aristotle's doctrine that heavier objects fall faster to the ground. However, in those days, it was likely that many people believed the false claim, not because they read Aristotle or because some expert told them of this, but simply because so many of their neighbors claimed it. It was these people who committed the Fallacy of *Argumentum ad Populum*. (80)

Did many people believe, in Aristotle's time, that heavier objects fall faster to the ground? This question is an empirical one, possibly not easy for historians to answer, because the case is about "pre-Galilean people." But it does not matter. The question is: If many people accepted, at the time, that heavier things fall faster, then does it follow, by logical reasoning, that it is plausible that heavier things fall faster?

The problem with this case is that if many people, at the time, believed that heavier objects fall faster because it was the conventional wisdom of the time, backed up by what was accepted as the learned views of the time, then in that context, at that time, it would have been reasonable to accept the opinion that heavier objects fall faster (unless, like Galileo, you did an experiment and found empirical evidence to the contrary). In other words, it seems on the surface anyway, that if some proposition is accepted as conventional wisdom of the time, and you have no particular reason to doubt it, or have found evidence showing it is false, then it is *prima facie* justifiable for you to (at least provisionally) accept that proposition. The expression "on the surface" is used to qualify this principle, however, because the problem is to come to know why it is an acceptable principle. This difficulty of knowing how to prove (or disprove) this principle is the problem of the *ad populum* argument in a nutshell. The particular problem for Dauer's analysis of his case is that, in general, it seems to be a reasonable enough principle, other things being equal, that if something is accepted by "conventional wisdom," or is generally accepted by most or many people, and you have no reason to doubt it, then it is probably (or plausibly) a good idea to accept it (as a working presumption).

Now we come to the heart of the problem. In Case 2.5, the popularly accepted opinion turned out to be false, as shown by Galileo's experiment. Does that not show that the *argumentum ad populum* in this case is a fallacy? The answer is "No." Just because a proposition that you once accepted because everyone (or many people) accepted it turned out to be false (as shown by new evidence), it does not mean (necessarily) that you committed a fallacy simply because of what you formerly accepted. It would be a fallacy, or logical error, if you refused to change your belief once the new evidence came in and was verified as true. But simply having a false belief, because you accepted something as true that many people accepted as true, is not a fallacy (in my opinion).

Case 2.5, then, suffers from a fundamental problem. It also poses some basic questions about the *argumentum ad populum* that have not yet been answered. Is it always wrong to accept something on the basis that it represents "conventional wisdom" or because many people accept it? And if not, and if it is sometimes right to accept something for such a reason, what, in general, is the reason why such an inference can sometimes be reasonable? If it is sometimes a fallacy to accept something just because many people accept it, what is a clear case of such a fallacious inference? And if the inference is fallacious, what is it about it that specifically represents a kind of erroneous inference that can be identified and explained? None of these questions have been answered yet.

6. The Inquisition Case

Another case that reveals some interesting aspects of the *ad populum* argument is also from Copi (1986, 105), as cited by Wreen (1993, 66).

Case 2.6   The Inquisition must have been justified and beneficial, if whole peoples invoked and defended it, if men of the loftiest souls founded and created it severally and impartially, and its very adversaries applied it on their own account, pyre answering to pyre (Croce 1913, 69–70).

The basis for this *ad populum* argument is, presumably, that the series of tribunals that lasted for a long period in Europe and other countries, called the Inquisition, was instituted and defended by "men of the loftiest souls." The Inquisition, at least during the period of its heyday in Europe, was supported by the established Church and was widely accepted, or did have a certain acceptance, among populations in Europe as a way of supporting religious values by forcing heretics to recant.

Here again, however, the premise is an empirical one. During the time when the Inquisition was a force to be reckoned with, was it, in fact, supported by the majority or did it have widespread popular support? Was it, in fact, invoked and defended by all people who had lofty souls or good values, or was there significant opposition to it? Perhaps not. However, if we can presume that it was supported by a lot of people who had thoughtfully deliberated about it, then that would be some grounds for arguing that, as an institution, the Inquisition was based on public judgment. But, of course, the current presumption is that a popular audience would reject the Inquisition and see it as representing something very bad or something that should definitely be avoided. In fact, the Inquisition is the very paradigm of what we in Western culture consider to be bad and unfair deliberation. That is indeed why Copi uses this particular case as an example of the *argumentum ad populum*, which the student readers of his textbook can be counted on to immediately categorize as fallacious.

And we can easily see that the argument is a weak and highly questionable one, for even if it were true that whole peoples invoked and defended the Inquisition as an institution, and even if it were true that men of the loftiest souls founded and supported this institution, it hardly follows that the Inquisition can be justified as a beneficial institution on these bases. True, these premises give us a weak or small argument in support of the Inquisition being a justified and beneficial institution, but given what we know about the institution of the Inquisition—that is, given all the other facts we know about how horrible the Inquisition was—there is a considerable weight of evidence already in place to the effect that the Inquisition was, indeed, not a justified and beneficial institution.

Quite to the contrary, we can all be counted on to accept the judgment that the Inquisition was an unjustified and very nonbeneficial institution. And as part of what we accept as a matter of historical fact and moral judgment about the institution, we think that the individuals who founded and created the Inquisition were either misguided or evil people who were using it to further their own ends for political power. This evaluation, at any rate, represents the conventional judgment supported by the conventional historical treatments of the Inquisition as a historical institution. Hence, even though men who did a certain amount of moral deliberation were responsible for the Inquisition, and the Inquisition itself did have a certain amount of public acceptance that made it possible for it to be carried out on such a wide scale, these facts by themselves, on the basis of a public-judgment type of argument, give only a small weight of evidence in favor of the conclusion that the Inquisition was justified and beneficial. Given what we know about the Inquisition, this argument is ludicrous because the appeal-to-popular-opinion argument gives such a small weight of evidence to support the conclusion that, on the contrary, we reject the conclusion.

Also, we should note that, in Copi's statement of Croce's example, the word "must" is used. The conclusion is to the effect that the Inquisition "must have been justified and beneficial." To put the conclusion in this very strong way means there is a high burden of proof required to establish the conclusion as true. This very high burden of proof, coupled with the inherent implausibility of the conclusion, makes it so difficult to mount any kind of reasonable argument that would give any kind of strong support for the conclusion that the example seems ludicrous, and it seems quite easy to dismiss it as fallacious.

So, this particular example represents the flip side of the other two types of cases of moral justification *ad populum* arguments discussed in sections 3 and 4, above. In these cases, even though the premises only gave a small weight of support in favor of the conclusion, the conclusion was fairly acceptable or plausible, or at least it was not outrageously implausible, so that the argument did not seem completely fallacious. However, in this case, the conclusion is so implausible, and the burden of proof required to establish it so high, that a very strong case would have to be made to even give some support to it. And, in fact, the premise that is used, although it is based on an appeal to popular support, is of a quite weak kind, which would be subject to considerable critical questioning. On the whole, the argument is so weak in relation to what it is required to prove that it is pathetically weak, and virtually anyone who knows about the Inquisition would find it highly implausible.

Even so, in this case, the premise is not entirely irrelevant to the conclusion, even if the premise is quite dubious and the conclusion it is supposed to prove is almost ridiculously difficult to prove. Given these observations, then, it is somewhat questionable whether the inference from the premise to the conclusion is of a type that would justify our categorizing it as an instance of the *ad populum* fallacy. It certainly does seem to be such an implausible and weak argument—even ludicrously so—that, in some sense, it certainly is a bad argument. But, the precise grounds on which it can be categorized as an *ad populum* fallacy are somewhat unclear. It does seem to be an appeal-to-public-support or acceptance type of argument, but just one that is so implausible in relation to the premise used and the conclusion that needs to be established that it seems to be ridiculously weak and unpersuasive. This might, perhaps, provide some grounds for classifying this case as an instance of the *ad populum* fallacy, although it is not altogether clear exactly what the fallacy consists of. But the problem is that Copi classifies the *ad populum* fallacy as a failure of relevance and, as we shall see in Chapter 3, defines the *ad populum* fallacy as the attempt to win popular assent to a conclusion by arousing the feelings and enthusiasms of the multitude.

It is not clear, however, that Case 2.6 is an *ad populum* argument of this type; indeed, Wreen does not classify it as being of this subtype (1993, 66). But also, as mentioned above, the other point is that the error in this case is not a fallacy of relevance in the sense that the premise is irrelevant to the conclusion. The failure is more one of simply not fulfilling a very high burden of proof because the premise used gives very little weight of evidence to support that conclusion, given that it is so implausible. But, the premise is relevant in the sense that, if it were true, it would certainly give some significant weight of evidence to support the conclusion, even though the conclusion is, in itself, highly implausible.

In section 2 above, it was shown that an argument with a false or implausible premise that appeals to popular opinion is not necessarily an instance of the *ad populum* fallacy. The fallacy resides in the structure of the inference from the premise to the conclusion. By the same token, an argument with a false or implausible conclusion is not necessarily an instance of the *ad populum* fallacy. Copi has evidently used this example to encourage his readers to dismiss the argument in it as an *ad populum* fallacy without having to go into the difficult questions involved in evaluating whether or why the argument is really fallacious or not—for example, by evaluating whether or in what sense the premise is relevant to the conclusion.

7. The Mark Antony Case

One of the most popular examples of the *ad populum* fallacy cited by the logic textbooks is the funeral oration of Mark Antony in Shakespeare's Julius Caesar. In this speech, Antony makes a passionate speech to those assembled at Caesar's funeral, just after he has been murdered by a group of conspirators. By appealing to the feelings of the crowd, Antony is able to provoke mob violence. The use of this example to illustrate the *ad populum* appeal by W. Ward Fearnside and William B. Holther is quoted below (1959, 95).

Case 2.7: The issues that the Roman public was called upon to face were (1) Had Caesar been guilty of conspiring to overthrow the Republic? and (2) Should any action be taken against the assassins? Mark Antony's speech says nothing of the issues. Instead, he reminds the audience that they once loved Caesar:

> *You all did love him once, not without cause.*
> *What cause withholds you then to mourn for him?*

exhibits Caesar's blood-stained-mantle,

> *Through this the well-beloved Brutus stabb'd;*

implies the conspirator's motives were personal,

> *What private griefs they have, alas, I know not, that made them do it:*

assures the audience he, Antony, is a guileless man,

> *I am no orator, as Brutus is:*
> *But, as you know me all, a plain blunt man,*

and, to cap his case, alleges Caesar's will leaves his property to public uses,

> *To every Roman citizen he gives,*
> *To every several man, seventy-five drachmas.*

This persuades the mob; they troop off ready to avenge Caesar. Incidentally, by saying over and over again, "But Brutus is an honorable man," Antony raises the issue of the conspirator's honor which, otherwise, would not be in question.

Fearnside and Holther classify the argument in this case as an instance of the fallacy of "popular passions," or the *ad populum* appeal. The basis of their evaluation of the argument as fallacious is that there were two "issues that the Roman public was called upon to face," but that Antony's speech "says nothing of the issues." In other words, the appeal to popular passions given in the speech is irrelevant, in the sense that it does not materially bear (as evidence, one way or the other) on these issues.

This evaluation is a little confusing because Antony's speech was a funeral oration. A funeral oration is a type of speech where emotional issues, or appeal to popular passions, would be perfectly appropriate. In this speech context, the *ad populum* argument does seem to be relevant, in other words.[2] But Fearnside and Holther treat the setting, or context of the speech, as that of a political deliberation or perhaps even that of a criminal trial, where the issues are whether Caesar was guilty of conspiring to overthrow the Republic, and whether any action should be taken against the assassins. Presumably, then, the allegation of a failure of relevance resides in the requirement that, in one or both of these contexts of argument, certain kinds of (factual) evidence would be the relevant considerations, whereas Antony's speech fails to provide any of this sort of evidence. Instead, it provides only unsubstantiated allegations about motives, a suggestion that Brutus is an orator (as opposed to a "plain blunt man"), that he is not a trustworthy person, and that there is a financial incentive to have sympathy for Caesar. Hence, Antony's arguments can be evaluated as irrelevant, and therefore fallacious.

If Antony's speech is supposed to be a collective deliberation on public policy (like some sort of town hall meeting), or a criminal trial or legal proceeding of some sort, then Fearnside and Holther's evaluation of Antony's speech as irrelevant to the two issues stated in Case 2.7 seems reasonable enough. But the deeper basis for their classification of this argument as a fallacious case of "popular passions" is that it is a rabble-rousing emotional appeal to the crowd by Antony, who tries to portray himself as a member of the crowd—"a plain blunt man." And it is not clear that this type of emotional appeal is entirely out of place in a political debate or even a criminal trial. It is, indeed, the sort of tactic that politicians and lawyers use to argue before juries or mass audiences all the time. The use of such mass appeal *ad populum* arguments by those who want to influence public opinion was as widespread in ancient times as it is now. So, the other side of this case is that (depending on how you postulate the context of the argument) it is hard to exclude the assumption that Antony's populist remarks may have some relevance. What Fearnside and Holther's example really poses as dangerous (if not fallacious) is the whipping up of a crowd to precipitous, violent action. The fallacy, or at least the danger, is not so much one of irrelevance as one of provoking mob violence by inflammatory speech-making.

Although the Mark Antony case is not a particularly good one to use for an introductory textbook for modern students, it is representative of a type of case of *ad populum* argument that truly is worrisome and problematic for twentieth-century readers. It represents the very real danger of the use of inflammatory

---

2. Any evaluation of this case is slightly complicated by its occurrence in a work of fiction.

crowd rhetoric by the demagogue, cited in section 1 above. If there is a fallacy in this type of case, it is well worth being seriously concerned about.

8. Inflammatory Language

Another type of *ad populum* argument that is frequently cited by the standard treatment in the textbooks is the kind of case where inflammatory language is used. The fallacy here, like that in Case 2.7, seems to be a species of mob-appeal argument because it is an attempt to arouse enthusiasms by appealing to deeply held values that an audience has. But, in this type of case, the inflammatory rhetoric is used in a way that manipulates the audience to either support something that reflects values that they themselves hold dear or attack something on the grounds that the supporters of the proposition hold bad values that should be morally condemned. One example of this sort is Case 2.8, quoted below from Copi (1986, 107), where it was used as an example of the *ad populum* fallacy. Copi quotes a nominating speech said to have been made by Robert G. Ingersoll at the 1876 Republican National Convention.

Case 2.8 Like an armed warrior, like a plumed knight, James G. Blaine marched down the halls of the American Congress and threw his shining lances full and fair against the brazen foreheads of every defamer of his country and maligner of its honor.

For the Republican party to desert a gallant man now is worse than if an army should desert their general upon the field of battle.

Somewhat like Mark Antony in the previous case, the speaker in this case is trying to evoke a quarrelsome or divisive response that identifies his own side as so good that anyone opposing it is put in the position of being a despicable enemy.

In this case, the speaker uses somewhat flowery language that he presumes his audience approves of. He compares James G. Blaine to a "plumed knight" and compares his actions to throwing a shining lance against the foreheads of his defamers. The use of this picturesque language invokes romantic associations with chivalry. Of course, popular audiences would now (probably) be inclined to strongly reject these associations, but the presumption is that, at the time when Ingersoll gave this speech in 1876 at the Republican National Convention, his audience would have very been much inclined to accept them.

Hence, we can see that Ingersoll's use of this (then) emotionally favorable language would be powerful rhetoric in winning the sympathy of the audience to support his case.

Here, the form of the argument is that of comparison or analogy but, basically, it seems to be an *ad populum* type of appeal because the speaker is using language that would invoke favorable attitudes, and on this basis, it could be classified as a species of appeal-to-popular-opinion argument. The speaker is trying to frame the argument in a confrontational way, so that James G. Blaine is a knight in shining armor; in other words, a force for good, and his opponents are portrayed as bad people who are opposed to this good person. Using the language of armed warriors and shining lances is a way of fanning the enthusiasm of the audience so that their favorable attitudes are used to inflame the confrontational stance that the speaker is wishing to put forward, and to solidify the group against "enemies," who would automatically be categorized as a force against good (or for evil).

A comparable case is the speech cited by S. Morris Engel (1976, 114), attributed to Westbrook Pegler, a syndicated columnist, at the time Fiorello LaGuardia was mayor of New York City.

Case 2.9   Mayor LaGuardia, who himself is a very noisy member of the crowd known as the labor movement, certainly must know that the worst parasites, thieves, and bread robbers now in active practice in the United States, and specifically in the city of New York, are the union racketeers. The waterfront is crawling with them; they are even preying on men employed to produce entertainment for troops under auspices of the USO and thus filching from the fighters for whose benefits the USO funds are raised. Throughout the country, they are reaching their dirty hands into the homes of the poor and stealing bread and shoes from children of the helpless American toiler. LaGuardia has never said a word against such robbery and, by his association with the union movement, he has given approval of this predatory system.

Engel categorizes Pegler's speech as an instance of the fallacious *argumentum ad populum* on the grounds that Pegler fails to address the point at issue in his speech, namely, the question of whether and how the union movement is predatory. To cover up this irrelevance, according to Engel, Pegler "employs explosive language which is well-adapted to lead towards the conclusion he wishes to draw" (114). So Mayor LaGuardia is described by using the adjective "noisy," and the movement he is associated with is described as a "crowd of racketeers" who are "stealing from the helpless American toiler and his children." Many other expressions used in the speech, like "reaching their dirty hands into the homes of the poor," are inflammatory and confrontational in nature. As opposed to the previous case, this argument explicitly invokes negative associations by using terms that are derogatory. So, the argument in this kind of case can be classified as a crowd-appeal type of *ad populum* on the grounds that the language used is meant to invoke certain attitudes in a target audience by appealing to values that the audience holds dearly and would react to enthusiastically.

In this case, however, it might be unwise to leap too quickly to the conclusion that Pegler's argument is fallacious on the grounds that it fails to address the point at issue. It is true that Pegler does not give specific details exactly on whether and how the union movement is being predatory in its actions, but let us ask: What is the context of the speech? From what I am told, the quotation given was a part of a syndicated column. Presumably, this would be an opinion column where Pegler was representing a particular opinion or political point of view. But in a political speech column of this sort—which is, after all, different from a news report—it is a legitimate part of the argumentation to attack one's political opponents using *ad hominem* arguments or negative-character-attack arguments that claim that one's opponents are acting unethically. This partisan type of argument is perfectly normal in a political speech and, in the context of an opinion column on a political issue, an attack of an ethical sort on one's political opponents (of the kind represented by the argumentation in this case) is not altogether inappropriate or irrelevant. Of course, if the context were that of a court case, where criminal charges had been made against Mayor LaGuardia, then the particular actions in the charge criticized would have to be made clear in much more specific detail in order to be judged relevant. Perhaps Pegler's arguments could be criticized on the grounds that they are not very specific. But should we go so far as to say that his argument is a fallacious *ad populum* on the grounds that his premises are completely irrelevant to the conclusion he is supposed to establish? It seems to be a stretch to get to this conclusion, precisely because the context is that of a political speech or opinion column, which could have the legitimate purpose of provoking indignation in the readers by raising an issue for discussion.

What is characteristic of the *ad populum* argument in this case and the previous one is the speaker's tactic of dividing up the world into good guys and bad guys, and then using inflammatory rhetoric to bond with the audience in the presumed group of good guys. It is the rhetoric and language of a "cause"—a set of group values that is portrayed as so good, so noble, or so holy that anyone opposed to it must automatically be discounted as bad, by being demonized or portrayed as enemies of the good cause.

9. How the *Ad Populum* Is Used to Manipulate Opinions

The cases studied in this chapter fall into two classes. The Mark Antony case and the following two cases of inflammatory language (Cases 2.8 and 2.9) are examples of the use of a special kind of rhetoric that appeals in a one-sided way to the interests of the crowd, audience, or group that is addressed. Instead of considering the arguments on the issue in a balanced or two-sided way that might be thought to be characteristic of reasoned deliberation to assess an issue, the speaker tries to solidify group interests and bias by hammering away at the one side and portraying the argumentation on that side in enthusiastic and even glowing terms. The failure in these cases does not seem to be in the argument itself but in how it is used in a certain rhetorical way to appeal to mass enthusiasm in a closed, group-oriented, partisan fashion.

All the other cases, studied in the first part of the chapter—that is, up to the end of section 7—fall into a different class. The arguments used in these cases all share a particular format. First, they postulate a premise stating that everyone, or everyone in a particular group, or anyone who has some particular property, accepts or has accepted a particular proposition A as true. Second, this type of argument draws an inference to a conclusion that, therefore, you (the respondent of the argument) should accept this proposition as true (or at least, as plausible, or as something that is reasonable for you to accept). All of the arguments used in the first group of cases up to and including the Inquisition case (section 6) have this general format.

It could be, as well, that the three rhetorical cases in the first class of arguments also have this format or pattern of argument. But if they do, the precise location of the format in the given case is more difficult to identify, and much of the argumentation used in the case is more broadly rhetorical in nature. The *ad populum* technique used in both types of cases works in a particular way to manipulate opinions. In both kinds of cases, the premise of supposed public opinion or sentiment is used to infer the acceptability of a particular course of action, or to suggest adopting a particular viewpoint. Such an inference typically arises because the statement of public opinion is joined to some kind of supportive generalization or inference warrant that leads toward a conclusion. The typical kind of case is one where the public opinion expressed is on some public policy issue, so that the conclusion suggested is that there is a public consensus that the statement expressed represents the "correct" or officially approved way of doing things now. The implication is that some ethical rule or general policy has now been approved or sanctioned as representing a social norm based on public consensus expressing the approved way to behave. Such a conclusion is not stated explicitly but suggested in the context of an issue of controversy, a dialectical context, by a process of implicature (Grice 1975). The suggested conclusion is that a certain policy has now been approved by the public as a societal consensus opinion that implies that anyone not following the approved norm of social conduct is behaving in a "deviant" or antisocial way.

The problem arising from this kind of implicature, drawn by inference from a premise of public opinion is that it can be used by politicians, ideologues, corporations, governments, or by anyone who wants to manipulate or influence mass conduct. It is, in fact, the main instrument of propaganda. It is the utilization of (supposed) public opinion to influence mass behavior.

It is easy to see how peer pressure is a powerful influence on the behavior of adolescents. They want to belong to particular groups because they feel that their goals can be achieved, or made more possible to achieve, by belonging to such a popular group. But all of us are just as susceptible to this kind of appeal, even though it may be less evident in the behavior of adults than in adolescents. To be perceived as being left out of a powerful, trend-setting, dominant group is stressful and deeply upsetting to anyone. So the implication that one is somehow out of step with public opinion, on some important matter of public policy that binds ethical codes of everyday behavior, is a powerful form of persuasion, suggesting how prudent a change in one's commitments would be.

The second problem is not just one of determining what public opinion is on some issue. It is a deeper and more subtle problem of determining what conclusions should be drawn from such a premise of the statement of a public opinion. There are two ways of manipulating public opinion or using it as a tool of deception. One is to give a false impression or wrong statement of what public opinion is; for example, by using a poll that looks scientific but has a hidden bias. The pollsters who do this could be called the pretenders to public opinion. But the other way of manipulating public opinion to commit fallacies—by misleading people through deceptive use of argumentation—is to use the claim to have determined what public opinion is, in order to get anyone who can be influenced by a poll to draw conclusions and, in particular, conclusions on how they ought to act, or to adopt certain viewpoints and policies. The cases studied in this chapter give a rough, initial idea of how this strategy works, and how it can be used in different ways, to suggest to an audience or respondent that following the crowd would be a good idea.

10. Appeal to Expert Opinion

Not all the cases studied above are (at least completely) fallacious arguments, however. Both the Gore Vidal case (Case 2.1) and the Falling Objects case (Case 2.5), in particular, suggest that in some instances, general popular acceptance of a proposition could be some small weight of evidence that could give one a reason to at least tentatively accept that proposition. This observation rekindles the view already expressed in Chapter 1, that an argument having the *ad populum* format could be reasonable as a basis for accepting a conclusion.

But, one might ask, how could such an argument in this format be reasonable or even appear plausible? Just because everyone once accepted the view that all the planets revolve around the earth, surely it does not follow that we should accept this proposition as true. In general, popular opinion and group acceptance of a proposition do not provide much of an evidential basis, if any at all, to support the conclusion that this proposition is true. To explore this question a bit, it is useful to contrast the *ad populum* argument (of the kind identified with the above format) with another type of argument called the appeal to expert opinion.

Appeal to expert opinion has been recognized (for example, in Walton 1996b, 65) as a reasonable kind of argument where the testimony of an expert in a domain of knowledge is cited as support for a proposition advocated by an arguer. The problem posed by appeal to expert opinion as a type of argument has been solved by modeling it as a kind of inference that shifts a burden of proof in a balance of considerations in a case.

It appears initially that appeal to popular opinion presents pretty much the same kind of problem as appeal to expert opinion, as a type of argument. Both types of argumentation have traditionally been treated as fallacies, and both have often been perceived as being subjective in nature and therefore hard to justify as an argument that could be used to give good reasons to support a conclusion. Charles Hamblin writes that appeal-to-expert-opinion arguments, traditionally classed as being appeals to authority, have been especially disliked during various historical periods (1970, 43). Although they have often been conceded to be nonfallacious in some cases, there has generally been an air of uncertainty, suspicion, and ambiguity about them. Appeal to popular opinion, like appeal to expert opinion, appears to be a potentially dangerous and misleading kind of argumentation that is difficult to evaluate in any objective fashion.

However, this parallel becomes questionable once it is appreciated that the analysis of appeal to expert opinion shows how this type of argument has a definite form that can be justified as meeting standards of correct use in some cases. In Walton (1997), it is shown that the appeal to expert opinion is reasonable in a given case if the argument in that case has been put forward by its proponent in the following form (where E is an expert source cited by the proponent and A is a proposition) (258).

(G7) E is an expert in domain D.
        E asserts that A is known to be true.
        A is within D.
        Therefore, A may (plausibly) be taken to be true.

The three premises in (G7) represent assumptions that, if met in a given case, license the drawing of the conclusion as a presumptive inference—meaning that the argument is correct insofar as it shifts a weight of presumption from the proponent's side onto the respondent's side in a dialogue.

To shift the weight of presumption back the other way, the respondent must ask one or more of the six types of critical questions (25).

Critical Questions for Appeal to Expert Opinion

1. *Expertise Question*   How credible is E as an expert source?
2. *Field Question*   Is E an expert in the field that A is in?
3. *Opinion Question*   What did E assert that implies A?
4. *Trustworthiness Question*   Is E personally reliable as a source?
5. *Consistency Question*   Is A consistent with what other experts assert?
6. *Backup Evidence Question*   Is A's assertion based on evidence?

The appeal-to-expert-opinion form of argument (G7) has only a presumptive or provisional bindingness on the participants in a dialogue. Once an argument of the form (G7) is put forward, the burden of proof is shifted on to the respondent to either accept the conclusion of the argument or ask an appropriate critical question. But if he does ask a critical question, then the argument defaults unless the proponent can produce an adequate answer.

The *argumentum ad verecundiam* (appeal to respect) is the fallacy of misusing an argument of the form (G7) by pushing ahead with the argument too aggressively in a dialogue exchange, by trying to browbeat the respondent to defer to the respect that should be accorded to an expert or the opinion of an expert. *Argumentum ad verecundiam* has been traditionally taken to be a fallacy. But according to the analysis sketched out above, it can be seen to be a type of argument that can be used correctly in some cases to shift a weight of presumption from one side to the other of a contested argument. Seen in this presumptive way, as a defeasible kind of argument that has some weight of presumption behind it but is open to critical questioning, the appeal to expert opinion can be evaluated in a balanced way that is appropriate for an argument that has some standing but that can also be abused. So it would seem, then, that there could be a parallel between the appeal to expert opinion and the appeal to popular opinion as types of argument. The weight of justification lying behind the appeal to expert opinion is comparable to that which could be seen as justifying the appeal to popular opinion as an argument. Both are based on the testimony or opinion of a group.

One might try to offer a group-based analysis of the *ad populum* arguments in the cases that are cited throughout this chapter, but this type of argument appears much weaker generally than the appeal to expert opinion. Appeal to expert opinion, when used correctly, is based on expert opinion, so the ultimate justification of this type of argument is that it is based on scientific evidence in a domain of knowledge, or at least on the skill of someone who is master of a craft or practical technique. Appeal to popular opinion is a much weaker form of argument because it lacks this basis of a group having access to organized knowledge. The apparent parallel vanishes as soon as it is realized that the reason that the appeal to expert opinion is correct in some cases, and can be justified generally as having presumptive weight, is that an expert in a domain of knowledge (or skill) is in a position to know. When a layperson consults an expert for an opinion, it is presumably because he, the layperson, is not himself an expert in the domain of knowledge in question. But he can legitimately appeal to the expert for an opinion and give weight to that opinion as a presumptive consideration precisely because the expert is in a position to know what is true or reasonably acceptable in that specialized domain of knowledge. Therefore, appeal to expert opinion is justified as a reasonable type of argument because the expert is in a position to know.

But what about appeal to popular opinion? Just because everybody, or everybody in some culture or country, accepts some proposition is true, does it follow that such popular acceptance is, by itself, a good reason to conclude that this proposition is true, or that there is a weight of presumption in favor of accepting it? The answer appears to be "No."

If the appeal to popular opinion were based on a premise of the form, "Everybody in a certain group accepts proposition A, and all the individuals in this group referred to above are experts in domain D," then it would be a fairly strong type of argument. It would, in fact, be a kind of combination of appeal to popular (or at least group) opinion with (G7). But the cases of the *ad populum* argument studied above do not appear to fit this format. They are merely appeals to popular opinion, of a kind that does not seem to represent any appeal to expert scientific opinion. They are not knowledge-based arguments at all, but merely appeals to the popular opinion of a group who has thought about, deliberated upon, or discussed an issue.

The general population are not experts in any particular domain of knowledge that the proposition in question falls into. Are they in a position to know in a way in which the user of the solicited opinion is not? It seems not. All of us are members of the general population, or the majority. The majority, or the broad population that holds the popular opinion, has no special standing or no more guarantee of being right than any particular individual who is a member of that population.

There is a very special problem about appeals to popular opinion as a type of argument. It is not easy to see how they could be justified at all. And it appears that they cannot be justified, or evaluated generally, in the same way that appeal to expert opinion is. As such, they are very weak arguments, and one might well wonder—if we give them any credence at all—what would be the basis on which we could say that the premise in such an argument gives any kind of rational support to the conclusion? This question is a tough one to answer, but one does get a glimpse, particularly in the Golden Rule case and the Democratic Civilization case, and even more specifically in the Inquisition case, of some sort of possible rational basis that may be present. In these cases, it is alleged that intelligent, democratic, and lofty-souled people had intelligent discussions where they considered the issue, or deliberated on it with some presumed rationality, and came to the conclusion that the practice or institution in question was a worthwhile one to adopt and support. Operating from this premise might give us some reason to move toward acceptance of the conclusion that there is some reason for us to accept the proposition that this practice might be a good one for us to follow. Or does it? It seems to provide perhaps, at best, a partial reason, but one that could certainly be challenged in many cases, such as the Inquisition case. But we seem to be a long way from understanding the logic of how such an inference works, and from being in a position to evaluate it as reasonable or fallacious in a given case.

Indeed, even before such a project of evaluation could begin, a prior requirement is the identification of the form of the *ad populum* as a distinctive type of argument. The problem revealed by the cases studied so far is that there seems to be significant variations between the cases, as one compares them, so that it is even less than clear whether we are dealing with one distinctive type of argument, or with a cluster of variants that have something (but something rather elusive) in common. To work toward a richer and more focused target for analysis of the *ad populum* argument, we turn toward a survey of how the argument has been defined or understood in logic textbooks.

Chapter Three

THE STANDARD TREATMENT

The *argumentum ad populum*, usually translated as "appeal to the people" is treated by logic textbooks under the heading of fallacies. Most logic textbooks have only a short section on this type of argument, and most (or nearly all) either define it as fallacious (usually on grounds of irrelevance) or concern themselves exclusively with its fallacious uses. This chapter is an account of the standard treatment of the *ad populum* fallacy in textbooks spanning the one-hundred-year period between 1895 and 1995. Some consideration is also given to the historical questions of where and how the *ad populum* originated from prior sources.

Many logic textbooks do not mention the *argumentum ad populum* at all. It is probably fair to say that of those textbooks that do have a section on fallacies, approximately half of them have only a short paragraph or brief mention of the *ad populum* treating it as a distinct fallacy.[1]

---

1. The survey in this chapter covered all the logic textbooks in the author's personal library, and in the University of Winnipeg Library. While not complete, it is fairly comprehensive.

1. Origins of the *Ad Populum*

There is an ancient history of the recognition of appeal to popular (majority, common) opinion as a premise for a distinctive type of argument. The notion of endoxic argument was an important part of Aristotelian dialectic (see Chapter 5, section 2). Ancient notions of probable inference would have been compatible with recognizing arguments based on what is accepted by popular opinion as a distinctive type of argument. In his commentary on Aristotle's *Physics*, Thomas Aquinas cited a species of probable argument that referred to an opinion as "probable among all" or as "probably held by many" (Byrne 1968, 107). It might be noted here that "probable" is meant in its ancient use of "plausible" or "accepted," as opposed to its statistical use current since the advent of probability and statistics.

There is also a passage toward the end of the *Topics*—quoted and commented on in Chapter 5, section 3—where Aristotle explicitly recognized a type of argument that is very similar to, or even perhaps identical to, the modern *argumentum ad populum*. In this passage, Aristotle gave advice on how the proponent of an argument can use generally accepted or customary opinion to allay an opponent's doubts about whether to challenge her (the proponent's) argument in a dialectical exchange. But this particular passage has not been previously noted or commented on in the historical study of the development of informal fallacies, as far as I know. There is no known connection between this passage in Aristotle and the later emergence of the *argumentum ad populum* as an informal fallacy in the modern logic textbooks.

But the more immediate problem is this: How did the *ad populum* as a fallacy get into the standard treatment of fallacies in the modern logic textbooks? The answer is that it seems to have come from Antoine Arnauld's *Port-Royal Logic* (also called *The Art of Thinking*), and from there found its way into Isaac Watts's textbook *Logick* (1772), where it got the name *argumentum ad populum*.

In part 3 of *The Art of Thinking* (1662), Arnauld has a long chapter (chapter 20), entitled "Concerning Faulty Arguments Advanced in Public Life and Everyday Affairs." Here Arnauld cites a particular sophism under the general heading of sophisms of authority and manner. He gives no name to this sophism, but it is clear that his description of it corresponds to a leading conception of the *argumentum ad populum* in the textbook treatments.

> Men follow the ridiculous procedure of believing a thing true according to the number of witnesses to its truth. A contemporary

author has wisely pointed out that in difficult matters that are left to the province of reason, it is more likely that an individual will discover the truth than that many will. The following is not a valid inference: The majority hold this opinion; therefore, it is the truest. Men are far too often persuaded by inessential characteristics having nothing to do with the position's truth. (1964, 287)

Arnauld even expresses the pattern or form of this type of argument quite clearly: the majority hold opinion *O*; therefore *O* is the truest opinion (among the available alternatives, presumably). This form of argument corresponds to the type of *ad populum* frequently cited in the standard treatment of the modern textbooks, called the "bandwagon" type of *ad populum* argument.[2]

In Watts's *Logick*, there is a section (5) in chapter 2 of part 3, where Watts lists a number of *ad* fallacies, including *ad judicium, ad verecundiam, ad hominem,* and *ad ignorantiam*. This group of four arguments *ad* originates from the account in John Locke's *An Essay Concerning Human Understanding* (1690) (quoted in Hamblin [1970, 159–60]). Locke is credited by Hamblin with introducing the *ad verecundiam* and *ad ignorantiam* types of arguments, although the *ad hominem* had previously been known. What is important here, however, is that Locke did not have the *argumentum ad populum* on his list. It is interesting to see Watts's inclusion of the following item just at the end of his own list.

> I add finally, When an Argument is borrowed from any Topics which are suited to engage the Inclinations and Passions of the Hearers on the Side of the Speaker, rather than to convince the Judgment, this is *Argumentum ad Passiones*, an Address to the Passions; or if it be made publickly, it is called ad populum, or an *Appeal to the People*. (1772, 311)

---

2. Arnauld (1662; 1964) also cites a form of "delusion" that corresponds fairly well to the subtype of *ad populum* cited in several textbooks as "appeal to snobbery," when he writes of errors of deference to those of high birth (p. 289):

> Obsequiousness and flattery account for much of the approbation bestowed on the words and actions of men of rank; but some of this approbation is prompted by a certain outward grace, a noble, free, and natural bearing, inimitable by those of lower birth. Many approve of whatever is said or done by the great. The outward pomp surrounding grandeur always commands attention and makes some impression even on the best of minds.

This passage is the first mention, to my knowledge, of the *argumentum ad populum*, by that name.[3]

Richard Whately (1870, 142) has a passage in his *Elements of Logic* (book 3, section 16) where he refers to the set of *ad* arguments derived from Locke's account (142).

> There are certain kinds of argument recounted and named by Logical writers, which we should by no means universally call Fallacies; but which *when unfairly* used, and *so far as they are* fallacious, may very well be referred to the present head; such as the "*argumentum ad hominem*," ["or personal argument,"] "*argumentum ad verecundiam*," "*argumentum ad populum*," &c. all of them regarded as contradistinguished from "*argumentum ad rem*;" or, according to others (meaning probably the very same thing) "*ad judicium.*" These have all been described in the lax and popular language before alluded to, but not scientifically: the "*argumentum ad hominem*," they say, "is addressed to the peculiar circumstances, character, avowed opinions, or past conduct of the individual, and therefore has a reference to him only, and does not bear directly and absolutely on the real question, as the '*argumentum ad rem*' does:" in like manner, the "*argumentum ad verecundiam*" is described as an appeal to our reverence for some respected authority, some venerable institution, &c. and the "*argumentum ad populum*," as an appeal to the prejudices, passions, &c. of the multitude; and so of the rest. Along with these is usually enumerated "*argumentum ad ignorantiam*," which is here omitted, as being evidently nothing more than the employment of *some* kind of Fallacy, in the widest sense of that word, towards such as are likely to be deceived by it.

Locke did not describe these different types of *ad* arguments as fallacious. As Hamblin put it, "Locke does not clearly condemn any of the argument-types, but stands poised between acceptance and disapproval" (1970, 161). So, it is interesting to see Whately state very carefully here that these arguments should "by no means" be "universally" called fallacies but only when they are "unfairly used." This care may stem from Whately's expertise in the field of rhetoric, and

---

3. The author would like to thank Robert Binkley for drawing my attention to this passage in Watts's *Logick*, on October 2, 1995, in response to a request for information on the ARGTHRY network.

from his analysis of the concept of presumption. Whately was in an unusually good position among logic textbook writers to be aware of the uses of these *ad* arguments in everyday presumptive reasoning in nonfallacious inferences.

In his *Elements of Rhetoric*, Whately noted, "Aristotle, and many other writers, have spoken of appeals to the passions as an unfair mode of influencing the hearers." But he adds, "Aristotle by no means overlooked the necessity with a view to Persuasion" of calling into action passions that may properly influence the will (1863, 114). Note that in the passage in the *Elements of Logic* quoted above, Whately also specifically describes the *ad populum* as "appeal to the prejudices, passions, &c of the multitude," which could suggest either Arnauld or Watts as the source of his idea of it. However, the word "passions" and the absence of any mention of the form of argument cited in Arnauld, suggests that Whately's conception of the *ad populum* is closer to that of Watts.

But what were really the historical connections, if any? Did Watts really get the *ad populum* type of argument from Arnauld's treatment of sophisms? One factor suggesting he may not have is that Watts seems to have a different idea of it from that of Arnauld. Arnauld's version of the *ad populum* fallacy was the bandwagon type of argument (arguing from what the majority believe). Watts's notion of the *argumentum ad populum* is one of appeal to the passions (*argumentum ad passiones*), suggesting more the "mob appeal" or "emotional appeal to the crowd" as the basic idea.

This difference of basic conceptions suggests a hypothesis of twin roots of the *ad populum* as a way of accounting for how the *ad populum* got into the standard treatment of the *ad populum* fallacy in modern textbooks. As will be shown in the subsequent survey of the standard treatment, there is definitely a dual approach running through the treatments of this fallacy, culminating especially in some of the later treatments.

2. Early Modern Textbooks

W. Stanley Jevons has only a short paragraph on the *argumentum ad populum*, in which he characterizes as a species of the more general fallacy of irrelevant conclusion. According to Jevons, the fallacy of irrelevant conclusion (also called *ignoratio elenchi*, or ignorance of refutation) is "arguing to the wrong point, or proving one thing in such a manner that it is supposed to be something else that is proved" (1878, 178). *Argumentum ad populum* is then characterized as a special subtype of the fallacy of irrelevant conclusion.

> The *argumentum ad populum* is another form of Irrelevant Conclusion, and consists in addressing arguments to a body of people calculated to excite their feelings and prevent them from forming a dispassionate judgment upon the matter in hand. It is the great weapon of rhetoricians and demagogues. (179)

The reference to "rhetoricians and demagogues," as well as a reference to "long harangues" in connection with the fallacy of irrelevant conclusion suggests a context of an emotional speech to a crowd (178). The *ad populum* fallacy seems to be characterized by the contrast between the exciting of feelings in such a body of people and the need for "dispassionate judgment."

While Jevons treats the *argumentum ad populum* as inherently fallacious, James McCosh (1879) treats this type of argument as allowable (reasonable) in some cases. McCosh sees it as only fallacious or wrong in some cases, as contrasted with Jevons, who defines it as a species of arguing to the wrong point. McCosh also defines the *ad populum* in a somewhat different way from Jevons.

> *Argumentum ad Populum*, or an appeal to principles cherished by the great body of the people. It is allowable only when the principles are right and proper in themselves, and are conscientiously entertained by those who advocate them. It is not legitimate when they are wrong in themselves, or when he who argues them is doing so hypocritically. It will commonly happen in the end that such a deceitful use of the argument will turn against the person employing it. In no case is it allowable to employ this argument to stir up a malignant spirit or violent acts. (1879, 188)

McCosh defines the *ad populum* argument as "an appeal to principles cherished by the great body of the people," suggesting that it could be reasonable, and that it does not have to be characterized by its illegitimate uses in the exciting of feelings in a mob or massed group. However, by mentioning the stirring up of violent acts, he indicates an awareness of the potential for such a misuse.

John Veitch, like Jevons, treats the *ad populum* as an inherently fallacious type of argument, but diagnoses the error differently. According to Veitch, the *fallacia ad populum* is the "appeal to the passions, prejudices, interests of a mob, sect, or political party, in virtue of which they are led to accept an unsifted or unproved conclusion." Veitch's account is similar to Jevons's in his mentioning passions and the mob setting, but his classification of the type of argument is different. He sees the *ad populum* as a subspecies of the argument from ignorance (*argumentum ad ignorantiam*), where one person tries to exploit the ignorance of another by arguing, "Here is my opinion. Here is my argument. If you admit you can't refute the argument, then you must accept the conclusion" (1885, 547). This account of the argument from ignorance derives from Locke's analysis of the *argumentum ad ignorantiam*.

Like the accounts of Jevons, McCosh and Veitch, James Hyslop's is very brief.

> The *argumentum ad populum* is an appeal to public opinion, or to the passions and prejudices of the people rather than to their intelligence. Thus, if the issue be the justice of protection or free trade, we may appeal to the interests and political passions of men rather than to reason and fact. (1899, 175)

This description of the *ad populum* attributes the fallaciousness of an appeal to "interests and political passions" as opposed to appeal to "reason and fact." We see here the contrast between passion and reason also present in Jevons's treatment, and common to many accounts of the *ad populum*. But Hyslop makes no further attempt to diagnose or analyze the precise nature of the error. He simply defines the *ad populum* type of argument as a fallacious appeal to passions and prejudices.

James E. Creighton takes pretty much the same approach, devoting only one sentence to the *ad populum*.

> The *argumentum ad populum* is an argument addressed to the feelings, passions, and prejudices of people rather than an unbiased discussion addressed to the intellect. (1904, 169)

The key word "unbiased" is notable, as well as the contrast cited between "passions and prejudices" on the one hand, and "intellect" on the other.

John G. Hibben gives an equally brief account of the *ad populum*, defining it as a fallacy, in a manner quite comparable to that of Creighton.

> *Argumentum ad populum*.—This is the fallacy of appealing to the passion or prejudice of an audience, rather than to their reason. It is essentially the argument of the demagogue. (1906, 163)

W. R. Boyce Gibson also defines *argumentum ad populum* as inherently fallacious, diagnosing the fallacy like Jevons, as a failure of relevance, but stressing the aspect of "passions" like Creighton and Hyslop. Gibson defines the *argumentum ad populum* (or *argumentum ad passiones*) as an argument that is "irrelevant" because "it is not the judgment that is convinced, but the inclinations and passions" (1908, 288).

Carveth Read also classifies the *ad populum* as a fallacy of relevance but, like McCosh, does not see this type of argument as always being fallacious. Read characterizes *argumentum ad populum* by the sentence: "This measure is favorable to such or such a class; let them vote for it." But then he adds: "An appeal to private greed, however base, is not fallacious, as long as the interest of the class is not *fraudulently* substituted for the good of the nation." (1920, 399). In other words, Read makes the point that appeal to financial or class interests can be relevant in some arguments. It follows that the *ad populum* type of argument is not fallacious in all cases.

Among these early accounts, there are disagreements on how exactly to define the *argumentum ad populum* and whether it is inherently fallacious or not. Also, there are differences of opinion on what is the precise nature of the fallacy. There seems to be wide agreement that this type of argument involves an appeal to passions or emotions, and that this aspect is important to understanding the fallacy. There is also broad agreement—McCosh and Read excepted—that this type of argument, if not inherently wrong, at least has a strong tendency to be used wrongly.

3. The Middle Period: 1935–1959

The early accounts of the *ad populum* as a fallacy set the tone for subsequent accounts, as logic textbooks after 1935 started to devote a little more space to the fallacies. However, during this second period of our study, most of the textbook accounts of the *ad populum* remained brief (generally one paragraph).

A few of the textbooks began to treat the *ad populum* at greater length, introducing a greater variety of examples and elaboration. The accounts of this period, however, uniformly treat the *ad populum* as a fallacious type of argument. Accounts of why it is deemed fallacious differ significantly, but the majority continue to classify it as a failure of relevance. Many of these textbooks draw a sharp contrast between emotion and reason, following the trend already well established by Jevons (1878), Veitch (1885) Hyslop (1899), Creighton (1904), Hibben (1906) and Gibson (1908). And the majority of this second wave of texts identify *ad populum* as a mob appeal device of the demagogue or propagandist, following Jevons and Hibben.

Alburey Castell follows the line of the previous texts by treating the *ad populum* as a species of the more general fallacy he calls irrelevant evidence, which means the tactic of presenting facts as "evidence or grounds" for a proposition that are "actually irrelevant to" that proposition (1935, 22). *Ad populum* is specifically "an appeal to popular feelings, popular sentiments, popular prejudices" (24), that should take the form of an appeal to the relevant facts but does not. A much-followed innovation (already quoted as Case 2.7), introduced by Castell, was a lengthy case study, quoting from Shakespeare's *Julius Caesar* the passage where Mark Antony addresses the citizens gathered around the coffin containing Caesar's body (25–30). Antony turns the crowd against Brutus by making him appear to be the leading culprit, but, as Castell stresses, nothing in the emotional speech is really relevant to this claim.

William Werkmeister also describes *ad populum* as a type of argument that is inherently fallacious because it is an emotional appeal that fails to argue to the point at issue.

> *Argument ad Populum.*—This argument is actually an emotional appeal addressed to the "gallery." Instead of arguing to the point at issue, one appeals to the passions and prejudices of the populace. Instead of presenting empirical evidence and logical argument, one attempts to win the masses by appealing to their emotions. During political campaigns such appeals are made quite frequently. Propagandists of all types employ them. (1948, 57–58)

Although Werkmeister does not use the term "relevant" above, it is clear that he, like Castell, sees the *ad populum* fallacy as a failure of relevance. And, in fact, he classifies the *ad populum* under the general heading of "irrelevant evidence" (56).

Giving a comparable account of the *ad populum*, Lionel Ruby also cites the case of Mark Antony's speech as his example of this fallacy.

> [One form of appeal to emotion is] the appeal is to the emotions of other persons, when a speaker substitutes emotional appeals for evidence. In traditional logic this is called the "Argumentum ad Populum," the appeal to the people, or, in less flattering terms, to the mob. The masses of men are often moved by emotion rather

than by reason. Speakers inflame crowds of people with emotionally loaded language, rabble-rousing and prejudiced appeals, by spellbinding, pulling the heart strings, and appeals to popular sentiment. But the truth is not always one with our emotions. (1950, 130)

This idea of mob appeal, or "masses of men" being "inflamed" by "emotionally loaded language" is well expressed here.

The same pattern is followed by Romane Clark and Paul Welsh, who include *ad populum*, along with several other *ad* fallacies, as species of "irrelevant conclusion." The *ad populum* is specifically defined as "demagogic appeal to stereotyped sentiment," frequently used in political speeches, where "all support the rightness of home and motherhood" (1962, 141).

Stuart Chase takes much the same approach of describing the *argumentum ad populum* as a fallacy: "The fallacy is an attempt to win an argument by an appeal to the crowd, the mass, the mob, rather than by reason." Chase classifies the *ad populum* as a type of "propaganda" that appeals emotionally to the "popular credos, myths, and systems of belief" of a "subgroup" within a society (1956, 109). Chase gives a speech of William Jennings Bryan as an example.

Robert Latta and Alexander MacBeath strongly describe *ad populum* as a fallacious type of argument, defining it as "appealing to people's passions and prejudices rather than to their intelligence" (1956, 380). Explicit here is a strong contrast between reason and emotion.

Bernard Huppé and Jack Kaminsky stress the mob appeal aspect of the *ad populum*, citing the "stirring up" of "strong emotions" by "demagogues," or even "lynch mobs" (1957, 198). However, they also cite another key aspect of the *ad populum* or "appeal to the people" argument: the speaker attempts to win over the group he himself is addressing by identifying with them, e.g., depicting himself as "one of the boys," as a fellow American, or as a "fellow worker" (197). This aspect could be called empathic identification with an audience, or the common-folks appeal.

John Blyth takes a somewhat different approach to defining the *ad populum*, seeing it as the fallacy of appealing to the bias or prejudice of an audience. "Since we are equipped with many prejudices and biases, there are many ways in which a speaker may appeal to our prejudices" (1957, 38). Blyth specifically mentions flattery as a method of making such an appeal for the purpose of cultivating a favorable attitude.

Case 3.1   For instance, a real-estate salesman might say to a prospective customer, "A man of your high standing in the community cannot afford to live in a cheap neighborhood." A man taken in by such flattery would be inclined to buy a much more expensive house than he could afford.

The context of the sales pitch makes this case interesting, and also the fact that the argument could be described as an appeal to snobbery.

The account of the *argumentum ad populum*, translated as "popular passions," given in the influential textbook by W. Ward Fearnside and William B. Holther is a typical "mob-appeal" characterization.

> The man who conjures with racial or religious hatred, the agitator who stirs passions by pointing to the evils of colonial government without acknowledging any of its accomplishments, the demagogue who resorts to name calling and in this country brands proposals which he does not like as "communist" or "fascist" or in the USSR similarly applies the word "capitalist"—all these are either relying on popular passion or invoking the self-interest of the crowd. (1959, 95)

Fearnside and Holther cite the Mark Antony case as their first example, describing it as an argument that "says nothing about the issue" (95). They classify the *ad populum* under the heading of "stirring up prejudice" (94), describing it as an appeal to the strong bias an audience has toward its own interests.

Edith Schipper and Edward Schuh define the *argumentum ad populum*, which they translate as "appeal to the crowd," as inherently fallacious.

> When the premises of an argument contain an appeal to popular attitudes or feelings in order to support the truth of some unrelated conclusion, that argument is said to commit the fallacy of "appeal to the crowd." (1959, 34)

A common means of "arousing popular enthusiasms or prejudices," according to their account, is "the propagandist's device of using emotionally toned words," This suggestion, interestingly, links the *ad populum* to the expressive function of connotation in language, which, Schipper and Schuh tell us, is "irrelevant" to the "informational content" of an argument (35).

These remarks indicate a condemnation of emotion in argument typical of many of the textbook accounts of the *ad populum*, set in place during the early period and continued through this next period. In emphasizing the appeal to "passion" and "prejudice" in a crowd situation, and diagnosing the failure as one of irrelevance, these textbooks are building on the basic framework put in place by the earlier texts.

4. Multiplicity of Types: 1961–1968

The next group of textbook treatments of the *ad populum* fallacy covers the period from 1961 to 1968. These textbooks continue (with only one exception) to treat the *argumentum ad populum* as inherently fallacious. And even the exception (seen below) concedes only that "rarely if ever" is this type of argument sufficient to establish any conclusion. These textbooks continue to treat the *ad populum* along the lines of the previous ones in general spirit and outline, stressing the emotional appeal aspect, the appeal to prejudice, the mob-appeal idea, and the diagnosis of the fallacy as a failure of relevance.

The new direction taken in this group of treatments is toward a proliferation of multiple types of *ad populum* arguments. Aspects implicit in the prior treatments are emphasized and brought out as distinctive types of *ad populum* appeals and even given different names as fallacies. The account of the *ad populum* given by Robert Kreyche emphasizes the "mob-appeal" aspect. Kreyche describes the *ad populum* as an attempt by a speaker to "sell a cause" to the people by "addressing himself to their prejudices [and] their emotions," in a "rabble-rousing" speech that plays up to "the instincts of the mob." This type of argument is classified as "ignoring the issue" (1961, 278).

A comparable account is given by John Mourant, who describes the fallacy as "an appeal to popular passion or prejudice," as used by "demagogues and politicians" to "sway the sentiments of a crowd," instead of using rational argument (1963, 192).

Quite a different approach is taken by Philip Wheelwright, who classifies *ad populum* under the heading of "appeal to prestige" (1962, 329). It seems that the *ad populum* fallacy Kreyche and Mourant have in mind is quite a different one from that of Wheelwright.

Nicholas Rescher explains this duality of the *ad populum*, however, by indicating how the prestige type of argument may be related to the mob-appeal type. Rescher defines the *ad populum* generally as "an argument that seeks to secure acceptance of its conclusion by appealing to the passions or prejudices of a group of people" (1964, 79). Rescher describes the mob-appeal variant by citing "speeches of rabble-rousing orators," and Mark Antony's funeral speech in particular. But then he describes another variant. "On the other hand, an *argumentum ad populum* may appeal not to the attitudes of '*the* crowd,' but to those of '*our* crowd,' substituting snob appeal for mob appeal." Rescher gives the following example.

Case 3.2   The hats made by Stovepipe and Co. must be the best, since their services are widely used by the nobility and gentry, and this establishment is hatter "by appointment to His Majesty, the King." (80)

Citing some comparable kinds of examples, Rescher adds, "Sales people who sell clothes to women on the recommendation that "it's exclusive," and to men by saying, "Everybody's wearing it," are using complementary versions of the same *argumentum ad populum*." This treatment suggests that the mob-appeal and snob-appeal types of *ad populum* are variants of a more general type that appeals to "the passions or prejudices of a group of people."

The most popular, and probably the most influential logic textbook for many years has been Irving M. Copi's *Introduction to Logic* (1972). The first edition appeared in 1953, and the seventh edition in 1986. The eighth and ninth editions, co-authored with Carl Cohen, appeared in 1990 and 1994. The one-page section on the *ad populum* fallacy has remained the same in subsequent editions. The *ad populum* fallacy is defined as "the attempt to win popular assent to a conclusion by arousing the feelings and enthusiasms of the multitude" (1972, 79). Copi uses much the same type of approach as Rescher, first describing the mob-appeal variant (citing the Mark Antony case), and then going on to something comparable to the snob-appeal variant.

What is remarkable about Copi's account of the *ad populum* is that he blasts commercial advertisements for committing this fallacy in a passage that is poetically memorable, and well worth quoting in full.

> It is to the huckster, the ballyhoo artist, the twentieth-century advertiser that we may look to see the *argumentum ad populum* elevated almost to the status of a fine art. Here every attempt is made to set up associations between the product being advertised and objects of which we can be expected to approve strongly. To eat a certain brand of processed cereal is proclaimed a patriotic duty. To bathe with a certain brand of soap is described as a thrilling experience. Strains of

symphonic music precede and follow the mention of a certain dentifrice on the radio and television programs sponsored by its manufacturer. In pictorial advertisements, the people using the products advertised are always pictured as wearing the kind of clothing and living in the kind of houses calculated to arouse the approval and admiration of the average consumer. The young men pictured as delightedly using the products are clear-eyed and broad-shouldered, the older men are invariably "of distinction." The women are all slim and lovely, either very well dressed or hardly dressed at all. Whether you are interested in economical transportation or in high-speed driving, you will be assured by each automobile manufacturer that his product is "best," and he will "prove" his assertion by displaying his car surrounded by pretty girls. Advertisers "glamorize" their products and sell us daydreams and delusions of grandeur with every package of pink pills or garbage disposal unit. (79–80)

Logic textbook sections on the fallacies tend to be pretty hard on advertisers, but this passage is a critical blast that approaches satire, making the advertisements appear to be logically defective and deceptive, on the grounds that they do not prove what they assert. One wonders here, however, whether the purpose of the advertisement is to "prove" anything. Questions are raised here on what is "relevant" in commercial ads.

Thomas Vernon and Lowell Nissen make a radical departure from previous treatments of the *argumentum ad populum*. Something they call "the bandwagon fallacy" appears to be similar to the *argumentum ad populum*, but is not quite the same type of argument described by the prior textbooks we have examined. Interestingly, Vernon and Nissen even offer a form or "pattern" of the argument.

> The bandwagon fallacy consists in urging the acceptance or rejection of a proposal on the ground that the majority is doing so.
>
> The general pattern followed by this type of argument is
>
> *The majority believes p (or does x).*
> ———————————————
> *p is true (or x should be done).*
>
> Rarely, if ever, is the fact that the majority believes or does *p* or *x* sufficient to establish any conclusion beyond the conclusion that

the majority does as claimed. However, few people like to think of themselves as part of a minority, as "oddballs." Most of us are therefore vulnerable to the type of argument that leaves us with the feeling that we are pariahs if we do not agree with the writer or speaker, however good our own reasoning may be. (1968, 148)

This form of argument, which could perhaps be called the bandwagon argument, as Vernon and Nissen suggest, could also be called *argument from popular opinion* (or *argument from popularity*, or *argument from popular belief*). It is not quite the same thing as the mob-appeal argument or the snob-appeal argument, although it does seem to be related to these two versions of *ad populum*. It corresponds to the type of argument cited by Arnauld (1964), noted in section 1 above.

Copi also cites this type of argument.

> Here, if they are trying to prove that their products adequately serve their ostensible functions, their procedures are glorified examples of the *argumentum ad populum*. Besides the "snob appeal" already referred to, we may include under this heading the familiar "bandwagon argument." The campaigning politician "argues" that he should receive our votes because "everybody" is voting that way. We are told that such and such a breakfast food, or cigarette, or motor car is "best" because it is America's largest seller. A certain belief "must be true" because "everyone knows it." But popular acceptance of a policy does not prove it to be wise; widespread use of certain products does not prove them to be satisfactory; general assent to a claim does not prove it to be true. To argue in this way is to commit the *ad populum fallacy*. (1972, 80)

At this point then, three different (although related) types of *ad populum* argument seem to be emerging—the bandwagon, the mob-appeal, and the snob-appeal arguments.

This multiplicity is made explicit in the treatment by William Kilgore, who cites three distinct fallacies of this general kind under the heading of "fallacies of misuse of appeal to emotions." The "bandwagon fallacy" is defined as "following the crowd and doing as they do" instead of appealing to "adequate evidence" to justify a conclusion (1968, 47–49). Two examples are given.

Case 3.3   You ought to learn the bugaloo, as everyone bugaloos, and you will be left out if you don't.

Case 3.4   You ought to buy a small European sports car as all members of the smart crowd now own one of these cars.

The first case does resemble the pattern called the bandwagon fallacy by Nissen and Vernon, but it also has an additional element appealed to, namely, exclusion from a group. The second case looks more like appeal to snobbery, perhaps combined with an element of the bandwagon fallacy (indicated by the word "all").

The second fallacy cited by Kilgore of this group is "the common-folks appeal," defined as the attempt to "secure acceptance of a conclusion by the speaker's identification with the everyday concerns and feelings of an audience rather than on the basis of adequate evidence" (49). Kilgore gives the following example:

Case 3.5   I'm sure you will recognize that I am more competent than my opponent. When I was in high school I had to get up at four-thirty every morning to deliver papers. In college I was barely able to make C's and had to do janitorial work in order to make ends meet to put myself through school. Therefore, I would make a better congressman.

This common-folks type of argument seems different from the mob-appeal type of *ad populum*, but the third type cited by Kilgore, called "appeal to the gallery," seems closer to the mob-appeal type. According to Kilgore, *appeal to the gallery* "seeks acceptance of a point of view by an emotional reaffirmation of a speaker's support of values, traditions, interests, prejudices, or provincial concerns shared widely by members of an audience" (49). This account seems to cover a lot of territory, but Kilgore gives an example.

Case 3.6   A speaker at a political rally might try to secure acceptance of his program not by offering evidence of its support, but by appealing to the prejudices against "big business" or "vested interests" or "outside groups."

This type of argument could certainly have elements of mob appeal, but what Kilgore seems more to be referring to is the kind of case where a speaker targets on the particular values, positions, or prejudices of the group he is addressing (in place of giving evidence that would really support his argument).

Both appeal to the gallery and the common-folks appeal seem to be different from the mob-appeal, snob-appeal, or bandwagon arguments.

5. Cracks in the Surface

The treatment of the following five years followed broadly along in the same pattern, but more cracks in the surface came to be revealed in a view of the *ad populum* that has now been stretched to cover different things. Some accounts conflict with others, or appear to be defining a different type of argument (or fallacy). Some straddle the border of two or more of the types of *ad populum* appeals identified by the prior treatments. Some suggest connections with other types of arguments that have traditionally been classified under names of fallacies other than *ad populum*.

John Kozy Jr. (1974) even challenges the assumption that *ad populum* arguments are fallacious, arguing that, in many cases, they can be reasonable arguments. This disquieting possibility had been mentioned by a small minority in the early textbook treatments, as noted in section 2. But in the modern books prior to 1974, it had been ignored.

Albert Frye and Albert Levi give a classic account of the mob appeal version of the *ad populum*, even translating *argumentum ad populum* as "appeal to the mob." They characterize the fallacy as "an address to the *mob* calculated to arouse its passions . . . to act as the nonrational cause of belief," citing "rabble-rousing" orators (1969, 221). Mark Antony's speech is their example. Alex Michalos, who calls *ad populum* the fallacy of popular sentiments, treats it as a distinctly different type of argument, more like a common-folks appeal, but his version shares the aspect of feelings or emotions with the version of Frye and Levi.

> *Popular Sentiments.* The fallacy of appealing to popular sentiments (*argumentum ad populum*; i.e., to the people) is committed when, in the absence of a plausible argument for some view, the *feelings* or *attitudes* of a group of people are appealed to to win acceptance. Suppose, for example, that a prosecutor is unable to prove that a defendant is guilty of treason. He reminds the jury that anyone who would aid or comfort an enemy of his own country ought to be severely punished; that anyone who would sell out his own people

> belongs behind bars; that treason is a sin against God and country; that a jury which would acquit such a man would surely face the judgment of their consciences; etc. By skillfully tugging at the emotional heartstrings of the jury and by appealing to the *sentiments* of the people, the prosecutor may be able to have his view accepted. (1969, 372)

One might ask here: What is wrong with appealing to the attitudes or feelings of a group of people to win acceptance for your view? The answer that Frye and Levi give, along with Michalos and many of the other authors of textbooks, is that such an argument is a fallacious *ad populum* when it is irrelevant to the proposition at issue. Or, as Michalos puts it, the fallacy occurs when the emotional appeal is made in the absence of a plausible argument for the view in question.

The key difference between the accounts of Frye and Levi and that of Michalos is that the latter's idea of the *ad populum* is broader. It could include the mob-appeal type of argument cited by Frye and Levi but it does not require "rabble-rousing" arousing of passions. The appeal to the feelings or attitudes of the group could be cool and calculated, in some instances. Indeed, the example given by Michalos suggests more of a moral appeal to conscience than a rousing mob appeal.

A fallacy cited by David Fisher called "the fallacy of the prevalent proof," is described as a species of "deference to popular opinion" (1970, 51, 52). It seems to fall into the area of the *argumentum ad populum*, as Fisher suggests.

Case 3.7   A historian has written, for example, "While the role of dope in damping social unrest in early industrial England has not been extensively investigated, every historian of the period knows that it was common practice at the time for working mothers to start the habit in the cradle by dosing their hungry babies on laudanum ('mother's blessing,' it was called)." This statement is often made, and widely believed. But it has never, to my knowledge, been established by empirical evidence. The reader should note the hyperbole in the first sentence. When an historian asserts that "X has not been extensively investigated," he sometimes means, "I have not investigated X at all."

This case does seem to be an instance of the bandwagon type of *ad populum* because the premise states that *every* historian of the period knows the alleged fact. However, one has to be careful in classifying the argument in this case, as well as comparable cases, because it is, at least partly, based on an appeal to expert opinion. Here we seem to have a combination of *argumentum ad populum* with *argumentum ad verecundiam*, or appeal to expert opinion (or authority, more generally).

Henry Byerly translates *argumentum ad populum* as "appeal to the gallery." By stressing the speaker's support of the values shared by the audience, his account comes quite close to that of Kilgore's category of appeal to the gallery.

> We include under this fallacy a variety of vague appeals to loyalties, fears, and hopes of the audience. Appeals to super-patriotism, sympathy for the underdog, virtue, motherhood, and progress are not uncommon in political speeches. The following example makes appeals that may be of little relevance in deciding the worthiness of the candidate to hold public office. (1973, 50)

This account of appeal to the gallery is distinctive, however, in that there is an element in it of what is often called "glittering generalities." The appeals cited by Byerly are vague and of little relevance in proving anything, but they strike a positive note with the audience (perhaps partly because they are abstract and general). The appeal is to shared principles (between the speaker and the audience), but what these principles amount to or require in the specific case at issue may be unclear.

Kozy defines *argumentum ad populum*, or "appeal to the people" (1974, 212), by using a general form or pattern of argument similar to the form of the "bandwagon fallacy" represented by Vernon and Nissen: "Because many or most people believe A, A must be true" (1968, 148). Recall that Vernon and Nissen cited as premise, "The majority believes A." Both proposals for the form of argument are stated in terms of "belief." However, the most radical and interesting development in Kozy's treatment of the *ad populum* is that he does not define it as fallacious, or even presume that it is always a fallacious type of argument. Instead, he proposes that some *ad populum* arguments are fallacies, while others are "valid," and still others are "of questionable validity" (1974, 212). As his example of the fallacious category, Kozy cites the following case (211).

Case 3.8   As time goes on, fewer and fewer Americans believe that capital punishment is morally acceptable; therefore, capital punishment is immoral.

Kozy's comment on this case is that the proper conclusion is only "more and more Americans believe that capital punishment is immoral."

As his example of the "valid" *ad populum* argument, Kozy cites the following case (211):

Case 3.9   A Democrat should be president because a majority of people in states with a majority of electoral votes believed that he should and so voted.

As his example of an *ad populum* argument of questionable validity, Kozy cites an argument based on the Mark Antony case (212).

Case 3.10   Mark Antony, in his funeral oration, made many people believe that Caesar was wrongly assassinated; so his assassination was wrong.

Interestingly, Kozy's evaluation of this case is expressed in the following comment.

> *Comment* The validity of this argument is questionable, because if the people believed that his assassination was wrong, it may very well have been wrong, for whether a ruler is fit to rule may very well depend on what people believe. This point can at least be argued.

Whatever we think of this comment as an evaluation of the argument in Case 3.10, the general point made that *ad populum* arguments can be weak (questionable, insufficiently supported) without being fallacious, is fascinating. Not only does it directly contravene the treatments of nearly all the prior texts (with the few exceptions noted), but it suggests that the policy of routinely dismissing *ad populum* arguments as fallacious could be an extremely simplistic way of evaluating them.

6. Broadening of the *Ad Populum*

The next two textbooks have both been popular and influential. Their impact on the treatment of the *ad populum* was to broaden the scope of this general type of argument considerably but in two different ways. S. Morris Engel (1976) offered quite a number of different kinds of examples, all treated under the heading of "the fallacy of mob appeal," citing seven different kinds of grounds for evaluating such arguments as fallacious. This citing of such a multiplicity of faults could be described as a kind of shotgun effect.

T. Edward Damer's approach was, on the one hand, to broaden the basic fallacy he called "appeal to the gallery" by citing some new subspecies of it, while at the same time adding several other fallacies under different names and classifications that tend to plausibly fall under the general heading of *ad populum* set into place by prior texts (1980; 1987).

Engel is pretty hard on the *argumentum ad populum*, calling it the "fallacy of mob appeal," a type of argument he castigates on numerous grounds.

> The *fallacy of mob appeal* is an argument in which an appeal is made to emotions, especially to powerful feelings that can sway people in large crowds. Also called *appeal to the masses*, this fallacy invites people's unthinking acceptance of ideas which are presented in a strong, theatrical manner. Mob appeals are often said to appeal to our lowest instincts, including violence. The language of such fallacious appeals tends to be strongly biased, making use of many of the linguistic fallacies we have examined previously in this book. Indeed, most instances of mob appeal incorporate other fallacies, melding them together into an argument that rests primarily on appeal to an emotional, rather than a reasoned, response. In so doing, such arguments commit a fallacy of irrelevance because they fail to address the point at issue, choosing instead to steer us toward a conclusion by means of passion rather than reason. (1976, 113–14)

Here, numerous grounds are given for condemning mob-appeal arguments as fallacious. They (1) appeal to "powerful feelings" that (2) invite "people's unthinking acceptance" by (3) appealing to "our lowest instincts," and (4) tend to be "biased," (5) incorporating numerous other fallacies, melding them into an argument that (6) depends on "an emotional rather than a reasoned response," and (7) thereby commit a fallacy of irrelevance. This heterogeneous account of *ad populum* allows Engel to condemn a broad and variable collection of examples (including the Bryan speech and the usual Mark Antony speech) as fallacious (115–21).

Damer (1980; 1987) also expands the *ad populum* argument beyond prior treatments. Damer includes various negative, as well as positive *ad populum* appeals, under the heading of the fallacy of "appeal to the gallery."

> The "gallery" to which an appeal is made refers to the undiscriminating public, which is often easily swayed through a manipulation of their strong feelings. Another name for this fallacy might be appeal to strong or popular sentiments or appeal to the crowd. Some of the strong emotions to which appeals are often made are fear, ethnic and social superiority, greed, and shame. Positive sentiments that are often exploited are familial concerns, patriotism, national security, group loyalty, and military superiority. Popular feelings against such groups as labor unions, certain religious or political associations, homosexuals, or even radical college students have also been manipulated as a means of persuasion. The arguer's choice of which sentiment to exploit is, of course, determined by the constituency of the gallery. (1980, 89)

Under this broad conception of the appeal to the gallery, Damer cites four subspecies of "distinctive types" that "deserve special attention" (89–90).

The first subtype cited is *appeal to flattery*, illustrated by the following example.

Case 3.11   Because you are a mature audience of highly educated professionals, I'm sure that you can see clearly the merit of my proposal.

This argument is said to be fallacious because "excessive praise" is "used as a substitute for evidence."

The second subtype is *appeal to shame*, which seeks to solicit a feeling of guilt from a person or group for holding an unpopular opinion or for acting in a particular way, without demonstrating why guilt would be warranted. Interestingly, this is a negative type of argument or attack that would more likely be treated traditionally under the category of *ad hominem* (personal attack) or a subspecies called "guilt by association."

The third subtype cited by Damer, "involves the manipulation of negative feelings, by pointing out that the opposing view is held by people or groups with negative prestige." Here again, *ad populum* is linked with prestige (see the account of Wheelwright 1962, in section 4), but this time it is negative prestige that is cited. One might wonder what kind of argument Damer exactly has in mind here, but fortunately, he offers an example.

Case 3.12   PROFESSOR SMITH: You are going to vote with *us* on this issue at next week's faculty meeting, aren't you?

PROFESSOR JACKSON: No, I really don't think it is a very good idea.
PROFESSOR SMITH: Really? Well, neither does Professor Hart or Professor Carter. They're voting against us too.

According to Damer, Professor Smith's strategy is to cite Professors Hart and Carter, because these are "people with whom Professor Jackson has always disagreed or predictably opposes." This case is quite a stretch for the *ad populum*, or appeal to the gallery fallacy. The case represents a distinctive and interesting type of argument (or perhaps fallacy), but it goes well beyond what the traditional approach had staked out as the borders of *argumentum ad populum* or appeal to the gallery.

Damer's fourth subtype is *appeal to group loyalty*, where the basis of the appeal is the person's "identification with a particular social group." This subtype is much more familiar, and is quite consistent with the idea of the *ad populum* appeal commonly found in the prior textbook accounts.

Damer also cites another fallacy, which he calls "appeal to popular opinion," adding that it is also called "the bandwagon fallacy" and *consensus gentium*, which he translates as "consent of the people."

> DEFINITION: This fallacy consists in urging the acceptance of a position simply on the grounds that most or at least great numbers of people accept it. Conversely, the fallacy consists in urging the rejection of a position on the grounds that very few people accept it. (1987, 124)

The appeal to common opinion is discounted by Damer as fallacious on the grounds that "an argument that uses the number of people that accept or reject an idea as a premise for accepting its truth or falsity uses an irrelevant premise" (125).

The *ad populum* (or what amounts to it, under other names) thus has been broadened considerably. But Damer goes even further. He has another fallacy, called "appeal to tradition," defined as "attempting to persuade others of one's point of view by appealing to their feelings of reverence or respect for some tradition that supports that view rather than presenting appropriate evidence." This type of argument could be related to the *ad populum* if expressed in the form: "The long established view of the group to which we belong has always been in favor of such-and-such." Thus there could be considerable overlap between appeal to tradition and the *ad populum* argument (1987, 119).

Yet another fallacy is introduced by Damer, that which appears to be related to, or could even be a subspecies of, *argumentum ad populum* (broadly conceived), and is what he calls the "is-ought fallacy" (1980, 57–59):

> DEFINITION: This fallacy consists in assuming that because something is now the practice it *ought* to be the practice. Conversely, it consists in assuming that because something *is not* the practice it *ought not* to be the practice.
>
> The is-ought fallacy is permeated by moral or value overtones. The "way things are" is regarded as ideal or morally proper simply because "things" are as they are. No good reasons are given for the appropriateness of a thing's being the way it is; it is simply assumed that if it *is*, it must be right, and the possibility of changing it is not seriously entertained.

Damer gives the following example (58).

Case 3.13   EXAMPLE: "Public school teachers and professors should not seek to engage in collective bargaining. After all, very few teachers are presently involved in such practices. There is simply very little interest in that sort of thing in our profession." The fact that very few teachers are currently members of labor unions is not a sufficient reason for concluding that such involvement is inappropriate.

This case seems like it could come under the heading of the appeal-to-common-opinion type of fallacy cited by Damer (see above), but Damer specifically denies it.

> This is-ought fallacy can also be confused with the fallacious appeal to common opinion. The appeal to common opinion is usually used in an attempt to establish the truth of a claim, that is, an opinion or judgment is erroneously assumed to be true because it is held by a large number of people. The is-ought fallacy, however, is used to establish the rightness or appropriateness of a particular kind of behavior or practice, simply because it is presently engaged in by a large number of people. Although the two may be easily confused the appeal to common opinion should be understood as a faulty method of establishing the *truth* of a *claim*, while the is-ought

fallacy should be understood as a faulty method of establishing the *rightness* of a *practice*. (59)

Despite Damer's disclaimer, however, it seems that what he calls the is-ought fallacy really is a subspecies of the type of argument generally identified by the prior textbook accounts as *argumentum ad populum*. And it is a very interesting subtype at that.

Now we are confronted with an almost bewildering variety of *ad populum* subtypes or related varieties of arguments. This multiple approach has however been carried forward by a group of recent textbooks. Before going on to examine this development however, let us look at a group of texts that emphasize two of these subtypes.

7. The Dual Approach

Among the more recent or "new wave" of textbooks, dating from the late 1970s to the mid- 1990s, there is a marked tendency to treat the *ad populum* not as a single fallacy. One approach is to distinguish two separate types of arguments, under two headings such as "bandwagon" or "mob appeal," and treat these as two distinct fallacies (sometimes calling one of them *ad populum*, sometimes both, or, in other instances, not using the Latin phrase at all).

The second group of textbooks could be called the "multipliers" or "proliferators"—they push forward with the trend for multiplicity, set by prior treatments of the *ad populum*. Again, they may call each of these fallacies *ad populum*, or use other terms, but what they have in common is that they cite three or more fallacies that would come under the heading of the general category normally called the *argumentum ad populum* by prior texts.

David Crossley and Peter Wilson cite two variants under the general heading of "fallacy of appeal to the masses" (appeal to the people). The first fallacy seems to evoke the common-folks or the mob-appeal idea. "The appeal to the masses is an attempt to win support by emotional appeal to the sentiments of the people in general, rather than by presenting evidence and reasoned arguments" (1979, 40). The second variant seems to be the bandwagon argument. "A common variant of this is to get someone to agree to something because everybody else does" (41).

W. Ward Fearnside also takes a dual approach, calling the one fallacy *ad populum* and the other "bandwagon" or "impressing by large numbers" (1980, 12). Fearnside describes what he calls the *ad populum* argument or "popular appeal" as the appeal that "seeks to win friends for an argument by playing upon the likes and dislikes of the audience" (14). Citing the Mark Antony case as his leading example (15), Fearnside seems to have the mob-appeal type of argument in mind. Under the separate category of "bandwagon" or "impressing with large numbers," Fearnside cites what amounts to the bandwagon type of argument as a fallacy. "This fallacy is the old bandwagon technique; lots of people believe this or do that, ergo, you may safely follow along" (12).

James Freeman also takes this dual approach, but uses the term "grandstand appeal" for the type of fallacy contrasted with the bandwagon appeal. The grandstand appeal is described as the appeal to the "gut emotions," as used by a political candidate addressing a large number of people in an assembly hall. The speaker "can't be sure that giving logically convincing arguments will work, but he can be sure the audience has "gut emotions."

> If those emotions can be aroused and played upon, you may be able to get those votes or at least to strengthen the audience's tendency to vote for you. How could you do this? Suppose you led your audience to "bask in a warm glow of self-congratulation and smugness." That certainly should make them receptive to our message. Suppose further that you identified yourself with the audience, adopting a "folksy" manner to bring this home. You are just one of these good, decent, down home folks. That would certainly arouse positive feelings toward you. Suppose you also know that your audience thinks of itself as bedrock conservative. You represent your party's policies and platform as being conservative, doctoring it up if necessary. This would raise those positive feelings further.
>
> Suppose in addition you portray the opposing party as scoundrels, deserving to be ignominiously thrown out of office. You arouse anger and hate. Now notice in all this, you may say nothing about your qualifications to hold office or the merit of our programs or party platform. You may not have given much hard information about the shortcomings of the opposition. But you have certainly fostered a very persuasive climate, and you have done it by appealing directly to various gut emotions. (1988, 69)

This account of the grandstand-appeal type of argument is quite inclusive, covering not only mob appeal, but also the common-folks appeal, appeal to the "prejudices" or special views favored by the audience, and negative appeals to the dislikes of the audience (or views or people they oppose). Freeman admits this inclusivity himself in his definition of the fallacy (69):

> Whenever a person attempts to make a point, get a view accepted, not by presenting cogent reasons, but by arousing the gut emotions of the audience, we have a *grandstand appeal* or the fallacy of *grandstanding*. Although the name "grandstand" derives from this setting of persuading the masses, we shall regard any argument whose persuasive force depends on arousing gut emotions and not on the cogency of its reasons as an instance of the grandstand appeal, whether or not it is addressed to a mass audience, a small group, or even a single person. (69)

What generally characterizes this fallacy for Freeman, then, is the arousal of the "gut emotions" of an audience in place of presenting good (cogent) reasons for a conclusion.

The second *ad populum* kind of fallacy identified by Freeman is called "the bandwagon appeal," or appeal to the "herd instinct," the need or urge to go along with the crowd. This fallacy is also described as an emotional appeal where someone "feels like getting on the bandwagon" and following "a crowd instinct" when "positive feelings" and "enthusiasm" are aroused, say in a "throng of happy supporters" at a political rally (70). The negative variant of the bandwagon appeal is called the *abandon ship fallacy*, where "the argument attempts to dissuade us from holding a belief or approving an action just because few or no people accept that belief or support that action" (70). Freeman cites the form of the bandwagon appeal as the argument pattern: "Most or all people accept a certain belief or approve a certain course of action, therefore the belief *must* be true or the action *must* be right." He sees the fallacy as the error of inflating the value of popularity as a reason "beyond all proportion." Interestingly, Freeman concedes that popularity is a reason for accepting a conclusion (71). He concedes, in other words, that bandwagon arguments are not totally worthless, but he sees the fallacy as the inflation of their value.

Gerald Runkle also acknowledges a duality, by citing a broader and a narrower sense of the *argumentum ad populum*. In the broad sense, he writes any argument "designed to appeal to the multitude," or "arouse the feelings of the masses" could be called *argumentum ad populum* (1991, 32). Runkle, however, also cites a narrower meaning of *ad populum* he calls the bandwagon argument:

> We shall, however, take the term in a narrower sense here and call the *argumentum ad populum* an attempt to create a "bandwagon" effect. This appeal works when addressed to timid people who do not want to be separated from the great majority, to people who derive comfort from being part of the crowd. Such people will take up backgammon (or anything else)—if that is what everyone else is doing. They will read Jacqueline Susann's latest book—if it is a best-seller. They are sure that 50,000 Frenchmen can't be wrong—unless 60,000 Frenchmen feel differently. They tend to identify with masses of people, perhaps proud of the fact that they are members of the "Pepsi generation." If a bandwagon is building up, they would rather be riding on it than trudging off alone in a different direction. (33)

Like Freeman, Runkle identifies the "herd instinct" or the emotional appeal of "going along with the crowd" as an important element of the bandwagon fallacy.

8. Multipliers

Perry Weddle cites three fallacies that could come under the area of *argumentum ad populum*—appeal to popular prejudice, appeal to gregariousness, and appeal to vanity. *Appeal to popular prejudice*, also identified by Weddle with "grandstanding," "demagoguery," and "playing to the gallery," is defined as "playing on culturally induced fears, likes, and aversions." Weddle is particularly critical of commercial ads for products such as mouthwash and cigarettes for "playing to the gallery" (1978, 38). *Appeal to gregariousness* is characterized by the phrase: "Everybody's doing it," exemplified by advertising claims such as "America's largest selling bourbon." *Appeal to vanity*, illustrated by the following example, "preys on our natural vanity" (37).

Case 3.14   You were probably born with a bigger share of intelligence than most of our fellow men and women . . . and taught how to use it. And you appreciate the difference. You aren't ashamed of having brains. You enjoy using them. That's why *The Hundred Greatest Classics* belong in your home.

According to Weddle, this sales pitch "butters us up and then asks us to buy" instead of arguing (36).

Stephen Toulmin, Richard Rieke, and Allan Janik define the *fallacy of appeal to the people* as "the fallacious attempt to justify a claim on the basis of its supposed popularity." Among the various types of appeals of this sort they cite are appeals to "class or national, religious or professional identity," appeal to predominant popular feeling in political arguments as "the ultimate court of appeal" (1984, 146), appeal to tradition, appeals by advertisers to the image of "the ideal American," and appeals to "conformity" and "snobbishness" (147).

Douglas Soccio and Vincent Barry cite five separate fallacies that would fall under the category of *argumentum ad populum* as established by prior textbook treatments. The *fallacy of popularity* "tries to justify something strictly by appeal to numbers." For example, a book advertisement is cited (1992, 68).

Case 3.15   Everyone is reading it: thousands of copies have been sold.

Soccio and Barry comment: "So what? Why should *you* read it?" (68), suggesting that the argument does not give a good reason for reading the book.

The *fallacy of common practice*, according to Soccio and Barry is "an argument that attempts to justify wrongdoing on the basis of some practice that has become commonly accepted" (129). The example given makes this appear to be similar to, or a variant of, what other textbooks call the bandwagon argument (130).

Case 3.16   Years ago, Regimen, manufacturers of weight-reducing tablets, was charged by the Justice Department with deliberate misrepresentation and falsehood in advertising its product. In fact, the U.S. Attorney General charged that Regimen's was "one of the most brazen frauds ever perpetrated on the public, mostly women." Regimen's reply: "Thousands of other advertisers and agencies are doing the same kind of thing." No matter how common the practice, misrepresentation is misrepresentation—hence, the irrelevancy of Regimen's defense.

However, the *bandwagon* fallacy is defined by Soccio and Barry as a mob-appeal type of argument. "Bandwagon mob appeals invoke inclusive feelings of belonging to a group" (132). This characterization confuses two distinct types of appeals (as recognized by prior texts) under one heading. To add to the confusion, Soccio and Barry include the common-folks type of appeal under the same heading, writing, "One component of bandwagon mob appeals is a sense of basic values," typified by "folksy" or "country" ways of talking like "regular folks"(133).

The fourth fallacy, called *mob appeal* by Soccio and Barry is "an argument that attempts to persuade groups or individuals by arousing their deepest emotions, beliefs, and values" (130). This type of appeal, typified by "crowd infection" in large audiences, conforms fairly well to the mob-appeal type of *ad populum* cited by prior texts. But the overlap with their third (bandwagon) category, which also involves aspects of mob appeal, is confusing.

The fifth fallacy cited by Soccio and Barry is called *snob appeal*, an appeal that "invokes feelings of superiority and exclusivity" (132). According to Soccio and Barry, both bandwagon and snob appeal "invoke a sense of identity with a group, and therefore sometimes the borderline between the two fallacies is blurred" (133).

Patrick Hurley proposes a classification of the different types of *ad populum* appeals, citing a total of four subtypes (1994, 118–20). The "appeal to the people" (*argumentum ad populum*) uses the desires of wanting to be "loved, esteemed, admired, valued, recognized, and accepted by others . . . to get a reader or listener to accept a conclusion" (118).

Hurley's *direct approach*, which "excites the emotions and enthusiasm of the crowd to win acceptance for [a] conclusion," corresponds to the mob-appeal type of *ad populum* argument. The *indirect approach*, instead of directing the appeal to the crowd as a whole, "directs it to one or more individuals separately, focusing upon some aspect of their relationship to the crowd." According to Hurley, the direct approach is characterized by "the arousal of a mob mentality" that produces a "feeling of belonging" for those in a crowd, especially when the crowd "roars its approval." Anyone who does not go along "cuts himself or herself off from the crowd" and risks a loss of security. The "same thing happens in the indirect approach," according to Hurley but it is more subtle (120). Hurley cites three specific forms of the indirect approach, adding that all are "standard techniques of the advertising industry." The *bandwagon argument* says "you will be left out of the group if you do not use the product" (119).

Case 3.17   Of course you want to buy Zest toothpaste. Why, 90 percent of America brushes with Zest.

The *appeal to vanity* associates the product with a celebrity who is admired and pursued.

Case 3.18 Only the ultimate in fashion could complement the face of Christie Brinkley. Spectrum sunglasses—for the beautiful people in the jet set.

The *appeal to snobbery* is not defined by Hurley, but an example is given.

Case 3.19 A Rolls Royce is not for everyone. If you qualify as one of the select few, this distinguished classic may be seen and driven at British Motor Cars, Ltd. (By appointment only, please).

Hurley's account seems to be the first textbook treatment to seriously attempt to bring in a system of classification to organize the various subtypes of *ad populum* arguments.

One way of dealing with the multiplicity of types of *ad populum* arguments now being recognized is to treat the mob-appeal type as central or basic, as Hurley does, and then classify other subtypes in relation to it. But another approach favored by other leading new wave textbooks is to treat the bandwagon appeal as central, by proposing a general pattern or form of this argument.

9. The Unifying Form

A candidate for the form or pattern of (at least one variant) of the *argumentum ad populum* had already been offered by prior textbooks. Vernon and Nissen (1968), it will be recalled, analyzed the general pattern of the bandwagon fallacy as the argument form "The majority believes p (or does x); therefore p is true (or x should be done)." A group of later "new wave" texts have centered their account of the *ad populum* around this form. By seeing this form of argument as the central *ad populum*, these textbooks could be called "unifiers," as opposed to the previous group classified as "proliferators" or "multipliers."

Robert Yanal defines the *argumentum ad populum*, or "appeal to the people," as the argument having the form: "Everyone says that P; therefore P is true." Curiously, however, Yanal sees this argument as "actually a kind of appeal to authority" (1988, 389). This classification is curious because the form of argument represented by Yanal would normally be taken to be different from the type of argument called appeal to expert opinion or, more generally, appeal to authority. However, a number of other texts also make the claim that the *argumentum ad populum* should be treated as a species of appeal to authority. These include Anthony Weston (1987, 85) and Bruce Waller (1988, 133).

Ralph Johnson and J. Anthony Blair define the *fallacy of popularity* as the error of "thinking that if most people or the majority believe something, then it is true." They go on to introduce two forms of this argument, representing "its purest and most blatant (and rarest) form" (1983, 125).

> (*F1*) Everyone believes Q.
>   Therefore Q is true.
>
> (*F2*) No one believes Q.
>   Therefore Q is false.

Johnson and Blair's analysis of how the *argumentum ad populum* works as a fallacy is that (*F1*) and (*F2*) are blatantly or obviously fallacious as arguments, so real *ad populum* arguments are not stated so "baldly," but concealed beneath the surface.

> This move [represented by (*F1*) or (*F2*)] is so outrageous, when baldly stated, that *popularity* rarely occurs in this blatant formulation. You often have to dig below the surface to find it. For example, M expresses the belief that drugs are harmful and that people shouldn't rely on them. N counters, "Oh, come off it! Nobody believes that nowadays!" N has not actually said that because nobody believes it, it is false; but that is the clear implication. Or M says that women are inferior to men. N responds, "Surely you must be joking; that crazy idea went out with the '60s! Where have you been hibernating?" Again, N stops short of the explicit statement of the inference that because no one believes it, the view is false. The best way to counter such moves is to ask, point-blank, "Hold on, are you saying that because everyone (or no one) believes it, therefore it is true (or false)?" (125)

Johnson and Blair do not claim, however, that the (*F1*) and (*F2*) are inherently fallacious forms of argument. They state, "We are not about to propose that the popular acceptance of a belief is never any reason for thinking it is true" (129). But they write, "Mere acceptance by numbers of people of a belief is usually not a very good reason for you to believe it" (158). Further, they write, "Most of the time [arguing from popular opinion] is a tool of intimidation, an attempt to browbeat a person into accepting some claim" (128). Accordingly, Johnson and Blair's account of the fallacy of popularity cites the type of argument (a) that has the form (F_1) or (F_2), and (b) the popularity of the proposition Q (or lack of it) "is not an adequate reason for accepting or rejecting Q" (159).

A comparable view of the *ad populum* fallacy is conveyed by the treatment of Barbara Warnick and Edward Inch, except that their account is much briefer than that of Johnson and Blair, and goes into the *ad populum* in less depth. Warnick and Inch, however, see the basic *ad populum* fallacy, like Johnson and Blair, as starting with the premise that a claim is made to acceptance by numbers of people, and inferring to a conclusion that the claim is true. Warnick and Inch describe the *ad populum* as having the form: "If enough people believe something, it must be true." They add that they "are not suggesting that arguments based on popular opinion are fallacious *per se*," but they think that "just because many people agree about something, does not mean it is necessarily true" (1989, 133). They see the basis of the fallacy as the use of popular opinion to avoid discussion of an issue (134).

A comparable, but also very brief, treatment is that of Josina Makau, who calls the fallacy "appeal to popular prejudice," citing as the type of argument, "Typically, the advocate claims that because most people believe a claim to be true it is true" (1990, 194). Makau adds that while arguments based on what the majority or most people believe (or do, or want) are very common, and very powerful, they should be "scrutinized carefully" by asking critical questions (195). As the prior two textbook treatments emphasize, appeal to popular opinion (or "prejudice" as Makau calls it) is often an inadequate basis for accepting a conclusion.

Merrilee Salmon seems to fit into the same category as the three textbook treatments above. She postulates roughly the same type of argument as the defining characteristic of the *ad populum*, and like Johnson and Blair, she even presents an explicit pattern or form for the argument. However, her slant on the *ad populum* is slightly (but significantly) different. She emphasizes the element of consensus or agreement of the people. Salmon defines the *argument from consensus* (or *ad populem / sic*) as the argument where "some assertion is held to be correct, or incorrect, on the grounds that most people believe, or reject, the assertion." She proposes that such arguments have the form of a "statistical syllogism" (1995, 111):

> When most people agree on a claim about a subject matter *S*, the claim is true.
>
> *p* is a claim about *S* that most people agree on.
> _____
> *p* is true.

Presumably, this form of argument is said to be a *statistical syllogism* in the sense that the major premise has a warrant ("most people") that can be filled in with some statistical generalization, and the other premise is an instance of this general statement. Salmon, like others noted above, sees this type of argument as similar to arguments from authority. In these respects, her account of the *ad populum* appears to be different from that of Johnson and Blair. But in emphasizing the centrality of the form of argument cited above, a form she calls a statistical syllogism, her account of the *ad populum* is similar in basic outline to the other unifying accounts treated in this section.

10. Summary of Developments

As we look over the whole history of development of the *ad populum* as a fallacy in the textbook treatments, we see a trend to greater complexity and sophistication through (a) the making of distinctions between various types and (b) the attempt to present the form or pattern of the argument (or its central paradigm) in an abstract and general way. However, in some ways, these two trends appear to run counter to each other and produce conflicting accounts. The impression of confusion is enhanced by the use of a bewildering variety of labels for each type of argument and some overlaps in categories.

The first, early wave of accounts was simple and brief, with only a minimal attempt to offer examples. As realistic cases began to be introduced as examples for the students (readers), complications and the discovery of new and different varieties of *ad populum* arguments led to somewhat lengthier and more sophisticated treatments. Among the early modern textbooks, *argumentum ad populum* was treated as a fallacy. Only two of these textbooks, McCosh (1879) and Read (1920), specifically mention or allow for the possibility that *ad populum* arguments could be reasonable in some cases. Most of these textbooks diagnose the *ad populum* fallacy as a failure of relevance, classifying it under the Aristotelian fallacy of *ignoratio elenchi*, or misconception of refutation (often also called "wrong conclusion" or "ignoring the issue").

Many of these textbooks contrast emotion and reason, seeing the *ad populum* as an appeal to passion or emotion. These include Jevons (1878), Veitch (1885), Hyslop (1899), Creighton (1904), Hibben (1906) and Gibson (1908). Some of the textbooks also specifically cite bias or prejudice as part of the problem or error, namely Veitch (1885), Creighton (1904), and Hibben (1906). Some also cite "interests" of the audience, as being opposed to reason, namely, Veitch (1885), Hyslop (1899) and Read (1920).

A phrase used by some of these early textbooks is "body of people," suggesting a mass audience; Jevons (1878) and McCosh (1879) use this expression. Some of these textbooks even mention "demagogues" suggesting a mob-appeal idea as part of the fallacy, namely, Jevons (1978) and Hibben (1906).

Generally, these early textbooks set the basic elements of the *ad populum* in place. Although all of them are very brief treatments, they set the framework in place that would provide a basis of development for subsequent textbooks to pursue and elaborate on.

The second wave of texts, from 1935 to 1959, continued to follow the basic pattern of treating the *ad populum* fallacy as a failure of relevance. However, this generation of textbooks began to lay more emphasis on the mob-appeal aspect, by citing emotional speeches like the Mark Antony speech. Such examples include a "stirring up of emotions" in a mass audience by "demagogues" and "propaganda." It could be that this aspect came to be seen as important because of the prominence of the widespread, effective use of propaganda and mass-appeal rhetorical techniques by political leaders during this period.

However, we also see the beginnings of some variants of the *ad populum* begin to appear during this period. Huppé and Kaminsky (1957) introduce the idea of the *ad populum* as a "common-folks" appeal. Blyth (1957) cites appeal to flattery, or the cultivation of vanity as a special subtype of *ad populum* argument. Schipper and Schuh (1959) draw attention to the use of emotionally loaded words. But it is not until the third period of 1961–68 that a more explicit multiplicity of different subtypes of *ad populum* appeals begins to proliferate in the textbooks. Wheelwright (1962) classifies the *ad populum* under the heading of "appeal to prestige." Rescher (1964) contrasts mob appeal and snob appeal. Copi (1972) distinguishes between bandwagon and mob-appeal arguments. Vernon and Nissen propose an Arnauld-like form of the bandwagon argument—a theme later taken up by new wave textbooks of the 1990s. Kilgore (1968) cites three distinct *ad populum* fallacies—bandwagon appeal, common-folks appeal and appeal to the gallery (none of which seems to be the same, exactly, as either mob appeal or snob appeal).

In the next wave, a number of hybrids are proposed that seem to combine elements previously treated as distinct subtypes of *ad populum*. Now we get "appeal to popular sentiments" (Michalos, 1969), which seems more like the common-folks appeal than the mob appeal, but combines elements of both while not being exactly identical to either. Fischer's (1970) fallacy of the prevalent proof seems to be partly the bandwagon argument, but contains elements of appeal to expert opinion. Byerly (1973), like Kilgore (1968) sees *ad populum* as an appeal to values shared by the audience. Only Kozy (1974) of this group admits or states the possibility that *ad populum* need not always be fallacious.

Then in Engel (1976) and Damer (1980) the multiplier approach really gets underway, Engel alluding to seven different grounds for judging mob-appeal arguments to be fallacious, and Damer citing five distinct subtypes that can be identified with the general type of argument now established as *ad populum*: (1) appeal to flattery, (2) appeal to shame, (3) appeal to a negatively perceived party who disagrees, (4) appeal to group loyalty, and (5) appeal to consent of the people (which seems to be similar to or the same as what most label the bandwagon argument). Damer also alludes to *ad populum* aspects of appeal to tradition and the is-ought fallacy, potentially adding two other *ad populum* subtypes.

Among one group of recent or new wave textbooks, one group takes a binary approach by citing two subtypes as the *ad populum* type of argument— the bandwagon and mob-appeal subtypes. This group includes Crossley and Wilson (1979), Fearnside (1980), and Freeman (1988). Like Damer, Freeman also cites a negative variant, which he calls the "abandon ship fallacy" (a kind of opposite of the bandwagon argument). Runkle (1991) also cites two types of *ad populum*, corresponding to what are usually called the mob-appeal and bandwagon arguments.

A more recent group of multipliers (1978–95) does not add much in the way of new varieties, but do recognize the multiplicity of subtypes such as mob appeal, bandwagon argument, appeal to snobbery, vanity, and so forth. The unifiers, on the other hand, try to bring these varieties under the general umbrella of the bandwagon pattern or form of argument as the central paradigm of the *ad populum*.

Chapter Four

PRESUMPTIONS, COMMON STARTING POINTS, AND PUBLIC JUDGMENT

Research on many of the traditional informal fallacies has discovered that the form of argument (argumentation scheme) underlying the so-called fallacy has turned out to represent a species of argument that is often nonfallacious (reasonable), and is only fallacious in some cases (Walton 1995). The problem, then, is to find justifiable and useful general criteria for distinguishing between the reasonable and the fallacious (or erroneous) cases.

As shown in Chapter 1, even when the *ad populum* type of argument appears in cases where it does appear somewhat reasonable, it still seems such a weak and fallible type of argument that it is hard to fathom what basis of justification it could have. In Chapter 2, section 10, the best that could be done was to grope toward the elusive basis of this argument in a conjectural way. Hence, it is understandable why logic textbooks have found it so easy to routinely dismiss *argumentum ad populum* as fallacious.

However, as we look over the recent scholarly literature on the appeal to popular opinion as a type of argument, we find a conflict with the standard treatment. These scholarly treatments not only assume that this type of argument is, or can be, reasonable, they also offer several different explanations and theories that give accounts of why and how the appeal to popular opinion can be used as a type of reasonable argument.

1. Bandwagon and Mob-Appeal Arguments

As we survey the standard treatment, broadly speaking, two main types of *ad populum* arguments stand out as being recurrent in central patterns. One is called the "mob-appeal" type of argument. Characteristic of this type of *ad populum* argument is the group dynamic with a speaker who, addressing a mass audience, often typifies a demagogue who arouses the enthusiasms of that mass audience. There are other elements, as we have seen, frequently mixed in with this idea of the enthusiasms of the multitude.

One of these elements is that of a speaker homing in on the so-called prejudices or dearly-held views that are important to the multitude as a focus of his persuasion. Another element often cited by the textbooks is what we call the "common-folks appeal." This kind of appeal seems to be related to empathy. The speaker is trying to reach the audience at their level. Whatever the defining characteristics of this type of argument are, what seems centrally important is the idea of a mass of people assembled and a speaker trying to arouse their enthusiasms in an emotional way.

No doubt one historical factor that caused so many of the post–World War II textbooks to use "demagogue" in their description of the mob-appeal argument as a rhetorical tactic was the influence of Hitler's rhetoric in Nazi Germany. Hitler's rhetoric appealed to "a deep sense of community" (Duncan 1962, 226), and the primary rhetorical method of the Nazi propaganda was the public mass meeting, staged carefully for the audience. According to Hugh Duncan, these mass meetings were artfully staged to represent a "drama of struggle between good and evil" (229). The orator portrayed the struggle in extremes, using strong appeals to emotion—especially a feeling of belonging to a powerful group—instead of using more rational or objective arguments of the kind that would appeal more to intellectuals than to the common people.

As noted in Chapter 1, the fear that democracy could be extinguished by the rise of a crowd orator like Hitler is by no means unreasonable. But should this fear of the possible consequences of inflammatory rhetoric lead us to declare that appealing to the emotions or group interests or loyalties of an audience is a fallacious type of argumentation? In section 2, below, I reject this approach as a simplistic solution.

The other main type of *ad populum* argument is called the "bandwagon" argument. This type of argument is more clearly defined in the textbook treatments by virtue of its cited logical form: "Everybody believes proposition *A*; therefore, proposition *A* is true." In general, this type of argument is distinct from the mob-appeal argument, although the two could certainly be related in some cases. It does not appear to be essential to the bandwagon type of argument that there be a speaker's appeal to the enthusiasm of some assembled multitude. Instead, it is more typical of the bandwagon type of argument that there are two parties involved, a speaker and a hearer, and the speaker is trying to persuade the hearer to accept some proposition A and, in order to do that, the speaker is arguing to the hearer, "Everybody accepts A; therefore, you, the hearer, should also accept A." The presumption with this type of argument is that the hearer does not presently accept proposition A or is doubtful about proposition A. With this type of argument, then, the speaker tries to get the hearer to accept A by referring to the views of other people saying, "Everybody else except you accepts A," so, therefore, the conclusion suggested is that the hearer also should go along and accept proposition A because everyone else already accepts it.

The structure of this argument appears to be inherently different from that of the mob-appeal type. In the mob-appeal type of argument, the premise is that the speaker appeals to some deeply-held belief, view, or cause of the assembled multitude, and then tries to get the audience to move on or accept something else that he, the speaker, wants them to accept. It is not that the speaker is saying to this multitude, "Everybody else accepts proposition A; therefore you should accept it, too." Instead, the speaker is addressing the mob internally, so to speak, and trying to appeal to common values that they all share, thereby getting them whipped up into such a state of enthusiasm that they will go on to accept some proposition that he wants them to come to accept.

Walton's treatment of the *ad populum* argument shows an awareness of this difference between the two basic types of argument that have often been lumped together under the *ad populum* heading (1989, 84–93). The *ad populum* argument is traditionally characterized as "the use of appeal to mass enthusiasms or popular sentiments in order to win assent for the conclusion of an argument" (84). This description indicates the mob-appeal type of argument. In contrast, what we are now calling the bandwagon type of argument is called "argument from popularity" by Walton, suggesting that it may not itself be an *ad populum* argument. The two inference forms characteristic of the bandwagon argument are presented and these basic forms are called the "argument from popularity" (89).

A comparable treatment is given in Walton (1992b, 77) where the type of inference characteristic of the bandwagon argument is, again, called argument from popularity, following the treatment of Johnson and Blair (1983, 175), who give it the same name (see Chapter 3, section 9).[1] Again, the assumption is that the argument from popularity may not be exactly the same thing as the *argumentum ad populum* generally, which is taken to be identified with an appeal to mass enthusiasms in a crowd setting. However, the assumption in both these previous treatments is that the bandwagon argument and the *ad populum* and mob-appeal argument are closely connected to each other, and that the argument from popularity is somehow a part of or connected to the mob-appeal type of *ad populum* argument.

Given the difficulties of defining the mob-appeal argument in any very precise way, however, the question remains open as to what the exact relationship between these two types of argument really is. Wreen also thinks that there are two separate types of arguments that can be distinguished under the heading of *ad populum* (1993, 64). He typifies one of these *ad populum* types of argument as the kind that appeals to widespread sentiment, emotion, or enthusiasm, or what we have called the mob-appeal type of argument.

The other kind of *ad populum* argument is typified by Wreen as an appeal to widespread belief. This type appears to correspond fairly well to what was identified above as the argument from popularity. The best generic names for these two distinctively different, basic types of arguments so often identified with *ad populum* are the "bandwagon argument" and the "mob-appeal argument." Let us adopt these terms provisionally for use in subsequent discussion as the names for the two broad subtypes of *ad populum* arguments.

2. Are *Ad Populum* Arguments Fallacious?

The considerations raised in Chapter 1 suggest that, despite the standard treatments surveyed in Chapter 3, neither the bandwagon argument nor the mob-appeal argument is fallacious in every case in which it might be used. For example, political and economic decisions are often influenced by public opinion polls in democratic countries, and despite the very real abuses and potential for deception and error in these polls, it would hardly seem defensible to condemn them as inherently fallacious, even when conducted and used with care and good judgment.[2]

---

1. Johnson and Blair actually call it the "fallacy of popularity," but for our purposes it is important not to judge just yet whether it is always a fallacious argument.
2. On public judgment and mass opinion, see section 9 below.

But what kind of logical basis can justify or explain such a correct use of appeal to popular opinion as an argument? Here we turn to the small but growing literature on the *argumentum ad populum* for some answers.

In the treatments in Walton (1989) and Walton (1992b), it is assumed that the argument from popularity, or bandwagon argument as we now tentatively propose to call it, is a weak but inherently legitimate type of presumptive argument that can shift a burden of proof one way or another in a situation where a person does not have much access to knowledge as a basis for accepting or rejecting a conclusion. For example, in Walton (1992b, 94), a case is given where a man is getting off a train in the central station of a foreign city. He does not know in which direction he should set off to get to the exit where the street is. Carrying heavy bags, he steps off the train and notices that all the other people are pouring toward one particular exit. Operating on the presumption that this popular route is probably, or at least presumably, the way to the exit, he follows the crowd. Now, normally, what one would do in a case like this is to ask the train attendant or ask one of the other passengers, perhaps, which way is the way to go to the street exit. However, the presumption in this case is that the person does not speak the language (therefore, trying to find the information by asking other people is problematic) or he thinks that he will not get the information this way. In the absence of any access to very reliable information, he simply follows the others even though it is possible that this route could be the wrong direction for him and these people could be going in some other direction; for example, toward a football game that would not get him to the exit he needs to get to. In Walton (1992b, chap. 3), this bandwagon type of argument is treated as one that is presumptively reasonable in some cases but is nevertheless fallible. It is treated as a weak type of argument that provides only some basis of presumption for acting on or going tentatively ahead with accepting a conclusion in the absence of some hard knowledge that might more conclusively affirm or refute the conclusion.

In fact, however, one must be very careful to see that, in many instances, the bare form of the bandwagon argument is tacitly supplemented by an appeal to another type of argument called "position to know." In other words, in many cases, the argument that seems to be a bandwagon type of argument is combined with an appeal to the knowledgeability or access to information of the individuals who are cited under the heading of "everybody." In this particular case, it is presumed by the traveler that all these people on the train are regular travelers and know this city and train station, so he infers that they are going in the direction of the exit when they all move in one particular direction after the train stops. The assumption is, in other words, that these people are in a position to know where the exit is or where the right direction is and that, therefore, it would be reasonable to follow them. So, in this case, what we want to carefully note is that it is not simply the fact that all these people are doing such-and-such that makes our traveler think that following the same course would be a reasonable thing to do.

There is another factor: This traveler has reason to think or presume that all these people are in a better position to know where the exit is than he is. It is not that these people are experts on this particular station but simply because they are familiar, or presumed familiar, with the area that they are in a special position to know which way to go. Nevertheless, arguments of the bandwagon type are often bolstered by appeal to expertise as well, suggesting an important link between the *ad populum* argument and the type of argument often categorized in logic textbooks as the *argumentum ad verecundiam* or "appeal to expert opinion" (Chapter 2, section 10).

In the textbook treatments of the *ad populum*, by far the most common reason for rejecting this type of argument as fallacious is that of relevance. But there are two problems with this reasoning. One is that the textbooks do not agree on any abstract definition of what relevance is—in a sense that could be helpful in analyzing the fallacies. The other problem is that the notion of relevance appealed to in the textbook treatment of the *ad populum* is highly contextual. An argument that could be highly relevant in a political speech addressed to a mass audience, for example, could be highly irrelevant in the context of a scientific investigation or inquiry. Although many different semantical theories of relevance have been proposed in logic in recent years, none of them has ever proved to be useful or applicable in analyzing fallacies of relevance like the *ad populum*.

Although relevance of various kinds can be defined in precise semantical formalisms that are applicable to arguments in natural language discourse (Epstein 1979; 1995), these semantic models are of limited usefulness in determining failure of relevance of a kind associated with informal fallacies of irrelevance (Walton 1982). Hence, in Walton (1995, chap. 6), a dialectical conception of relevance—meaning relevance as defined within the context of a conversational exchange of arguments between two parties—is advocated as the best tool for studying fallacies.

This move to a dialectical definition of relevance still does not, by itself, solve the evaluation problem of the *ad populum* argument, however. As noted in Chapter 1, section 6, Billig cited Aristotle as making the point that basing one's premises on the values or commitments of one's audience is relevant and appropriate in a rhetorical speech (1987, 194). Billig goes on to suggest that Aristotle was not committing any fallacy when he urged the orator to emphasize the similarity between himself and his audience. In other words, what is being stressed here is the need in successful rhetoric for the speaker to empathetically enter into the point of view of the audience and then, in his speech, identify with the values of the audience, drawing his premises from propositions that express those values so that these premises will be propositions that the audience will accept and agree with. In the context of a persuasive speech this sort of *ad populum* appeal is not only relevant, it is essential to making the speech successful.

Billig goes on to suggest that, to the extent that orators adapt themselves to their audiences in this empathetic way, the image of the powerful fallacy-committing orator, dominating the emotions of the helpless crowd, is a myth (195). A more realistic view, according to Billig, is that the crowd controls the orator because the orator's argumentation needs to be based on the commitments of the audience. It is a more balanced view, according to Billig, to see the orator and the audience as linked together in a social activity so that the orator's success is only possible, at least to a considerable extent, because the audience colludes with him in sharing certain values (196). Blaming the orator for committing an *ad populum* fallacy whenever he appeals to the views of the crowd is one-sided. Billig's thesis about rhetorical argumentation also seems to be applicable to persuasion dialogue generally and, in particular, even to the dialectical type of persuasion dialogue one might have in any reasoned discussion.

3. Premise Adequacy of Dialectical Arguments

It is characteristic of the dialectical systems proposed by Hamblin (1970; 1971) that argumentation in a reasoned discussion, or dialogue between two parties, has the characteristic that the arguments of each party should be based on premises that are commitments of the other party. In other words, the basic idea is that, if you and I are arguing together in a dialogue exchange, then my arguments should be judged successful only to the extent that they are based on premises that are commitments or, at least at some further point, could be commitments of yours. Of course, such arguments will also have to meet structural requirements of inference in order to be judged correct or successful, that is, they will have to be deductively valid, inductively strong, or, at least, presumptively acceptable in that they have certain types of argument structures or argumentation schemes of which they are instances. However, a main requirement for the correctness or adequacy of an argument in dialectic, as stressed by Hamblin, is that the argument of a given party must be based on premises that are accepted by or are commitments of the other party.

This account of correctness of dialectical arguments is also an integral part of the analysis of commitment presented in Walton and Krabbe (1995). One important type of dialectical framework of argument is the persuasion dialogue. Generally, in a persuasion dialogue, an argument is judged adequate or successful according to the appropriate standards for that type of dialogue if it is based on premises that are acceptable to, i.e., commitments of the party to whom it was addressed as an argument. Indeed, we could say that this requirement of acceptability of premises as being commitments of the respondent is the key defining characteristic of persuasion dialogue generally, and since the critical discussion is a subspecies of the persuasion dialogue, this premise requirement will also be a leading characteristic of the critical discussion as a type of dialogue framework for argument (see section 5 below).

J. Anthony Blair and Ralph Johnson see the notion of premise adequacy as a key aspect of their dialectical notion of argumentation (1987, 48). According to their account, the requirement of premise adequacy in a reasonable dialectical argument is that the proposition cited as premise by the proponent must be accepted by the respondent to whom it was addressed as an argument. As they put it, "If he is to succeed in gaining the adherence of the audience to the proposition by using arguments, the proponent must begin with premises that the audience is willing to grant, to concede, to admit, to allow, to believe, to endorse, to agree with, to subscribe to, and to approve of, to consider—in a word, to 'accept'" (49).

The dialectical structure Blair and Johnson have in mind, and in which this principle is embedded, takes the form of an argument as a verbal exchange between two parties. One party takes the role of proponent and the other party resists. This second party is described by Blair and Johnson as the critic, doubter, or questioner (48). Blair and Johnson also, in some situations, describe the latter party as being the audience of the argument, with the first party being the speaker. In some cases of argument, the audience may be insulated from the proponent so that the proponent or orator is doing all the speaking (49), whereas, in other cases, the audience may intercede actively with verbal objections and criticisms made each time the speaker puts forward an argument (48). Whether the context is one of a rhetorical speech or more one of a personal critical discussion type of dialectical exchange where two parties are arguing together, Blair and Johnson think that the same principle of premise adequacy applies in both contexts. The success of an argument or its correctness should depend on whether the premises used by the proponent are accepted or are acceptable to the respondent.

Blair and Johnson are, however, quite alert to the possibility that there will be strong traditional objections raised to their thesis (49). In fact, from a traditional viewpoint, their dialectical account of premise adequacy would be seen by traditional logicians as a highly objectionable form of relativism. As Blair and Johnson note, the twentieth-century logician's response would be that it is crucial to distinguish between what the audience *does* accept and what the audience *ought* to accept as premises of an argument. Indeed, Christopher Tindale has criticized Blair and Johnson precisely on these grounds, arguing that theirs is a form of epistemological relativism.

> The possibility of epistemological relativism is a threat to any standard of premise acceptability that must consider the audience for which the premise is intended. What is at issue is how serious this threat is and whether all relativism related to audiences is necessarily impermissible. In the worse case it would seem that any particular premise, no matter how outrageous, should be allowed if the audience will accept it. We can imagine cases that would concern us, from the railings of the white supremacist delighting the ears of his sympathetic audience, to the advocate of corporal punishment in schools who addresses an audience of abused teachers. It also seems to follow that some audiences, because of the beliefs they hold, should be permitted to accept premises that are logically flawed. (1981, 288)

Quoting Aristotle's *Eudemian Ethics* (Book I, 1214b–1215a), Tindale notes that, when Aristotle writes that we do not need to examine the views of the many because they speak in an unreflective way, he is echoing the sentiments often expressed by Socrates in the Platonic dialogues (289). The problem Tindale notes in this connection is that, when a speaker uses as premises the shared views that bind his audience together, his speech is bound to exploit the prejudices of that audience by using arguments that are emotional appeals to the particular shared views of that audience. This observation, according to Tindale, shows how Johnson and Blair's requirement of premise adequacy allows for the exploitation of an audience in cases where the speaker uses premises that are acceptable to that audience but would be regarded as generally unreasonable from a more objective standpoint.

To meet the kind of objection of relativism posed by Tindale, Blair and Johnson argue that what is needed is an expansion of the notion of argumentation as dialectical to include the surrounding community in which the argument occurs (1987). In other words, even though the main argument is between the proponent and the respondent, nevertheless both are partly addressing a larger community of others in the exchange as well.

Blair and Johnson call this larger community the community of "interlocutors" (50), defining it as a body of individuals that has the following four characteristics (51). First, this body of individuals is knowledgeable in the sense that they are in possession of some body of knowledge so that they can check the knowledge claims of the principal arguers. Second, the community of interlocutors are reflective in the sense that they can challenge and probe the claims of the two main parties. Third, the community of interlocutors are regarded by Blair and Johnson as being open in the critical sense that they are willing to change their opinions and they are not locked into fixed ideas or biases. The fourth property of the community is their dialectical astuteness, meaning that they are alert to problems of relevance, and to possibilities of counterarguments and conflicting evidence.

4. Conflicts with Expert Opinion

Tindale sees a number of problems with Blair and Johnson's notion of the community of interlocutors. One question he poses is whether the entire community must agree (1991, 290), asking what happens, for example, when the community of interlocutors is split into two groups, and one group of experts accepts a particular proposition while the other group either doubts that proposition or even argues that the opposite proposition is true.

Another kind of problem cited by Tindale is a case where belief systems and knowledge systems are a source of disagreement (293). He cites a case where every member of a particular culture believes in witches, but an anthropologist who studies this culture is aware of other cultures that do not believe in witches. So, for an arguer who is addressing an audience composed exclusively of members of this witch-believing culture, it would be appropriate for her to use arguments that have premises expressing or presuming belief in witches. However, in judging such an argument as correct or reasonable in that context, there could be a conflict if, as a matter of fact, we know there is a scientific culture that is either skeptical about belief in witches or rejects propositions to the effect that witches exist. In such a case, if the argument is based on a premise that includes a premise depending upon beliefs about the existence of witches, should we evaluate this argument as being acceptable or not?

From one point of view, it is acceptable, but from another point of view, it is open to doubt. This kind of situation is definitely a problem for the Blair and Johnson dialectical model of argument, for how are we to weigh these two factors of expert opinion versus acceptance of the audience? It is clear that there could be conflicts of this kind apparent in many instances of argumentation in everyday conversation and, also, that it would be difficult to have a simple rule to decide such conflicts that would be applicable to all cases.

The problem, then, can be described as follows. Suppose we accept the notion that requirements for the success or correctness of an argument are, in part, based on the commitments of the respondent, or the willingness of the respondent to accept the premises of the argument. But suppose also that it is an accepted part of the context that both the respondent and the proponent are willing to take the word of a group of experts in a particular domain of knowledge and accept what these experts say as having a certain weight of evidence. What do we do, then, when there is a conflict between what the experts say and what the respondent is inclined to accept as being true? There seems to be no simple way out of this dilemma.

One solution could be to require that, at the opening stage of an argument, both the proponent and the respondent agree to certain outside sources of knowledge as being definitive. This agreement means that if an expert—who both the proponent and the respondent have agreed in advance is an expert whose word shall be given weight on propositions within her domain of expertise—vouches for a certain proposition, then the respondent would have to accept this proposition and retract his commitment to any other proposition that conflicts with the proposition vouched for by the expert. In other words, resolving the conflict depends on the prior acceptance of the source of expert knowledge by both parties to the dialogue, as well as the weight of evidence accorded to the source.

A similar solution appears to be advocated by Frans van Eemeren and Rob Grootendorst in their use of the concept of an intersubjective testing procedure (ITP) (1984, 167–73). The ITP is defined by van Eemeren and Grootendorst as a procedure used in a dialogue whereby both participants in the dialogue—that is, the proponent and the respondent—agree at the opening stage on how they will determine whether or not a particular proposition ought to be accepted.

According to van Eemeren and Grootendorst both parties in a dispute might agree at the outset that if a proposition can be found in a given written source, such as an encyclopedia or a dictionary, then both parties would accept that proposition as a commitment and not subject it to further disputation or questioning for the purposes of their dialogue exchange.

Another type of ITP suggested by van Eemeren and Grootendorst as applicable to some cases would be the joint conduct of observations or experiments by the two parties. Such an ITP we might propose here would be the consultation of a third-party expert or group of experts who make a pronouncement on some proposition that falls within their domain of scientific expertise. This type of input from expert sources or outside sources of information could make a critical discussion more informed, bringing it closer to the real world by bringing in facts that have been established independently by scientific observation, or by experts, and that would enrich the critical discussion's capability to explore the subject in depth.

This use of an ITP as a source of information means that, in a critical discussion, Blair and Johnson's requirement of premise adequacy would be met, in that the argument used by either party would have to be based on premises accepted by the other party in order to be a correct or acceptable argument in a given dialogue. However, if one of these premises was accepted by the respondent of the argument but then turned out to conflict with what the community of model interlocutors (or the ITP, in van Eemeren and Grootendorst's conception), then the respondent would have to retract his commitment to this proposition and bring his commitments into line with what was expressed by the ITP or community of model interlocutors. It might be added here that the word of the ITP or community of interlocutors might be regarded as fixed in some cases, while in other cases, it might be open to challenge—that is, there might be room in some types of dialogue for a respondent to pose critical questions. In particular, a case of this sort might arise where the experts disagreed, or where there was some question about the relevance of what the experts said, or where there might be certain critical questions about how what the experts said should be related to the proposition committed to by the respondent. So, there might be grounds for questioning the pronouncements of an ITP, but the set of such pronouncements would carry a certain presumptive weight depending upon the type of dialogue that the two participants were engaged in, and other circumstances.

Tindale's objections, then, are not completely answered. There remain many open questions about how clashes between the different constraints on premise adequacy might be resolved. Nevertheless, in principle, there seem to be ways open for resolving these conflicts. There seems to be room for both the *ad populum* type of argument, where the requirement of premise adequacy in terms of what the audience expects is one factor, and the pronouncements from another group of interlocutors, perhaps a group of experts or some source of knowledge that has been agreed upon by the proponent and the respondent at the opening stage of the dialogue.

These additional factors make the evaluation of argumentation in a critical discussion more complex, but they do seem to leave enough room open to preserve Johnson and Blair's requirement of premise adequacy. The critical discussion, and the persuasion type of dialogue generally, can still be based on a primary requirement of the respondent's acceptance of a premise as being an important part of the evaluation of whether or not an argument is correct or reasonable in a given case. If so, some room appears to be left open for justifying the rhetorical practice of the speaker's basing his reasonable arguments on values and commitments that the audience enthusiastically or warmly accepts. Certainly, to judge this type of audience—commitment-based argumentation as being inherently fallacious—would appear to be an inappropriate stance to take, given that the central basis for the requirement of premise adequacy in persuasion dialogue generally is the commitment of the respondent or audience to whom the argument was directed.

5. Common Starting Points

The foregoing considerations advanced by Blair and Johnson, Tindale, and van Eemeren and Grootendorst show that there can be different kinds of requirements for premise acceptability in an argument that is to be judged reasonable in a dialectical exchange of arguments. One central requirement is obviously the acceptability of the premise to the respondent, that is, the person to whom the argument was addressed in the dialogue exchange. Indeed, it has been postulated in Walton (1989, 6) that the primary characteristic of one type of dialogue, called persuasion dialogue, that the primary obligation of each party in the dialogue is to prove his or her own thesis from premises that are all commitments of the other party.

Van Eemeren and Grootendorst (1984) have defined one normative model of dialogue, which they call the critical discussion, where the purpose of the dialogue is to resolve a conflict of opinions. The critical discussion is a species of persuasion dialogue where the participants each try to resolve the conflict by rational means and through the use of arguments based on the concessions of the other party. But in the critical-discussion type of dialogue, the commitments of the other party are not the only source of premises an arguer can use for rational persuasion.

Another source of accepted premises in a persuasion dialogue is what van Eemeren and Grootendorst call "common starting points" in a critical discussion (1992, 9–11). Common starting points are propositions that both participants in a dialogue agree to accept in virtue of some mode of consensus for agreement at the opening stage of the dialogue. The intersubjective testing procedure (ITP) is a case in point. The ITP represents a body of propositions that both participants in a critical discussion agree to accept as common starting points, so that both will accept any propositions drawn from this source as commitments used in the role of acceptable premises for their arguments.

Obviously, one source of common starting points that would be very common in the kinds of persuasion dialogues found in everyday conversation are propositions accepted on the basis of expert opinion. In a critical discussion, the two participants could agree on some source of expert opinion, such as an encyclopedia or the say-so of some duly qualified expert. Both are bound by this prior agreement to accept propositions as premises during the course of their argumentation together that have been vouched for or can be documented as coming from the expert source. But the question should be raised whether common starting points other than appeals to expert opinion ought to be included as part of the premise requirements in a critical-discussion or persuasion type of dialogue. For example, ought we to include as common starting points propositions that everyone accepts in relation to the issue being discussed? In other words, ought we to take as presumptions propositions that neither party in the dialogue disputes and, moreover, are so widely accepted that most of the audience of observers or commentators on the critical discussion would accept them without question?

The issue of what presumptive propositions should have in argumentation is complicated by a number of factors. One is that many appeals to popular opinion have an epistemic component built in. In other words, many claims to popular opinion, when analyzed carefully, are not just claims that everybody believes such-and-such. They are implicitly or explicitly claims that everybody believes such-and-such because such-and-such proposition is common knowledge. Presumably, this type of intermixing of expert opinion and popular opinion as a basis for supporting premises in persuasion dialogue would be very commonplace because, in any modern setting, it would be widely assumed that the audience of a discussion would be scientifically literate and would be broadly inclined to accept or, at least not to challenge, propositions that they regard as well-established by science.

For example, scientists widely agree that the hole in the ozone layer, at the present time, is widening to an area the size of Antarctica. No reputable scientists have successfully disputed this claim to the extent that it has become controversial among scientists who are expert on the subject. The claim has also become widely reported and known and accepted by the public. It is thus just the sort of claim that could be expected to function as a premise in a critical discussion, for example, on the subject of the environment, where it is accepted by both sides because it is a proposition that is widely believed and that people generally do not doubt. But the reason for the acceptability of such a premise by both sides is that it has been recently announced and generally accepted as a result of scientific research. Reputable scientists have widely accepted it as such and, moreover, it has been reported as such in the popular media and not generally challenged by either experts or respected media commentators. So, in this case, the proposition that there is a hole in the ozone layer the size of Antarctica could be accepted by both sides as a premise in a critical discussion on the grounds that either everybody accepts it or most people accept it. But, of course, part of the reason that most people accept it is that it is accepted as having been verified by scientific research.

We have to be careful, then, in examining the requirements of premise adequacy in a critical discussion, to carefully distinguish between appeals to popular opinion that may be a possible basis for accepting premises, and appeals to expert opinion that are definitely recognized by all parties. The latter are recognized by Blair and Johnson, Tindale, and van Eemeren and Grootendorst as important classes of propositions to be included in requirements for premise adequacy arguments. But, even so, it makes a good deal of sense to allow premises to be accepted by all parties to a critical discussion as common starting points, provided that nobody disagrees with these premises and there is no evidence known to be strong enough to refute them. How could we have critical discussions on any subject important for deliberation in a democracy if we did not grant certain assumptions to a co-discussant who wants us to provisionally accept "for the sake of argument"? The purpose of granting a proposition that is widely accepted as true, even though it is not known to be true (or false) beyond all doubt, is to facilitate the dialogue—to make it possible to continue, even in the absence of hard knowledge, based on expert opinion.

6. The Status of Presumptions

The next question to be raised is: On what basis, in a critical discussion on some controversial issue in everyday conversation, would it be reasonable to accept as a requirement for premise adequacy in an argument that a proposition be one that is generally accepted by the majority or by all people? Of course, the participants in a critical discussion could be required by convention to accept such propositions and not challenge them when used as premises by the other party. But the question is also raised: What would be the basis on which we could say that the acceptance of such premises in a critical discussion would be justified and would reflect a rational procedure for resolving conflict of opinions in a reasonable way?

This question raises the whole issue of presumptions. What should be the status of presumptions, such as those based on the opinion of the majority or the opinion of everybody in a critical discussion? In persuasion dialogue, are premises that are based on presumptions of this kind frequently taken for granted by the participants and, if so, would this be an important source of premises for reasonably convincing arguments used in this type of dialogue exchange? But if such propositions are not based on expert opinion, or upon some other ITP source that was certified as a domain of knowledge and agreed upon as such by the participants, then what could be the justification for this type of premise adequacy characteristic of presumptions, which makes them different from propositions based on expert opinion, is that the latter have a burden of proof requirement?

In contrast, propositions accepted as presumptions are more conditional in nature. They are propositions that can be provisionally accepted by both parties without anyone having to prove them, provided both parties agree. In the case of propositions accepted on the basis of appeal to expert opinion, such propositions, however, would not be beyond challenge once accepted. They would have a defeasible status—that is, they would be premises that are tentatively accepted but subject to defeat if, during the subsequent course of the conversation, evidence or strong arguments come in that tend to refute them or make them questionable.

So, here we get into a trickier area: propositions accepted on the basis of expert opinion, certified by a source that both parties agree at the outset of the discussion is acceptable to them, do have a more solid basis than presumptions that are merely accepted because no one disagrees with them, or are widely accepted and would not be disputed by the audience or by anyone who is privy to the discussion.

Another type of premise requirement is more loose and more easily subject to defeat, and not so easy to justify. Many people would be quite skeptical about this type of basis for accepting propositions as premises in a critical discussion for the same reason that Blair and Johnson (1987) and Tindale (1991) worry about, namely, relativism. This sort of requirement for premise acceptability makes the argument highly relativistic in a way that acceptance in virtue of appeal to expert opinion would not be relativistic for many commentators. The reason is that expert opinion, if it is acceptable in a critical discussion, is presumably based on some domain of knowledge or scientific research (Chapter 2, section 10), whereas accepting a premise on the basis that it is generally accepted or not doubted is much more slender and has less of an epistemic basis, if any at all, behind it.

At any rate, these distinctions suggest that we need to be very careful to distinguish between accepting propositions in a critical discussion on the basis of expert opinion and accepting premises on some more slender basis of popular acceptance. Also, as noted above, this takes us into the whole area of presumptions and raises questions about how presumption could be justified as a source of propositions that would play some kind of role in requirements for premise adequacy in persuasion dialogue.

Nicholas Rescher ties presumption to the prior notion of burden of proof, which in turn he ties to the dialectical notion of the context of dialogue in which an argument is used. According to Rescher, there are probative asymmetries, as he calls them, in a dialogue, meaning that the weight of proof required to adequately support a proposition in a dialogue exchange between two parties is a function of the party's role in the dialogue and of the stage in the dialogue at which that proposition is maintained by a participant (1977, 17). Rescher illustrates this contention with its use in the legal context, where, for example, in a criminal case, the prosecution has the burden of proving the guilt of the defendant beyond a reasonable doubt, whereas the defense, in order to win its case, need only throw sufficient doubt on the case of the prosecution (26). What Rescher calls a *prima facie* case is one that succeeds in shifting the burden of proof in a dialogue from one side to the other (28).

To fill gaps needed in argumentation and, most notably, for example, in argumentation in a legal case, Rescher brings forward the concept of a presumption. According to his definition, a presumption "indicates that in the absence of specific counterindications, we are to accept how things as a rule are taken as standing, and it places the burden or proof upon the adversary's side" (30). Presumption is a kind of rule that enables us to put a proposition forward, even though there may be insufficient evidence to prove it; that is, to meet the burden of proof that would be required for its acceptance. Even so, in such a case, we may move forward to provisionally accept a proposition for the sake of argument, calling it a presumption, meaning that it is provisionally acceptable and there is no presently known evidence that refutes it or shows it to be false. Rescher gives the example of the standing presumption in favor of the usual normal or customary course of events, as we know them (31).

It is notable that Rescher's doctrine of presumption, as stated above, would support the idea that there could be a presumption in favor of a proposition in the context of a dialogue where it has been shown that the majority, or everyone, in the normal course of things, tends to accept a particular proposition as true, or tends to normally operate on the assumption that this proposition is true. Of course, Rescher stresses that a presumption of this kind would have the important property of defeasibility (32); that is, if new information comes in that shows, in a particular case, that this proposition that has been tentatively accepted as a presumption is now shown to be false then a rational participant in the dialogue must be prepared to give up that proposition, i.e., to retract it as a commitment from that point onward in the dialogue.

Rescher utilizes the rule that the notion of a defeasible presumption carries with it the idea of reversing the burden of proof in a dialogue, citing Richard Whately as his source. Quoting a well-known passage from Whately's *Elements of Rhetoric*, Rescher introduces the Whatelian idea that presumption is associated with preoccupation of a ground implying that the presumption stands good only until some sufficient reason is adduced against it (32). In this passage, Whately explicitly states that the burden of proof, in the case of a presumption, lies on the side of the party who would dispute that presumption.

Rescher's doctrine of presumption would seem generally to support the idea that the *ad populum* argument could be accepted as a presumptive type of argument that would have the function of shifting a burden of proof in a dialogue. As such, this type of argumentation could seem to be, in principle, reasonable as a dialectical form of argument. Rescher notably goes so far as to lend support to this idea by stating that a presumption of truth should be generally accorded to what he characterizes as the cognitive status quo or the domain of what is generally accepted or qualifies as common knowledge (36). Rescher cites Perelman and Olbrechts-Tyteca (1969) as supporting this notion of presumption, as well.

According to Perelman and Olbrechts-Tyteca, presumptions are connected with what is normal and likely (1969, 71). Moreover, they add that the concept of what is normal can be clarified by showing that it depends upon a reference group (72), that is, upon a particular audience to whom an argument was directed. This notion of presumption, like Rescher's, seems to allow the appeal to popular opinion as, in principle, a legitimate type of presumptive argument. Perelman and Olbrechts-Tyteca go even further when they refer to agreements of certain special audiences as a basis for a speaker's choosing premises that are acceptable on a basis of presumptive reasoning (99). Perelman and Olbrechts-Tyteca go on to add that the premises in argumentation generally consist of propositions accepted by the hearers, meaning that the speaker should generally choose his premises from propositions that he presumes are commitments of the audience (104). This form of reasoning is clearly meant by Perelman and Olbrechts-Tyteca to be presumptive in nature because they add that the interlocutors, i.e., the audience, can challenge the presumed agreement on the speaker's premises with a denial, if they see fit.

The concept of presumption as a basis of premise acceptance is also cited by James Freeman, who sees presumption as operating in what he calls a "dialectical situation" where two parties are involved in an exchange of arguments, and the one party is attacking or questioning a thesis proposed by the other party (1991, 339). Freeman writes that we call such a situation dialectical because there is a conflict or opposition between the two parties, and the one party has the role of raising critical questions about the theses and arguments put forward by the other side. He sees presumptions as being useful in a dialectical situation because there are generally cases where the proponent has made a good point and the challenger must either grant this point or rebut it, even though there may be insufficient evidence for either proving or refuting the proposition (340). In such a case, as Freeman sees it, the dialectical situation can be furthered by introducing the notion of presumption so that a proposition can be put forward by the one side and then tentatively accepted by the other side as a basis for carrying the argument further. Accordingly, he sees presumption as a basis for premise acceptability. According to Freeman, there are dialectical situations where we should find a statement rationally acceptable because there is a presumption in favor of it (342). Citing Rescher's notion of presumption noted above (Rescher 1977), he argues that there should be a presumption in favor of common knowledge (1991, 344).

7. Presumptive Reasoning in Dialectical Arguments

Several warrants for making a presumption in a context of dialogue are distinguished by Walton (1992a, 58–59). The first is facilitating actions. Provisional assumptions in practical reasoning often need to be made where there is absence of definite knowledge on how to proceed in a particular case. Clearly, in such cases, the bringing in of a presumption is a temporary way of allowing the reasoning to go ahead subject to feedback and correction.

A second kind of warrant for making a presumption is that of an accepted procedure. Presumptions are often based on familiar ways of doing things that have been found to be successful through practical experience. Standard examples would come from practical crafts and applied sciences like medicine and engineering.

A third basis for presumption is expert opinion. In any type of dialogue, such as critical discussion, it can improve the quality of the discussion as we have already seen, if propositions are accepted on the basis of expert opinion. Of course, such a proposition would be accepted on a tentative and defeasible basis. Nevertheless, it could help a critical discussion and make it go forward in a more informed way if this kind of presumptive reasoning is allowed.

A fourth basis of presumption is custom. There are ways of doing things that are widely accepted by a group, which often reflect the group's values. They are customs that are open to challenge and may not be mandatory but nevertheless represent usual ways of doing things that have a certain presumption in their favor.

A fifth kind of warrant, cited in Walton, is called "conventional wisdom." This type of presumptive reasoning is based on what are called "broad acceptance of common sense beliefs that are not generally or widely challenged because there has been no reason to question them" (58). Both the fourth and fifth categories of warrants for making a presumption can clearly be seen as representing types of *ad populum* arguments.

The sixth type of warrant for making a presumption cited is that of cooperation and politeness (59). These are the kinds of presumptions that make social activities proceed smoothly by facilitating actions requiring collaboration or tolerance. In other words, we may accept certain ways of doing things or beliefs or propositions even though we do not agree with them completely or would not do things that way ourselves. Nevertheless, we can go along with it because to do so would facilitate some activity we're involved in and there is very little cost to us to sacrifice our normal way of doing it.

A dialectical framework that can be used to analyze presumptive reasoning generally is presented in Walton (1992a, 55–56). According to this analysis, plausible reasoning is based on a defeasible framework that shifts a burden of proof to one side or the other in a dialogue as the dialogue proceeds through a sequence of argumentation. According to this analysis, presumptive reasoning is very closely related to the type of argumentation traditionally called the *argumentum ad ignorantiam* or argument from ignorance, sometimes also called appeal to ignorance. Using this form of argument, you can go ahead and presume that a proposition is true, provided that it has not been shown yet, according to the current evidence, that this proposition is false. Conversely, you could accept a proposition as false on the same kind of reasoning, provided it has not been shown yet in the dialogue that the proposition is true. So, this type of argument from ignorance could be described as a kind of flip-flop reasoning. You can go ahead and assume that the proposition has one truth value as long as your opponent in the dialogue has not shown, by bringing forward sufficient evidence and arguments at any given point, that this proposition has the other truth value.

According to the analysis given in Walton (1992a, 280–82), this pattern of reversal of burden of proof is also generally characteristic of presumptive reasoning. This analysis gives a set of speech act conditions to characterize the sequence of argumentation identified with presumptive reasoning in a context of dialogue. Presumption is a proposition put forward by one party in a dialogue, namely, the proponent, in a kind of situation where the proponent does not have adequate evidence yet to prove this proposition. So, the proponent puts forward the proposition, since he needs it for his argument, as an assumption, by asking the other party: "Will you provisionally agree to accept this proposition as a premise in my argument, even though there is insufficient evidence to definitely prove it yet?" This question leaves an opening or choice for the respondent: "No, I won't accept this proposition even provisionally" or "Well, yes, of course, I'll accept it tentatively even though it's not something that I'm going to assert or put forward as a commitment of my own. But, nevertheless, since you want me to grant it, I'll collaborate in the discussion, and go along for the sake of the argument and accept it provisionally."

There is a problem, as shown by Walton and Krabbe (1995), with the traditional Hamblin-type of dialogues (Hamblin 1970; 1971). Such a respondent could always just retort, "No commitment," thereby blocking the ability of the proponent to carry forward any further in the dialogue. In other words, the respondent could always adopt the role of skeptic and simply never accept any propositions as commitments that the proponent puts forward. Were such a tactic to be used, the respondent could get away with never granting any premises that could be used by the proponent as bases for proving anything to the respondent. This skeptical move would effectively stall the argument, somewhat unfairly, but nevertheless block the proponent's ability to ever prove anything to the respondent and, thereby, block any possibility of the proponent's making any progress in the dialogue at all. So, we have here a technical problem in analyzing the structure of a critical discussion. What we need generally to solve this problem is some kind of incentive that would make it attractive for the respondent to accept commitments, so that the proponent could use these commitments as premises instead of always having the respondent repeating "No commitment," "No commitment," "No commitment," in a dialogue.

The analysis of presumption given in Walton (1992a, 280–82) offers a structure of presumptive reasoning that fulfills this purpose. When a respondent is given this choice of whether to accept or not a proposition the opponent has put forward as a presumption, the burden of proof is reversed. What happens precisely in this kind of situation is that, instead of there being a burden of proof on the proponent to prove this proposition, which would be the normal allocation of burden of proof, the burden of proof shifts to the respondent. If the respondent does not want to accept this proposition as a commitment, then he must give some reason against it, that is, he must fulfill the burden of proof or present some kind of evidence that the proposition is false or is not acceptable to him as a commitment. Then, according to the analysis given by Walton, the proposition is put in place as a commitment of the respondent. That is, if the respondent can give no sufficient reason for his nonacceptance of this proposition then, automatically, this proposition is placed in his commitment store as a proposition that he accepts. It does not mean that he accepts it in the sense that it is part of his position or, if challenged, he would have to prove it. It means that he accepts it as a presumption; that is, he accepts it tentatively in order to make the argument go forward, so that it goes into his commitment set marked as a special kind of proposition that he accepts, not fully, but accepts for the sake of argument.

Another condition, called "condition 3" (Walton 1992a, 291), is one where the way is left open at some further point in the dialogue, so that if the respondent wants to reject this proposition, the burden of proof is then reversed. A way is left open for the respondent to reject this proposition at some subsequent point if sufficient evidence or information comes into the dialogue, so that the respondent can show that this proposition is false, given the evidence, and go ahead and reject that proposition. If, at some future point, both the proponent and the respondent agree that this presumption may now be rejected then another avenue for the respondent's retracting his commitment to this proposition is opened.

The basic point is that the proposition is accepted only tentatively by the respondent and lodged into place as a commitment of his on a tentative and defeasible basis. This analysis of presumptive reasoning bears out the thesis that this kind of reasoning is structurally similar to the argument from ignorance because, from the respondent's point of view in a dialogue, once a proposition is accepted as true as a presumption put in place by the other party it is tentatively accepted as true for some subsequent series of points in the dialogue exchange. But, it can be refuted if sufficient evidence is brought forward to show it is false. This general characteristic, then, expresses the general concept of how presumption works in dialectical argumentation.

8. Popular Opinion and Common Knowledge

The standard treatment account of the bandwagon argument expresses the form of this argument in terms of belief. The form given is: "Everybody believes that such-and-such a proposition is true, therefore, it follows that this proposition is true." In expressing the form of the *ad populum* argument this way, the presumption appealed to is that there is a distinction between knowledge and belief; that is, there is a distinction between saying a proposition is believed to be true and saying that a proposition is known to be true. Presumably, the key difference from a point of view of a logic textbook is that when a speaker says a particular proposition is known to be true it means that this proposition is based on some evidence.

Whereas, if the expression "It is believed that a proposition is true" is used, there may be, in fact, no evidence supporting this belief. Given this distinction, then, the bandwagon argument tends to be an inherently weak argument because such an appeal need not be based on any knowledge or evidence. In this respect, the bandwagon argument can be contrasted with appeal to expert opinion as a form of argument. Presumably, an expert who has been consulted is an expert in a particular domain of knowledge; therefore, if an expert says that a particular proposition is true then the expert has some evidence in a domain of knowledge to back up this assertion. Hence, appeal to expert opinion as a type of argument has a distinctly different and higher standing than appeal to popular opinion.

When one asks the question "What could the logical basis be for giving appeal to popular opinion in the form of the bandwagon argument a special standing, as an argument that commands our acceptance or has some kind of validity or structural correctness as a plausible or generally acceptable type of argument?" As long as one sticks to the bandwagon type of argument given as the form of argument in the standard treatment there seems to be no straightforward way to answer this question. For, even if it is found that everybody in a particular population of individuals believes proposition A, that does not mean that proposition A has to be true or is even likely true, or that there is any genuine evidence supporting the truth of acceptability of proposition A.

Of course, we could accept proposition A as a presumption if everybody believes that it is true, but the question still needs to be asked, "What would be the logical basis for this?," that is, on what specific kind of evidence would a rational acceptance of proposition A be based? An attempt to answer this question would be to argue that public opinion can, in some instances—such as in relation to some particular propositions—be well-informed and thoughtful. Therefore, one might argue, public opinion is not mere mass opinion but represents a kind of thinking through of an issue, resulting in a conclusion to accept a proposition that is based on a kind of knowledge or awareness of the evidence and circumstances surrounding this proposition.

Generally, as we have seen, there is often a tendency to bolster up the bandwagon type of argument by presuming or adding in assumptions to the effect that the public is in a position to know about a particular proposition and, therefore, in a sense, has knowledge of the truth of this proposition or is basing its acceptance of this proposition on evidence and thoughtful deliberation. Thus, some accounts of the requirement of premise acceptability would rephrase the *ad populum* argument and put its evidential thrust not in terms of popular opinion or mass opinion without any qualification but, instead, use a term such as "common knowledge" to express this kind of basis for premise acceptability.

For example, Trudy Govier states that a proposition should be allowed as an acceptable premise if it states something that is known to virtually everyone. "A premise in an argument is acceptable if it is a matter of common knowledge" (1985, 80). Govier cites as examples statements such as "Human beings have hearts" and "There are many trees in Canada" (81). According to Govier, these statements, while not necessarily true, are, in fact, true, and virtually all human adults know them to be true. Therefore, they are the kinds of propositions that should be accepted as premises in an argument without requiring further supporting evidence to back them up.

In Govier's opinion, we cannot realistically dispense with common knowledge as a condition of premise acceptability because arguments have to start somewhere, and people will generally accept premises based on common knowledge, and it is not generally reasonable to go on having to question propositions accepted on such a basis. Why exactly is common knowledge a rationally acceptable basis on which to ground a premise in argumentation, and how are we supposed to tell the difference, generally, between propositions that are merely based on popular opinion and those that may correctly be said to be based on common knowledge?

The answer given by James Freeman is that premise acceptability should be understood in terms of challenger presumption (1995, 270). For Freeman, this means that challengers in a dialectical exchange are also representatives of the "community of rational inquirers." This community is, of course, reminiscent of Blair and Johnson's community of rational interlocutors (1987, 50). An interlocutor is a participant in an argument, who is engaged in a dialectical exchange with another party, and needs to generally presume that the other party will share her background knowledge of a given situation. According to Freeman, then, this limitation means that a questioner is committed to continue probing the other party's case only to a certain limit. Such attempts to question the case of the other party must draw distinctions on which presumptions made by the other party are genuinely questionable and which ones can be taken for granted or should be set aside as presumptions that do not need to be questioned. If a particular proposition is a matter of common knowledge to both parties and to the general listeners or audience that are also part of the dialectical exchange then a questioner does not need to challenge them and can take them for granted as acceptable premises in the other party's argument.

But the question still has not been answered regarding the evidential status or logical basis of such presumptions as being based on evidence. Why should propositions, which are part of the background knowledge of the participants in the general community, be regarded as acceptable premises? Freeman gives two reasons that could supply such a logical basis (271–72). The first reason is that propositions that are part of common knowledge, such as the one cited by Govier, come to be known partly, at least, because they have been vouched for by authoritative sources. According to Freeman, such propositions have been vouched for by parents and teachers, for example, who give us instruction. Of course, these propositions are accepted on the basis of a presumption of trust, but later experience has given us no reason to undermine this trust if such a statement is to be counted as common knowledge, which is the basis for reasonably accepting such a proposition as a premise in a dialectical exchange.

Freeman's second reason is that matters of common knowledge are part of what he calls "our lived experience." This means that a questioner in a dialectical exchange will recognize a particular proposition as being based on common knowledge, at least partly because it arises out of her own experience. By recognizing that she shares this experience with her dialogue partner, she will find a basis through the lived experience of both parties for accepting it as having common-knowledge status. According to Freeman's account, then, common knowledge propositions are based on a kind of evidence. They are based on knowledge, because such propositions come to us through authoritative or expert sources who have, in turn, presumably based their reasoning on their scientific knowledge of some particular domain of knowledge or skill. But also, common knowledge propositions are based on our own individual experience that we share with others in dialogue who share a common situation, and because these propositions are singled out as common knowledge propositions because they are based on our experience, this means that there is a source of evidence and empirical verification behind them.

Following the route taken by Govier and Freeman, then, the so-called bandwagon argument can be seen to have two different forms (or at least, if we take the basic type of bandwagon argument found in the standard treatments, we can see that it has a counterpart, another type of argument that has a similar or comparable form, but that is nevertheless distinctively different in its logical properties from the first form). The first form of argument could be called the bandwagon, public opinion, or mass opinion argument, and it has the form "Everybody believes that proposition A is true, therefore, proposition A is true."

Both Govier and Freeman cite a comparable type of argument that they call the *common-knowledge argument*, that has a somewhat different form. This form of this argument is "Everybody accepts that A is based on common knowledge, therefore, A is true." So, the underlying form of this argument is epistemic rather than doxastic, that is, it is phrased in terms of knowledge rather than belief. Its underlying structure of argument takes the form "Everybody knows that proposition A is true, therefore, proposition A is true." But the philosophical objection to this way of proceeding is posed by the traditional division between knowledge and opinion, conjoined with the traditional view that mass or popular opinion is not knowledge but only that, namely, opinion. This view, based on a sharp division between knowledge and opinion, has been strongly prevalent in traditional philosophy since the time of the Greeks. In fact, Plato is perhaps best known for the view that knowledge is absolute and unchanging, whereas popular opinion is constantly changing.

Another question is whether, according to Govier and Freeman, the appeal to a common-knowledge type of argument is being viewed as a subspecies of *ad populum* argument or as a separate type of argument that is perhaps similar or related to the *ad populum* argument but is distinctively different in its structure. Govier, in fact, does not use the term *argumentum ad populum* in her section on common knowledge as a type of justification for premise acceptability (1985, 80–82), while Freeman goes further and drives a wedge between appeal to common knowledge and appeal to popularity (1995, 272).

According to Freeman, appeals to common knowledge are not appeals to popularity. "They are certainly not appeals by proponents that everybody accepts some claim." Appeals to popularity are seen as inherently fallacious. Freeman describes them as basically being *hasty conclusion fallacies*. "The data concerning the popularity of the belief are simply not sufficient to warrant accepting the belief." Appeal to popularity is a fallacy on the grounds that the error in this type of argument lies in "inflating the value of popularity as evidence." Freeman seems to be claiming, then, that the fallacy lies in the use of the very weak type of argument called *appeal to popularity*, while at the same time exploiting its resemblance to the very strong form of argument called *appeal to common knowledge*. The deceptiveness of the fallacy is apparently constituted by the possibility or plausibility that the respondent or the audience will mistakenly assume that the appeal to popular opinion is an appeal to common knowledge. "The claim that a belief is commonly held does not constitute proper grounds for recognizing it as common knowledge by some challenger" (272).

What Freeman seems to be saying is that we have an appeal to common-opinion type of argument—that is, the *ad populum* or appeal to popularity argument—that is either inherently very weak or even generally fallacious. He contrasts this with another type of argument, namely, appeal to common knowledge, which he sees as an inherently reasonable type of argument because it is based on knowledge. It is a knowledge-based type of argument because it is based partly on expert opinion as a source of evidence and partly on the lived experience of the arguers. However, according to Freeman's account, the mere appeal to popularity, that is, the argument that claims that a belief should be accepted because it is popularly accepted, is fallacious. Freeman describes exactly this form of argument as the fallacious appeal to popularity (273).

Freeman's account of the *ad populum* fallacy presents two general problems. One is the question, What are the criteria that enable us to distinguish between a proposition that is merely an appeal to popular opinion and an argument that is an appeal to common knowledge? The second problem raised is whether appeal to popular opinion is inherently fallacious; that is, is it as bad an argument, generally, as Freeman thinks? Could there be arguments based on popular opinion that might have some standing as presumptive reasoning for tentatively accepting a co-arguer's premise, even though these propositions are not, in some sense, based on hard knowledge or expert opinion? In other words, is it conceivable that the public could have access to some source of evidence, or plausible basis for reasoning, other than expert opinion? Perhaps it could be that, on some issues the public has a more sophisticated and informed view than the experts, while on other issues the experts might have a more informed and sophisticated view than the public. Thus, on whether public opinion has any evidential value or merit with regard to accepting the truth of a proposition may depend very much on what that particular proposition is.

9. Mass Opinion and Public Judgment

Daniel Yankelovich argues that public opinion has a distinctive value in its own right as a source of premises for argument apart from expert opinion. As he puts it, public opinion "is not merely a second-rate reflection of expert opinion. Each form of opinion—expert and public—has its own excellencies and its own failings, but public opinion is not, as is generally assumed, simply less well-informed expert opinion" (1991, 42). According to Yankelovich, public opinion can be a good source of evidence on some issues, but in other cases, polls taken to determine public opinion can be very misleading and can overinflate the value of public opinion.

To emphasize the distinction between these two types of appeal to public opinion, Yankelovich distinguishes between two types of appeal to public-opinion arguments. He uses the term *mass opinion* to refer to poor quality public-opinion appeals that have failed to take into account that the public has been poorly informed on an issue or is not in a good position to pronounce on it in a consistent way that gives the poll good value. In contrast to this poor type of appeal to public opinion, Yankelovich cites another type of *ad populum* he calls *appeal to public judgment* (42). To say that public judgment has been reached on an issue, according to Yankelovich, means that people have deliberated thoughtfully on the issue and have formed a judgment that they are willing to stand by. An example of the difference between these two types of appeal to popular opinion is the case of polls on the issue of protectionism (22).

In the opinion of Yankelovich, polls on protectionism indicated that 70 percent of people polled accepted the idea that the United States should have protectionist legislation in order to protect American jobs. He points out, however, that when you dig behind these data, it turns out that the people who answered these polls were not fully aware of the consequences of the protectionist policy. When it was pointed out that protectionist legislation would have the consequence of less choice in the products you can buy, and more cost for certain products, then the 70 percent support for protection policies declined in the polls to about 26 percent to 28 percent. This example shows a radical change once people had become aware of the consequences of the protectionist policy. The problem in this kind of case, according to Yankelovich, is that people may simply not be informed about the consequences of an issue they are asked about in a public opinion poll (42).

As Yankelovich views the picture, the people who are the respondents in the poll should not be held responsible for this failure of information. The problem, as he sees it (1991, 42), is that, in many cases, the public is not given an opportunity to take these possible consequences into account because of both the way the questions in the poll are asked and the way they are reported in the findings of the poll. However, for Yankelovich to say that public judgment has been reached does not mean that the people polled have to be aware of all the relevant facts. What it means is that the issue is one that the public has had the time and opportunity to deliberate about, so that their opinion on the matter has reached a mature state. As Yankelovich describes it, a public opinion poll is like a snapshot or a piece of information reporting only one particular time or one particular point in an extended sequence of developments on an issue. But opinion, in his view, is formed in a dynamic process (23). This process could be described as a sequence of practical reasoning on an issue that is being deliberated about as circumstances change over a period of time.

Yankelovich describes this dynamic sequence of reasoning as a journey that has seven steps (1991, 24). The first two steps he calls consciousness-raising steps, where first people become aware of the problem and record a sense of urgency about it. At this initial stage, the issue surfaces as a problem which requires a decision about a course of action to be taken. The third step occurs where policymakers offer initial proposals for change and test public reactions to these proposals, often by means of public opinion polls. In the fourth step, problems are encountered when negative consequences become apparent, and it becomes clear that trade-offs have to be made. At this fourth step, conflict and opposition begin to appear. The fifth step consists in the working through of these trade-offs to reconcile conflicting values. This fifth step on an issue of public deliberation, can take not just weeks but even months or years for people to get through. The fifth step is called by Yankelovich the stage of intellectual resolution, where people reach a mental resolution of the problem as opposed to an emotional resolution of it. Then, at the seventh step, the stage of public judgment, people resolve the issue morally and emotionally as well as intellectually.

This analysis of the basis of *ad populum* arguments is quite different from those outlined above. It does not postulate the *ad populum* as an appeal to common knowledge or as any sort of knowledge-based reasoning or argument based on expert opinion. Instead, it sees the public-judgment argument as based on a kind of thinking called deliberation, bringing the basis of the *ad populum* much more in line with the examples studied in Chapter 1.

But what kind of dialectical framework of reasoned argument is a deliberation? In Chapter 5, some historical precedents for thinking about this important question already exist. Most of all, what needs to be appreciated at this point is that through Yankelovich's seven-stage model of reasoning needed to reach a public judgment we are given a framework in which the *ad populum* argument can be evaluated as a reasonable argument in some cases. The problem remains, however, that public judgment, even if based on a sequence of deliberation, may still seem too relativistic a basis on which to base the logical evaluation of arguments.

10. The Two Faces of the *Ad Populum*

Tindale's statement that the possibility of a worrisome epistemological relativism is a threat to an audience-based standard of premise acceptability expresses the key worry about *ad populum* arguments very well. This worry is not only reflected in the standard treatment of the *ad populum* as a fallacy but even as far back as ancient times, when Plato and Aristotle worried about accepting the views of the many who speak in an unreflective way. After all, if we accept premises merely because they are supported by popular opinion, are we not only accepting the prejudices of popular sentiment in an uncritical way but possibly even sanctioning appeals to mob instincts and prejudiced emotions of all sorts? Is not this mob appeal type of sanction just opening the way for the kind of bigoted, inflammatory rhetoric that is so dangerous, and that logic ought to criticize and condemn? Do not public deliberations have a bad track record of arriving at disastrous decisions, based more on emotions and short-term interests than on logical reasoning?

The answer suggested by the theories surveyed in this chapter is that if we want to evaluate arguments used in persuasion dialogue in all kinds of everyday conversational exchanges of argumentation, including political deliberation in a democracy, we need to accept popular opinion as a basis for premise adequacy of arguments. Moreover, we need to allow that, under the right conditions, popular opinion can be rational or reasonable, or a correct or justifiable type of argument, to draw conclusions by inference from such premises. But the structure of reasoning appropriate for serving as the logical basis for the drawing of such conclusions should be seen as presumptive in nature, a sequence of deliberations concluding to a prudent course of action, even if the outcome is not conclusive.

The problem seems to be that in so much of Western culture for so many years, the dominant view of logic and rational argument has emphasized reasoned logical inference as being airtight and conclusive. According to the deductive model of argument, for an argument to be valid, it must be logically impossible for the premises to be true and the conclusion false. Presumptive reasoning is not well served by this model. In a presumptively reasonable inference, it is possible that the premises are true and the conclusion is false.

To make persuasion dialogue possible, we need arguments based on common starting points, on premises that are presumed to be true, as a basis for drawing presumptive conclusions to make a deliberation or a persuasion dialogue move forward constructively and collaboratively, even where we cannot be sure of the truth of a matter.

But it seems that to make this kind of reasoning work, it is important not to be dogmatic about your arguments. What is crucial to a correct and justifiable account of presumptive reasoning is to realize that it is defeasible in nature and needs to be open-ended, as used in a dialogue. Where rhetorical mob appeal is a closed type of argumentation that targets the interests and prejudices of the audience, demonizing opponents and ruling out all possibilities of doubts or questioning by the other side, the danger of the fallacious use of the *ad populum* is real. But if reasoned deliberation comes to a judgment that is defeasible and open to revision in light of new information, it can be a reasoned guide to prudent action.

It is questionable whether there is such a thing as common knowledge at the basis of the *ad populum* argument. As we saw in Chapter 1, the appeal to expert opinion, a species of knowledge-based or knowledge-justified argument, is distinctively different as a type of argument from appeal to popular opinion. Instead, the examples of *ad populum* argument cited in Chapter 1 seem to be based on what Yankelovich calls public deliberation as a type of reasoning (1991; 1992). But the exact relationship between appeal to expert opinion (and position to know reasoning, generally) and the appeal to popular opinion type of argument, remains to be determined.

The subtlety about the appeal to popular opinion as a type of argument now revealed is that it has two faces: a good side and a nasty side. It is a fallible, defeasible, imperfect type of argument that can be an instrument of deception and rhetorical manipulation. But it is also a useful and important presumptive type of reasoning that can help to serve as a tentative guide to action in prudent deliberations, when used properly and in the right place in a dialogue exchange of viewpoints.

Curiously, outside the confines of the standard treatment in logic textbooks, the appeal to popular opinion has, from time to time, been recognized as a species of reasonable argument (when used for certain purposes). Most notably, as mentioned at the beginning of Chapter 3, Aristotle himself recognized a species of argument he called dialectical argument, based on premises drawn from the opinions of the many.

Chapter Five

THE OLD DIALECTIC

As noted in Chapter 1, section 10, there is a well-known and ancient history of the recognition of appeal to popular opinion as a reasonable (nonfallacious) type of argument. Aristotle recognized a particular type of argument he called dialectical, which was based on a so-called endoxic premise—meaning a proposition accepted by the many. Aristotle, Plato, and other leading thinkers in the ancient world saw dialectical argument as not only reasonable and useful but judged it to be fundamentally important in both philosophy and politics, as well as in any kind of attempt to reason about issues where opinions are divided.

So what happened to dialectic? How did we get from the viewpoint of Plato and Aristotle, where dialectic was thought to be so important to reasoned argument, to the modern viewpoint, where it is either not recognized at all or thought to be of little or no importance? How did we get the modern view that *ad populum* arguments are inherently fallacious, from an ancient and medieval view that was balanced between seeing them as reasonable in some cases and fallacious (or at least dangerous) in other cases?

1. Platonic Dialectic

The method used in Plato's earlier dialogues is called *elenchus*. Richard Robinson defines elenchus in both a wider and a narrower sense. According to Robinson, elenchus in the wider sense means "examining a person with regard to a statement he has made, by putting to him questions calling for further statements, in the hope that they will determine the meaning and the truth-value of his first statement" (1962, 7). As used by Socrates in the earlier dialogues, the elenchus typically has the outcome of turning up a falsehood. Robinson writes that elenchus in the narrower sense of the word refers to a form of cross-examination or refutation.

In the early Platonic dialogues, Socrates typically begins by putting some general question to an interlocutor. When he receives an answer, he asks another question, and then a series of further questions. Typically, the first question was a difficult or controversial one, but the answers to the subsequent questions tend to be obvious or not so controversial. As the culmination of this process of questioning, the interlocutor is led to a contradiction or to some statement that is clearly false.

The elenchus was one element in the method Plato called *dialectic*. However, it is difficult to define exactly what Plato meant by dialectic because he tended to change the meaning of this word from his earlier to his later dialogues. According to Robinson, Plato's use of "dialectic" has a tendency to mean "the ideal method, whatever that may be." (70). Some elements, however, are characteristic of dialectic. One of these is that dialectic was meant to be a form of conversation; in other words, a verbal, social activity that took place centrally between two parties. These two parties played the roles of questioner and answerer. The questioner led the sequence of argumentation and the answerer answered.

According to Robinson, another important characteristic of dialectic was that the elenchtic sequence drawn out by the questioner was based on the commitments of the answerer. "The answerer was expected to say what he himself really thought, and nothing else" (78). In other words, the assumption is that dialectic requires that the answerer, in replying to a question, say what he really thinks.

Two other requirements are also noted by Robinson. The first is that the answerer's opinions must agree with each other or, if not, the questioner should challenge this failure of consistency. The second requirement is that there should be agreement between the questioner and the answerer, that is, things that seem true to the one must also seem true to the other. So, the presumption of a dialectical conversation is that, in the end, the two participants will come to agreement and that they will not remain content with an inconsistency.

It is interesting that Robinson notes that dialectic is very much oriented to the commitments of the answerer. He goes so far as to say that the answerer must say what he really thinks and that this is part of the general principle that "dialectic recognizes no authority" (78). As Robinson puts it, "Neither party may accept a proposition from anyone else however near or great. The only authority is what seems true to us two here and now" (79). These remarks suggest that the sequence of reasoning in dialectic is based exclusively on premises that are propositions accepted by the questioner as well as the answerer in certain instances. Thus, it would seem that there is no place in the Platonic dialectic for propositions that are accepted as premises on the basis of what the majority believe or accept as true. In fact, Plato often seems to reject, or to place a low value on, the worth of *ad populum* arguments.

There are prominent passages in many of the Platonic dialogues where Socrates takes quite a negative view of the value of majority opinion in serious argumentation. For example, in the *Crito* (44c–44e), Crito is concerned whether people will think badly of Socrates' colleagues because they might think that the colleagues persuaded Socrates to stay around in Athens and, as a result, to meet his death instead of escaping from the city. Crito is worried (44c) that most people will never believe that it was Socrates who refused to leave Athens, even though his colleagues did their best to persuade him to leave.

In reply to this worry, Socrates suggests to Crito that he is paying too much attention to what most people think. Crito is not too easily convinced, however, and replies that one has to take popular opinion into account. Socrates insists on the point, however. He replies in turn that the majority opinions of ordinary people do not make a man either wise or stupid. This passage suggests a dismissive attitude toward propositions based on popular or majority opinion as premises in argument having some sort of rational value. A little later in the *Crito* (46e), however, Socrates takes a more balanced approach, suggesting that some of the popular opinions should be respected while others should not be.

In the *Laches* (184d–185a), Socrates compares popular opinion to expert opinion. Socrates asks his questioner whether he would follow the advice of the majority on a question concerning the gymnastic training of his son, or whether he would follow the opinion of an expert or, at least, someone who had been trained under an expert. According to Socrates' estimate (184e), the vote of the expert would be worth more than the vote of all four persons who were not experts. Socrates concludes (184e) that a good decision should be based on knowledge and not on majority opinion or numbers of respondents. This passage is interesting because there is a clear contrast drawn between the opinion of the majority and the opinion of the experts, and also because the relative worth of both in argument are compared and the expert opinion as a type of argument is given a considerably higher weight.

In an interesting passage in the *Protagoras* (352d–353c), Socrates says that dialectic must explain the opinions of the many. This passage is interesting because it suggests more of an Aristotelian approach whereby dialectic could be partly based on popular opinion as a kind of premise. Socrates says that most people do not believe the opinions of the philosophers and even find them paradoxical. Protagoras then replies that it is by no means uncommon for people to say what is not correct. This reply suggests a condemnation of popular opinion as a source of acceptance or insight. But Socrates replies that it is not enough to reply to such a person who is an outsider and whose opinion represents that of the majority: "You are wrong. What you say is false." Instead, it is better to explain how the philosophical view relates to that ordinary opinion.

Protagoras still does not accept this, however, and asks again why it is necessary for philosophers to look into the opinions of the common man. Socrates insists that he believes that this path will help us, that is, the philosophers, toward insight in finding out whether various philosophical positions can be justified and are reasonable or not. So, in this passage, Socrates is less negative about the place of popular opinion in argumentation and seems to take a balanced attitude toward it. It is not that he says it can be accepted at face value, and, indeed, he suggests that it is generally in conflict with what the philosophers say. But, nevertheless, he does accord it a certain presumptive status, provisionally, as a way of helping a dialectical argument to go forward. In this passage, Socrates does find a place for appeal to popular opinion in dialectical argument.

An interesting passage in the *Phaedrus*, starting at 260a, has Socrates discussing rhetoric and, in particular, commenting on the ability of the Sophists to persuade a mass audience to believe things that are not really true. At 260d, Socrates cites the case of the master of rhetoric who employs his power of persuasion, and, by studying the beliefs of the masses, persuades them to accept something as true that is really false. At 261d, Socrates cites the case of the Sophist who, in a public harangue, makes the same things seem to the community good at one time, and the reverse of good at another time. Here it seems, Socrates is very skeptical about the value of the opinions of the many in argumentation. He sees it as highly variable as well as highly vulnerable to the rhetorician or Sophist who can manipulate the community by, first of all, studying their beliefs, and then cleverly persuading them to accept propositions that are, in fact, false by haranguing them using clever techniques of rhetoric. Socrates suggests, at 262b, that people can hold beliefs contrary to fact and be misled by Sophists, so that, in such a case, a popular opinion can be mistaken.

Referring to the Sophists again, in the *Republic* (Book VI, 493a), Socrates warns about arguments that exploit the opinions of the multitude in rhetoric. Socrates compares the opinions of the multitude to a great, strong beast. It can be savage or gentle, depending on how its master handles and manipulates it. Socrates grants that such a speaker is skilled and that he has learned to "know the moods and pleasures of the motley multitude in their assembly." But Socrates censures such an individual, saying that he is giving too much "mob authority over himself" than is appropriate.

Thus the Platonic dialogues reveal a fairly balanced attitude toward argument based on popular opinion. Socrates is somewhat disdainful about according such arguments much worth, and he is aware of how they can be powerfully abused in mob appeal rhetoric. But he does concede that they should have a legitimate (if somewhat uncertain) place in dialectic.

2. Aristotelian Dialectic

In his *Prior and Posterior Analytics*, Aristotle studied a kind of reasoning that he called *demonstration*, which I have compared to the type of dialogue called the *inquiry* (Walton 1988). The type of reasoning used in the demonstration was deductive and formalistic in nature. Specifically, it was analyzed by Aristotle using his technique of syllogistic reasoning, a form of deductively valid inference. According to Aristotle's description, analytical reasoning of this kind is impersonal. The conclusion is a proposition that either follows deductively or does not from a given set of propositions called the *premises* of an inference. What is less well known, however, is that Aristotle also described a use of reasoning in argument he called *dialectical* in his writings *Topics, Rhetoric*, and *On Sophistical Refutations*.

At the beginning of his work *On Sophistical Refutations* (165a38), Aristotle describes four types of arguments used in discussion that he calls respectively, *didactic, dialectical, examination arguments*, and *contentious arguments*. Didactic arguments are arguments used in teaching, and, according to Aristotle, they reason from principles appropriate to a branch of learning, as opposed to starting from premises based on the opinions of the answerer (165b2). Dialectical arguments are "those which starting from generally accepted opinions, reason to establish a contradiction" (165b3). Examination arguments are those that are described by Aristotle as being based on opinions held by the answerer and "necessarily known to one who claims knowledge of the subject involved" (165b5). This type of argument seems somewhat similar to what was called above information-seeking dialogue.

Finally, contentious arguments are described by Aristotle as those which "reason or seem to reason from opinions which appear to be, but are not really, generally accepted" (165b8). Contentious arguments are similar to what were called above quarrelsome arguments, except that Aristotle adds an additional dimension to them here. They are arguments that seem to be dialectical arguments but are not really so. Hence, in Aristotle's view, contentious arguments also have an aspect of deception that is part of them. It would seem plausible to suggest that the contentious type of argument could represent the kind of argumentation warned about by Socrates, where the skilled sophist uses rhetorical appeals that are based on "the moods and pleasures of the motley multitude in their assembly" (*Republic*, Book IV, 493a).

The next question is: What did Aristotle mean exactly by dialectical arguments? This seems an unusual category to modern ears and we are hard-pressed to grasp exactly what Aristotle might have meant by this category of arguments, trying to put it into modern terms that might be familiar to us. Ernst Kapp described dialectic as "a curious kind of mental gymnastic" in which two persons argue about a proposed problem (1942, 12). It seems that what Aristotle describes as dialectical arguments are very similar to *ad populum* arguments because they are based on what he calls generally accepted opinions. But, on the other hand, what Aristotle calls dialectical arguments also seem different from *ad populum* arguments because the former, according to Aristotle, reason to establish a contradiction. In other words, dialectical arguments seem to be arguments that are based on what people generally accept or popularly accepted opinions but, unlike the *ad populum* argument, where such a premise is used to try to persuade somebody to accept a proposition or to do something, in a dialectical argument, we start from this generally accepted type of premise and then reason toward establishing a contradiction.

It seems then that dialectical argument must be a type of argument for Aristotle that somehow challenges popularly accepted opinions by showing how they lead to contradictions. Since any proposition that logically leads by a sequence of valid inferences to a contradiction cannot be true, a dialectical argument that proceeds from a premise that is a generally accepted opinion to a conclusion that is a contradiction would lead us to challenge this generally accepted opinion. In order to make it possible for such an opinion to be true, it would have to be revised or altered, or some part of the proposition retracted, in order to remove the contradiction from it. Dialectical arguments for Aristotle, then, would seem to be kinds of arguments that are brought to bear on topics of public controversy by taking some generally accepted opinion and challenging it by raising critical questions about it, through using reasoning or logic to show how the generally accepted opinion in its present form leads to a logical contradiction.

Of course, what comes to mind here immediately, for most people, would be the type of elenchtic argumentation used by Socrates in the Platonic dialogues, where Socrates starts from concessions made by an answerer and then uses these to reason toward a contradiction by eliciting other kinds of assumptions along the way from the answerer that are also used as premises.[1] Clarifying this question a little bit, Aristotle makes the distinction again between demonstrative reasoning and dialectical reasoning right at the beginning of the *Topics* (100a20). According to Aristotle, reasoning is called demonstration when it proceeds from premises that are described as being "true and primary or of such a kind that we derived our original knowledge of them through premises which are primary and true" (100a30).[2] So, demonstration is the kind of argumentation used in science.

But there is also a connection made by Aristotle between demonstrative reasoning and dialectical reasoning. Aristotle, when he explains the uses of dialectical reasoning, claims that one of its uses is the critical examination of the assumptions (axioms) of a science. In the *Topics* 101a25–101b4 he gives three uses of dialectic: (1) as a method of training (*gymnasia*) for teaching skills of argument, (2) for arguing in casual conversational encounters, and (3) for questioning the first principles (*archai*) of a science. This connection between dialectic and demonstration helps us to better understand the differences between these two types of reasoning in Aristotle.

In contrast to demonstrative reasoning, Aristotle describes reasoning as dialectical that starts from generally accepted opinions. He goes on to add that generally accepted opinions are those "which commend themselves to all or to the majority or to the wise—that is, to all of the wise or the majority or to the most famous and distinguished of them" (100b23). Here we should note, first

---

1. Referred to here is the elenchtic method outlined in section 1.
2. On Aristotle's epistemology, see the discussion in Hamblin (1970, 76).

of all, that Aristotle is distinguishing between the two types of reasoning—demonstrative and dialectical—on the basis of the kinds of premises used in the inference. In the case of dialectical reasoning, the premise is a proposition that is accepted by the majority of people or by the wise, that is, among the experts in the various fields of scientific knowledge or practical arts.

We should note that Aristotle is here combining what would now most likely be recognized or separated as two distinct types of arguments. One is the argument from expert opinion where the person interviewed is an expert in some domain of knowledge, most centrally, scientific knowledge. The other is the *ad populum* argument, or appeal to popular opinion, of what we have now recognized as the bandwagon subtype, where the appeal is to what the general population or the majority accept as true. But, interestingly, what Aristotle may be suggesting here is that there is an intrinsic connection between these two types of arguments, and it may be difficult or impossible to separate out the elements of appeal to expert opinion within the *ad populum* type of argument. The reasoning is that the general public or the majority will, of course, be inclined mostly to accept things that are told to them as representing the views of experts in the various scientific domains of knowledge. Generally speaking, to go against what the scientific experts say is quite difficult in argumentation, and has a high burden of proof attached to it, whereas to use premises accepted by what is taken to represent the consensus of scientific expertise in a domain of knowledge is quite an easy thing generally to support in argument, or to take for granted as a presumptive basis in everyday conversational argument.

So, let us return to our question. What exactly does Aristotle mean by the expression *dialectical argument*? According to Daniel Devereux, the exact purpose of dialectic in Aristotle's philosophy is not clear, and the array of different views held by recent commentators is "bewildering" (1990, 264). But the central theme is that of the *endoxon* as premise in a dialectical argument. It is a kind of argument based on a premise saying that a particular proposition is accepted by everyone or by the majority. But how is this premise being used? Dialectical argument seems to be different from the *ad populum* argument.

In the *ad populum* argument, a premise is being used to persuade another party to accept a proposition on the basis that the premise is representative of the views of what everyone accepts. However, in dialectical argument, the same kind of premise is used, but, somehow, it is shown that it leads to a contradiction. What are we to conclude from such an argument? Why would it be revealing to show that a generally accepted premise has led to a contradiction? Again, the direction here seems to be that a philosopher (or some questioner) might use this finding to challenge the original proposition, so that the kind of reasoning involved in dialectical reasoning would take the form of a *modus tollens* argument—that is, an argument that begins by establishing a contradiction as following from a certain premise and then arguing back to say that, since this premise implies a contradiction, the premise itself cannot possibly be true. Dialectical argument, then, would seem to be a way of challenging propositions that are generally or popularly accepted.

What could the central purpose of dialectical argument be? Could it be to persuade somebody that some proposition is true, that is, could it be a persuasion type of dialogue that is involved? (see Chapter 3, section 5). In the *Rhetoric* (1856b12), Aristotle tells us that something is persuasive if it is "persuasive in reference to someone, and is persuasive and convincing either at once and in and by itself, or because it appears to be proved by propositions that are convincing." An argument is persuasive when it is directed toward a particular respondent, and the purpose of the argument is to get that respondent to come to accept a particular proposition because a convincing argument for it can be given. By this description then, persuasion does seem to be the goal of rhetoric. But is it the goal of dialectic?

In the *Rhetoric* (1357a12), Aristotle tells us that rhetoric takes its material from what he describes as "common subjects of deliberation." But dialectical argument "takes its material from subjects which demand reasoned discussion" (1357a12). According to Aristotle's account of rhetorical argumentation then, the purpose of this type of argumentation is to persuade people to adopt a certain course of action or accept a proposition when a group of people is deliberating together. The rhetorical argument is designed to persuade such a group of people to accept a particular conclusion which the speaker is arguing for. But what about dialectical arguments? What really could the purpose of this type of argumentation be?

Aristotle gives us the clue that dialectical argument takes its material from subjects that demand reasoned discussion. So it would seem then that dialectical argument starts from some controversial subject or dispute where reasoned discussion would be appropriate to resolve the dispute or to throw some light on it. What is suggested here, then, is the kind of dispute that might arise through some subject of philosophical public or scientific controversy, where there are different points of view or conflicting points of view and where reasoned discussion would be an appropriate way of attempting to resolve the conflict—or at least would throw some light on the controversy as a way of suggesting how one might proceed toward resolving it.

3. Endoxic Premises

The Greek word that Aristotle uses for an opinion that is generally accepted is *endoxon*. Endoxic premises, as classified in the passages from Aristotle quoted above (*Topics* 100b 23), are propositions that seem to be true to the majority of people or to the wise (*sophoi*). What especially characterizes dialectical reasoning, according to Aristotle, is its use of endoxic premises. But what sort of use and status do endoxic premises have as propositions that are accepted, or acceptable, and what sort of use are they supposed to have in dialectical reasoning?

Aristotle's account seems to be somewhat ambivalent on these questions. On the one hand, endoxic premises, because they are accepted by the majority or by the wise, do seem to have a certain standing as presumptions or propositions that are generally acceptable as premises in an argument. On the other hand, as we have seen in *On Sophistical Refutations* (165b3), Aristotle suggests that the purpose of using endoxic premises in dialectical argument is to lead by a sequence of steps of reasoning to a contradiction, suggesting somehow that the endoxic proposition contains a contradiction and, therefore, must be false. This aspect suggests that endoxic propositions are deficient somehow, or illogical, or susceptible to logical refutation. So, there appears to be a certain ambivalence here. On the one hand, endoxic propositions have a certain standing as acceptable propositions. On the other hand, they seem eminently rejectable as propositions because they are the kinds of propositions that tend to lead to contradictions.

Some light is thrown on these questions by J. D. G. Evans, who points out that, for Aristotle, dialectical questions were concerned with matters about which there is difficulty and dispute (1977, 79). By their nature, endoxic propositions would belong to this class of controversial propositions about which dialectical dispute would be appropriate. According to Jonathan Barnes, "presumably" *endoxa* "may conflict among themselves," and as well, they may be vague and ambiguous (1980, 492). For Aristotle, dialectic is concerned with matters where there is *aporia* or puzzlement caused by the existence of conflicting arguments or by an unexplained matter (Evans 1977, 80). It seems, then, that the way to come to understand what Aristotle means by the concept of an endoxic proposition is to see how such propositions have a function in dialectical argumentation.

In the *Topics* (159a18–159a22), Aristotle writes that the aim of the questioner in dialectic is to lead the argument on in such a way as to make the answerer say things that are implausible (*adoxon*). In other words, in dialectical argumentation, there are two participants—a questioner and an answerer—and the answerer (or respondent) evidently makes certain concessions or states certain propositions at the starting point of the argument. Then the questioner, through asking a series of questions, leads the respondent to make several more concessions in the form of propositions that he concedes. Evidently, in this sequence of question-answer exchanges, the aim of the questioner is to get the respondent to begin by conceding certain propositions that are endoxic and then, by a sequence of reasonings, show how these propositions lead to certain propositions that are adoxic—for example, logical contradictions or propositions that go against what the majority believe or would accept as true. Evidently, the purpose of this exercise is to explore the arguments on both sides of a controversial issue.

It is evident from the subsequent discussion of Evans (1977, 82–85) as well, that when Aristotle postulated that an endoxic proposition was one that was accepted by everybody, he did not mean absolutely everybody. He evidently meant that an endoxic proposition was one that was accepted by the majority or that was generally accepted by a broad majority at a particular time.

Barnes, who traces the root meaning of *endoxon* in Greek as something that could be translated as "reputable" or "of good repute" (1980, 499), proposes as the best translation of *endoxa* "the reputable things" (500). He suggests that the scope of *endoxa* would include not only explicit public beliefs, but also "a large and important body of implicit beliefs," of three types (501): (1) propositions entailed by our explicit beliefs, (2) propositions "ascribed to us on the basis of our actions," and (3) "beliefs latent in language." According to Barnes' analysis, then, the *endoxa* are the "reputable" views accepted by the majority and the wise at any given time, as determined not only by explicit pronouncements but also by what is implied by those pronouncements, conjoined to the language used to state them, and the actions accompanying them. By this view, what is an *endoxon* is a relative matter, depending on what views are "reputable" at a particular time for a particular group. But questions remain about exactly how relative this notion of an endoxic proposition should be, because what is accepted by the majority or the wise tends to change over time and will be a function of different cultures and different groups that make up the majority at any given time.

According to Evans (1977, 82), Aristotle does not require of an endoxic proposition that it be one that is universally accepted. For as Evans notes, Aristotle frequently speaks of questions where there is a conflict between the views of the experts, or the *sophoi*, and the ordinary mass of people, or the broad majority of people (*Topics*, 104b4–105b5). On the other hand, the endoxic proposition is not so qualified that it refers to the view of any particular person or group at a particular time. Evidently, then, an endoxic premise in Aristotle's sense, is a proposition that is accepted by the broad mass of people at a given time and generally accepted by the experts.

But it is not the sort of proposition that has to be agreed to by absolutely everyone. In fact, it is normally to be expected that there will be some people who will not accept an endoxic proposition. What characterizes the endoxic proposition is the quality of being generally accepted by a broad enough mass of people so that it can be taken for granted as the kind of proposition that one would not normally have to argue for, or fulfill a burden of proof with respect to, in an ordinary conversation or argument. It is the kind of proposition that could be taken for granted as a premise without giving further justification, except by pointing out that it is broadly accepted by the majority at the present time.

Whatever else we might say about Aristotle's attitude toward arguments based on endoxic premises, he certainly does not think of them as being generally fallacious. In fact, he clearly thinks of them as being a normal and important part of dialectical argumentation, a type of argumentation he generally thinks is useful and reasonable as a kind of dialogue exchange. Still, if we define the *ad populum* argument as the argument to the effect that most people (or the majority or everyone) accept such-and-such a proposition, therefore this proposition is true, Aristotle would see this type of argumentation as being normally and even characteristically used in dialectical reasoning. Therefore, he would certainly not see it as inherently fallacious or classify it generally as a fallacy. In fact, we do not find the *ad populum* argument, or anything close to it or that would describe this type of argumentation, listed among his classification of the types of fallacies in his book on fallacies, *On Sophistical Refutations*.

Of course, Aristotle does have a fallacy called *misconception of refutation*, where an arguer uses an irrelevant premise or argues toward a wrong conclusion. And, of course, the *ad populum* is generally categorized in the standard treatment under the heading of a fallacy of relevance. So, *ad populum* would, quite naturally, fit under the general category of Aristotle's fallacy of misconception of refutation. Nevertheless, apart from this fallacy of misconception of refutation, Aristotle makes no specific mention in his classification and discussion of the various fallacies of the *argumentum ad populum*, or appeal to popular opinion, as a fallacious or sophistical type of argument. So, while in one way the classification of the *ad populum* argument as a fallacy does flow from Aristotle's treatment of fallacies in his book *On Sophistical Refutations*, nevertheless, it is quite clear from what Aristotle says about endoxic arguments, both in this book and in his other books on reasoning and persuasion, that, in general, arguing from a premise accepted by everyone or by the majority would not be regarded as a fallacious type of argument. Therefore, classifying the *ad populum* argument as a fallacy is a somewhat uncertain and variable, even contradictory, move as a development or extension of the Aristotelian theory of logic and argument. There are grounds, namely failure of relevance, on the one hand, for classifying such an argument as fallacious on the Aristotelian classification of fallacies generally. But, on the other hand, this same interpretation of *ad populum* as a fallacy goes strongly against Aristotle's treatment of endoxic arguments in the *Rhetoric*, the *Topics*, and even in certain key passages of his *On Sophistical Refutations*.

All this having been said, however, we must now go on to examine a previously ignored but very interesting passage that appears much later in the *Topics*, where Aristotle describes a type of argument that is based on appeal to popular—or at least customary—opinion, and could possibly be interpreted as recognition of the *ad populum* fallacy. In Book VIII of the *Topics*, Aristotle shows the reader how to use different kinds of argumentation tactics to persuade a respondent in a dialectical exchange. Many of these bits of advice are quite clever. For example, the reader is advised: "You should sometimes bring an objection against yourself; for answerers are unsuspicious when dealing with those who appear to them to be arguing fairly" (156b19–156b20). Aristotle is telling the proponent of an argument that if she occasionally brings an objection against her own argument, it will guard against the respondent's suspecting that she (the proponent) is biased by giving an appearance that she is arguing in a fair and balanced way. The advice is clever because Aristotle is telling us how to take advantage of appearances of a kind that can be quite important for purposes of persuasion when arguing with a respondent in a dialectical exchange.

The next piece of advice given by Aristotle sounds very much like he is telling the reader how to use the *argumentum ad populum* as a tactical move in a dialectical exchange for the purpose of persuading the other party to accept your thesis.

> It is useful also to add: "Such and such a view is that generally held and expressed (*sunethes kai legomenon*)"; for people shrink from

> trying to upset customary (*to eiothos*) opinions unless they have some objection to bring, and they are wary of trying to upset them at the same time they are themselves also making use of such things. (156b20–156b24)

Here Aristotle is advising that the questioner should tell the respondent that the thesis he is advocating is a view that is generally held and expressed (literally, a view that is customary and also spoken about). People hesitate to upset what is customary or usual (*to eiothos*) because they themselves also make use of such things in their arguments. It looks very much in this passage like Aristotle definitely recognized and clearly described the *argumentum ad populum* as a distinctive type of argument.

Note that Aristotle is not describing the *argumentum ad populum* as a fallacy. He is not saying it is inherently wrong or incorrect as a move in argument. But he is giving tactical advice on how to use it to get the best of an opponent in a dialectical exchange. He is telling us how to take advantage of the opponent's normal perceptions of how the argument will likely appear to him, as persuasive or not. There could be implications here on how such an argument strategy could be used in a sophistical or deceitful way. But he is not saying whether the argument is logically right or wrong. He is only saying how it can be used to persuade a respondent in a dialectical exchange.

Another important thing to note about this passage is that Aristotle does not use the word *endoxon*, but uses the expressions *to eiothos* and *sunethes*. One wonders whether he refers to the same kind of argumentation based on a premise of generally accepted opinion as he referred to in defining the notion of dialectical argument. Why would he use only the terms *sunethes* and *to eiothos* in the passage at the end of the *Topics*, and use only the term *endoxon* in the passage at the beginning of the *Topics*, if he is referring to the same type of argument in both instances? This question is perhaps best left to the Aristotle specialists, but a few remarks may be helpful.

In the Loeb Library editions of the *Topics* and *On Sophistical Refutations*, *endoxon* is translated as "generally accepted opinion." But Aristotle, as previously noted above, explicitly defined endoxic propositions as those "which commend themselves to all or to the majority or to the wise—that is, to all of the wise or the majority or to the most famous and distinguished of them" (*Topics* 100b23). This definition imposes a fairly high requirement on endoxic propositions. They represent not just popular opinions but generally accepted opinions in some stronger sense that also requires acceptance or backing by leading experts and authorities. On the one hand, Barnes, the reader will recall, prefers to translate *endoxon* as "reputable opinion," which again suggests something more than just popular opinion, or opinion of the majority, is involved. On the other hand, both *sunethes* and *to eiothos* suggest something more like "customary" or "usual," in a way that does not (at least so strongly) imply that the opinion should have to also include the acceptance or backing of "the wise" (*sophoi*)—the experts in the domain of knowledge in question.

These differences in terminology could have many explanations. One explanation occurs in the beginning passage of the *Topics*, where Aristotle emphasizes the correct use of *ad populum* (endoxic) argumentation in dialectic, whereas in the later passage he explains the tactical use of the *ad populum* argument to get the best of an opponent strategically in a dialectical exchange. So, if that is right, Aristotle could be talking about the *ad populum* argument in both instances but referring to different ways the same argument can be used. On the one hand, the endoxic type of argument should be seen as different because it explicitly includes the type of argument known as the appeal to expert opinion. But on the other hand, on our analysis of the *ad populum*, one of its subtypes turns out to include exactly this kind of premise of appeal to expert opinion as a component (see Chapter 7, section 3). These considerations raise provocative but difficult questions on whether or not Aristotle was referring to the same type of argument in both the earlier and later passages in the *Topics*.

Whatever one should conclude on such questions of how to interpret Aristotle, one does get a strong impression that, in this later passage in the *Topics*, he did recognize the *ad populum* type of argument and identify how it can be used strategically in argumentation. If this assumption is correct, one wonders why the *ad populum* seemed to appear out of nowhere in the modern logic textbooks, without there (apparently) being any prior tradition of the recognition of this type of argument as a fallacy. As I have already stressed, the *ad populum* was not listed by Aristotle as one of the famous fallacies in *On Sophistical Refutations*. And it was this list that proved to be so influential in the history of logic (Hamblin, 1970). Perhaps the later passage in the *Topics* just never played any role in the history of the fallacies. But if there were links between this passage and the much later emergence of the *ad populum* as a fallacy in the modern textbooks accounts, perhaps further historical research may uncover these missing connections.

4. Seneca on *Ad Populum* Arguments

Lucius Annaeus Seneca (ca. 2 B.C.–A.D. 65) was a Roman Stoic philosopher who was also administrator of the Roman Empire during the period A.D. 54–62. Seneca's moral letters explained and defended Stoic doctrines, although Seneca generally adhered to Stoic doctrines that had been laid down in earlier times (Seneca 1925). He frequently departed from orthodox stoicism and quarreled with earlier Stoics on point of doctrine. The moral letters are primarily concerned with points of Stoic ethics, and Seneca regarded wisdom as the key to goodness. Many of his arguments in these letters concern the relation of wisdom to goodness according to Stoic views.

In letter 117, during the course of an elaborate and subtle discussion of a particular Stoic doctrine concerning wisdom, Seneca introduces into his argument, and also formulates the type of argument known in the modern logic textbook treatments of the *ad populum* as the bandwagon or appeal to popularity argument. However, because of the subtle context of the argument, it is not a straightforward matter to try to determine whether Seneca is accepting this *ad populum* argument or rejecting it. In general, his attitude toward it seems to be mixed. He seems to hold that it is an argument that has some value, but he also appears to maintain that it is an inferior kind of argument.

The context is that Seneca is discussing the Stoic view that wisdom is a good, but being wise is not a good. Seneca first sets out the Stoic argument traditionally used to support this view, and then adds his own opinion on the issue. One of the problems that seems to concern Seneca is that this traditional Stoic view appears to depart from popular opinion. It seems to be a somewhat paradoxical view, for it would be popularly accepted that, if wisdom is a good, then being wise should also be a good. However, the Stoics have an elaborate argument, according to Seneca (letter 117), that good is corporeal because the good is active, and whatever is active is corporeal. But the Stoics, according to Seneca (line 3), do not think that being wise has this same property, because it has the property of being incorporeal. What the Stoics exactly meant by this doctrine is not very clear, but the point, for our purposes, is that it was a doctrine that was special to the Stoics but one that appears to depart from popular opinion.

Accordingly, the objection discussed by Seneca (letter 117, line 4) is the question, Why do we not say that being wise is a good, in studying this objection? Seneca states that, in fact, we do say that being wise is a good. But the basis of the argument (line 5) is that being wise is a good because it is a thing to be desired. Seneca then goes on to comment (line 6) on the meaning of the word "desire," and suggests that there could be a semantic confusion between this term and the term "desirable."[3] Seneca then goes on to question the premise to the effect that the desirable is sought as a good. The Stoics deny this premise, but Seneca indicates his disagreement with them in the following key passage.

> I myself do not hold the same view, and I judge that our philosophers have come down to this argument because they are already bound by the first link in the chain and for that reason may not alter their definition. People are wont to concede much to the things which all men take for granted; in our eyes the fact that all men agree upon something is a proof of its truth. For instance, we infer that the gods exist, for this reason, among others—that there is implanted in everyone an idea concerning deity, and there is no people so far beyond the reach of laws an customs that it does not believe at least in gods of some sort. And when we discuss the immortality of the soul, we are influenced in no small degree by the general opinion of mankind, who either fear or worship the spirits of the lower world. I make the most of this general belief: you can find no one who does not hold that wisdom is a Good, and *being wise* also. I shall not appeal to the populace, like a conquered gladiator; let us come to close quarters, using our own weapons. (Seneca 1925, 341)

When Seneca uses the expression "our philosophers" in this passage, he is referring to the Stoics with whom he is disagreeing. When he introduces the bandwagon type of argument, and cites it as a reason commonly given for inferring that the gods exist, it is difficult to be clear on exactly how this interjection fits in to the prior subtle discussion of the Stoic argument about wisdom and the good.

Whatever the precise nature of the connection here, Seneca is certainly introducing the basic structure of the bandwagon or appeal to popularity type of argument as a structure of inference. He writes that people are inclined to concede much to the things which all men take for granted, meaning that, if a

---

3. It seems that Seneca's comment throws some light on an ambiguity that was to become famous much later as John Stuart Mill's unintended pun on the word "desirable" (in the context of Mill's proof of the principle of utility) meaning "able to be desired," in the same way that "visible" means "able to be seen."

proposition is a universal belief of mankind, in the sense that everyone accepts it as true, then this premise warrants an inference to the conclusion that the truth of this proposition should be conceded as acceptable for purposes of argument. As Seneca puts it, "The fact that all men agree upon something is a proof of its truth." This statement is the first known explicit identification of the bandwagon, or appeal to popularity type of *ad populum* argument.

The examples Seneca cites as common instances of this type of argumentation are also interesting. The first example he gives is the argument for the existence of the gods. He writes that we infer that the gods exist on the grounds that "there is implanted in everyone an idea concerning deity." And he goes on to add the empirical premise that every people has laws and customs to such an advanced state, among which is included the belief in gods of some sort. In short, we have, here, an empirical premise to the effect that all past civilizations have included among their customs and beliefs the particular belief in supreme beings of some sort. The conclusion drawn from this premise is that, therefore, the gods exist. This type of argument was commonly employed by later philosophers and theologians and came to be known as the common consent argument for the existence of God, sometimes also called the *consensus gentium* argument.

Seneca goes on to cite another example of the use of the *ad populum* argument, namely, the proof of the immortality of the soul. He notes that, on this question, too, we are "influenced in no small degree by the general opinion of mankind." However, in citing this second argument, Seneca seems to take a somewhat negative attitude toward the argument, because when he cites the general opinion of mankind as a basis for the premise, he adds that the people in this general population "either fear or worship the spirits of the lower world." This remarks suggests that the popular belief in the immortality of the soul may be based on emotional factors, that is, either fear of the spirits of the lower world or an emotional attitude of worship or awe toward these spirits. In making this remark, then, Seneca seems to be indicating an attitude that this type of argument may be based more on an emotional than rational justification. He is not entirely rejecting the argument as unreasonable. Nevertheless, he is indicating that the argument may be based on only a slender type of emotional justification that might perhaps be best thought of as giving way at a deeper discussion to other kinds of evidence.

Seneca also applies the *ad populum* form of argument to the discussion of Stoic principles that is his principal topic, namely, the question of whether being wise is a good or not. In this connection, Seneca adds a puzzling remark to the effect that he is not going to appeal to the populace as he puts it "like a conquered gladiator." Instead, Seneca says that he is going to come to close quarters, using his own weapons. In other words, what he seems to be suggesting here is that appealing to the populace in using the bandwagon argument, of the form that he has indicated, is an inferior type of argument that depends on the goodwill of the audience. Just as in the case of a conquered gladiator, he appeals to the goodwill of the crowd to be spared.

In his final remark in the passage quoted, Seneca indicates that there is an alternative to this way of justifying his argument. Instead of depending on the goodwill of the crowd, one fights for one's own survival using one's own weapons. In other words, what he seems to be suggesting is that appealing to the populace is a weaker type of argument because it depends on the goodwill of the audience, whereas, on this question of whether being wise is a good, what is really needed is a dialectical analysis of the subtleties of the notions of wisdom of the good and being wise. And, in fact, this was just the very sort of discussion that Seneca was engaged in prior to his interjection of the *ad populum* argument, and that he continued for several pages with the various subtleties of Stoic doctrines right after the passage quoted (letter 117).

The passage quoted from Seneca above, and his use of it within this larger and more elaborate argument concerning the Stoic doctrines of wisdom, is very interesting with respect to the *ad populum* argument. For one thing, it is the first known clear articulation of the bandwagon or appeal to popularity type of argument of the form "Everybody believes that A, therefore A is true" as an explicit structure of logical inference. The other interesting thing is Seneca's ambivalent attitude toward this type of inference as an argument to be used in philosophical discussion. On the one hand, it is a type of argument that he does accord some credibility to, but, on the other hand, he appears to suggest that it is also an inferior kind of argument that should ultimately give way to a more close dialectical analysis of the concepts themselves. In other words, what he seems to be suggesting is that the *ad populum* is an indirect kind of argument that has some weight in a discussion but that, nevertheless, also has more direct considerations, more direct kinds of arguments, that should generally be given more weight in deciding an issue. He is suggesting that the appeal to popular opinion type of argument should be accorded a certain weight of presumption in a discussion, but it is a provisional type of argument in that it depends on the goodwill of the audience. In short, Seneca adopts the view the *argumentum ad populum* is a defeasible type of argument that can vary with the circumstances of a case.

What is striking is that all three leading ancient philosophers—Plato, Aristotle, and Seneca—take a balanced position with respect to the *ad populum* argument. Instead of rejecting this argument as fallacious, in the way the modern standard treatment in logic does, they seem to generally assume that it is a reasonable type of argument that has legitimate and important uses in reasoning.

5. Eikotic Arguments

If the *ad populum* argument has a legitimate place as a species of reasonable inference, it is (as shown in Chapter 4, section 7) as used in presumptive reasoning in dialectical argumentation. But what kind of reasoning is this? It seems unfamiliar to the modern mind and has no recognized place of importance in modern logic. But it was familiar in the ancient world.

The ancients recognized a species of argument based on what they called *eikos*, which we could perhaps translate as "plausibility." However, the usual translation of this type of argument given is "argument from probability." This terminology is misleading, however, because in modern usage, the term "probability" is generally taken to refer to the mathematical conception of probability, which is a scientific concept and is quantified by various numerical measures. The ancient argument from *eikos* did not mean probability in this modern or post-Enlightenment sense. As the ancients thought of it, according to George Kennedy, argument from probability or, as we might better call it, argument from plausibility, would be excluded from philosophy as claiming to be a scientific and exact notion. The reason is that, in a plausibilistic argument, as the ancients conceived it, it was often possible to demonstrate the probability of an exact opposite of the plausible proposition. The notion of argument from *eikos*, whether we call it probability or plausibility, comes from the Sophists, and this type of argument, as Kennedy points out, is inherently sophistic in its ambivalent nature (1963, 31). Leading Sophists, such as Protagoras and Gorgias, denied that absolute truth can be known and, instead, took the point of view that legitimate plausible arguments can be put forward on both sides of every question.

What exactly did the ancients mean, then, by plausible arguments, or arguments from *eikos*? The original idea was exemplified in rhetorical manuals written by the Sophists to help people write speeches and, in particular, to help people who had to argue before the courts to defend themselves against accusations. A Sophist named Antiphon (ca. 480 B.C.–411 B.C.) wrote a number of speeches called *Tetralogies*, which were meant to be used to illustrate how judicial oratory could be learned. In the first of the *Tetralogies*, Antiphon discusses the legal case concerning a man who had been killed in a lonely spot (Kennedy 1980, 26–27). The slave accompanying him was also killed, but before he died, he stated that the defendant was the murderer. In the prosecutor's speech, he uses the argument that the defendant had suffered great wrongs at the hands of the man who was killed, and that, therefore, this reason suggests that the defendant was the murderer.

In addition to this argument, Antiphon used several supplementary arguments that can be seen as arguments from *eikos* or plausibility. One of these arguments was that: "It is unlikely that muggers killed the man, for no one who ran the risk of his life would have abandoned the object of his robbery when he had it in his hands. Yet the victims were found with all their property intact" (27). Note that this argument is not based on any observation or empirical evidence because the man was killed in a lonely spot and there were no surviving witnesses. However, Antiphon used the argument to attempt to exclude the possibility that the murdered man was killed by muggers, on the grounds that the murdered man's property, that is, his cloak, was still there at the scene of the crime when the body was found. The inference drawn is that, if this man had been killed by muggers, their normal motivation would be to kill him in order to rob him of his property. But, since the property was not taken, the conclusion can be drawn that it was unlikely—that is improbable or implausible—that it was muggers who killed him. Indirectly then, this argument would provide some evidence, or at least a plausible basis for arguing for the hypothesis that it would be possible, or even somewhat probable, that the defendant killed him. By eliminating one alternative that might otherwise have been a plausible account of why the man died, this argument from plausibility shifts a greater weight onto the assumption that the man might have been killed by the defendant. We see that the argument is not an empirical argument based on probability in the modern sense but rather on a somewhat weak but plausible argument that has the function of shifting a weight of credibility of opinion from one hypothesis to another in the context of the case.

The works of Antiphon, and this example, in particular, illustrate the teachings of the rhetorical handbooks written by the Sophists in ancient Greece, and show how they relied on this type of argument, usually called argument from probability. The classic example of argument from probability in ancient times also concerns legal argumentation, and was cited by both Plato and Aristotle. This case concerns a weaker man who is accused in court of having assaulted a stronger man. His defense is that it is not probable (that is, not plausible) that he would attack a stronger man. But the argument has two sides, and could be used the other way around as well.

Supposing the case concerned an assault where a bigger or stronger man is accused of assaulting a weaker man. The stronger man could argue that the crime is not probable on the grounds that the stronger man would be aware that the perception of his being the perpetrator would be more plausible to a jury just because he is the stronger party and the other is the weaker. The conclusion of this use of the argument would be that the stronger man would be likely to desist from his intent to assault the other man. So, argument from plausibility is a two-edged sword that can be turned against its users, and the Sophists did generally recognize its ambivalent nature as a species of argumentation.

Discussion of this particular case in Plato's dialogue *Phaedrus* is very interesting. Socrates and Phaedrus are discussing the rhetorical manuals written by the Sophists, and Socrates discusses one of these manuals written by a Sophist called Tisias. Socrates asks Phaedrus, Does Tisias maintain "that the probable is anything other than that which commends itself to the multitude?" (273b1). Socrates' way of putting the question is interesting because he seems to be saying that Tisias equated his argument from *eikos* or probability with the kind of *ad populum* argument based on what is accepted by the multitude. Socrates, of course, ridicules this notion of argument from probability as being of very little or no importance in philosophy, on the grounds that it is only based on probability or appearances, and that consequently there is no relation between it and the real truth of a matter. In his subsequent discussion of this case of the man who was killed but not robbed of his property, Socrates describes the one man of having "recourse to the famous plea, 'How could a little fellow like me attack a big fellow like him?'" Socrates ironically remarks that the stronger man will "try to invent some fresh lie" (273c5) that will enable him to refute the other party in the lawsuit.

Aristotle also mentions this classic case in the *Rhetoric* (2 1402a11), citing it as a defense against the accusation of assault and battery on the grounds that such a crime would not be probable in a case where the weaker man is said to have attacked the stronger. This case, then, gives quite a good illustration of what the ancients meant by the argument from probability, or as it might more accurately and less misleadingly be called in modern terms the *argument from plausibility*. This type of argument is contrasted with the use of direct evidence in the form of empirical evidence or eyewitness testimony or contracts of the kind that might be used in a legal trial.

The argument from plausibility is more indirect in that, instead of being based on something that is observed, it is based on our normal expectations on how something would be expected to go in a kind of practical situation that we are all familiar with. It should generally be evaluated as a weak and defeasible type of argument that, if used by one side, could also be used in a somewhat different form by the other side.[4] But, nevertheless, one can easily appreciate how such an inherently weak argument can often be extremely powerful in a balance of considerations case, such as that of a legal case in court where there is evidence on both sides and the jury is weighing the evidence on one side against the evidence on the other.

In a case such as the one cited by Tisias, there were no surviving witnesses to the crime. In this type of situation of absence of firm knowledge that would definitely show that the accused is guilty or not, weaker arguments based on probability (plausibility) can play quite a considerable role in the jury's deliberations. Especially interesting is Socrates' statement in the *Phaedo* (273b1) that Tisias maintains that argument from probability or *eikos* is the same thing as the *ad populum* argument based on what the multitude accepts or what "commends itself to the multitude." It seems, then, that at least one of the Sophists identified the *ad populum* argument with the argument from probability or, at least, saw it as an important species of argument from probability (plausibility) or *eikos*.

The ancient idea of plausibility has been neglected since the Enlightenment, and in many ways it is an alien and incomprehensible concept to thinkers since the Enlightenment. The reason is that, since the Enlightenment, the concept of evidence has been dominated by the conception of scientific evidence centered around the all-important notions of deductive inference and inductive inference based on numerical conceptions of probability. The ancient idea of plausible argument, or argument based on *eikos*, was different from the objective post-Enlightenment notion of scientific evidence, in that the idea of argument from *eikos* is inherently dialectical in nature. As used in a dialectical context, argument from plausibility or *eikos* refers to a relationship between an opinion and an argument, where the argument is put forward in favor of the opinion, but not in a conclusive way.

Instead, the idea is that, in dialectical argumentation or disputation, there are two sides, and the evaluation of the argument always needs to be seen as a weighing of a balance of considerations on both sides. The function, then, of

---

4. On presumptive reasoning in dialectical argumentation, see Chapter 4, section 7.

an opinion-based argument from *eikos* is to shift a slight weight in this balance of considerations context toward one side of a dialogue and against the other side. This dialectical use of argument is contrasted with the notion of scientific demonstration, which is argument based essentially on mathematical calculations or on reproducible, empirical evidence.

6. The Medieval Period

The recognition of the *ad populum* as a reasonable type of dialectical argument, based on Aristotle's distinction between demonstrative and dialectical arguments, was carried forward into the manuals on reasoning in the Middle Ages. For example, in Boethius' book *De Topicis Differentiis* (before 523 A.D.),[5] the *ad populum* argument is accepted as a reasonable type of inference (1190a26–1190a34).

> The Topic comprised of judgment is of this sort. For example, if we say that things are as they are judged to be either by all people or most people, and also either by the wise or those deeply learned in any one of the arts. For example, the heaven is revolvable, since those who are wise and very learned astronomers have judged it to be so. The question has to do with accident. The maximal proposition: what seems true to everyone or the many or the wise should not be gain-said. The Topic: *from judgment*. (Boethius 1978, 54)

It is interesting that Boethius calls this type of inference warrant (topic or *topos*) "from judgment."

For Aquinas, who extended Aristotle's notion of dialectical argument further, the *ad populum* argument was tied to deliberation. The idea that the *ad populum* type of argument from common opinion could be a reasonable type of argument from probability in a dialectical context was not only accepted but even further developed by Aquinas. Edward Byrne cites Aquinas as recognizing that common opinions can be important in argumentation because they are widely accepted and, therefore, may be taken as a probable basis for drawing inferences. "Accordingly, arguments that proceed on the basis of what is commonly held are taken to be probable: If the premises are probable and widely accepted in this sense, then the argument is probable whether those premises

---

5. The date "before 523" is given by Stump (1978, 15).

are granted by an opponent or not" (1968, 106). Byrne refers here to Aristotle's reference to the use of probable propositions in disputation in the *Physics*, but he cites the commentary of Aquinas on this Aristotelian passage as recognizing probable arguments based on common opinions as indicating a direction toward the truth.

What is even more interesting is the extension of the Aristotelian notion of deliberation by Aquinas to include probable arguments within deliberation as a species of argumentation based on probability in the ancient sense. Aquinas, like Aristotle, sees human action as being concerned with the contingent and the probable and, therefore, sees an important place for argument from probability in both moral and political argumentation. Aquinas sees argument from probability in the ancient sense as being an important kind of argumentation in the courtroom, because testimony does not have infallible certainty but is itself only a probable kind of basis for argument. Therefore, Aquinas concludes, anything that gives probability to the contrary of an argument based on testimony can bring that argument from testimony into doubt.

What is remarkable about Aquinas' treatment of plausible inference is that one can find some kind of basis here for the *ad populum* type of bandwagon argument where the premise is based on what people generally accepted as having a place in reasonable deliberation. The key to the recognition of the acceptability of this type of argument is its dialectical and defeasible nature as a tentative type of argument useful in a balance of considerations type of situation. However, this type of situation is characteristic not only of argumentation in legal cases but also of deliberation in ordinary affairs. The reason is that, in much of our everyday situation where we need to resolve problems by deliberation, the circumstances are changing rapidly, therefore, we cannot have exact or scientific knowledge of all possible outcomes in time to make a prudent decision.

Aquinas, then, like Aristotle, takes prudence to involve the consideration of possible choices among the alternatives known to an agent in a given set of particular circumstances. So, Aquinas, like Aristotle, recognizes practical reasoning as a distinctive type of reasoning that is crucial to human deliberation. Unlike the exact knowledge-based reasoning characteristic of the ideals of scientific argumentation, prudential reasoning depends on judgment on an estimation concerning the weighing of alternative courses of action in a rational deliberation that is characteristic of coming to a judgment.

Aquinas asserts that deliberation on what one should do in a situation with many particular contingencies that are difficult to know about with reasonable certainty is best done by means of a conference involving more than one person. Instead of being primarily concerned with "knowledge of necessary and eternal truths," deliberation is based on probable estimates of future events, as a basis for deciding on a "serviceable action" (1970, Question 14, 149). Like Aristotle, Aquinas sees this type of deliberation on how to act as containing reasoning (what Aristotle called *phronesis*, or practical reasoning), based on probable estimates of what seems to be the case in a particular, but fluid situation.

The question, then, is whether in this context, the *argumentum ad populum* can have some role as an inherently weak and fallible argument that is, nevertheless, useful on a basis of probability (plausibility) for shifting a weight of evidence back and forth from one side to the other in a rational dialectical exchange of viewpoints. It seems that for Aquinas, like Aristotle, the purpose of dialectical deliberation is not to resolve the conflict of opinions definitively, at least not necessarily, nor is it to decide the outcome based on exact reasoning or mathematical calculation as would be appropriate in scientific argumentation, according to post-Enlightenment views. Rather, the purpose is to examine and articulate the strengths of the arguments on both sides of a contentious issue, in order to more deeply reveal the important, leading considerations on both sides of the issue as a basis for arriving at a prudent conclusion on how to proceed.

According to Aquinas the use of syllogism is involved both in deliberation and in scientific reasoning (see Byrne 1968, 219). However, this same syllogistic reasoning is put to a different use in these two different contexts of argument. Aquinas thought that, in deliberation, as in dialectical argumentation generally, one is faced with various alternatives and then one must look toward finding the most plausible arguments in favor of each alternative.

The problem with this type of argumentation, however, is that it can often happen that the arguments for the various alternatives might be so well-balanced that there is no conclusive way to opt for one as a reasonable course of action over the other. "A decision to act . . . need not and in fact cannot arrive at demonstration in the strict sense" (221). Hence, in deliberation, the opinion to which one ultimately becomes committed to in the concluding stage of the dialectical exchange of views should be regarded as the "best expression of truth obtainable under the circumstances" (222). Aquinas does then find a very important place for argument from probability and opinion (or plausibility, as we prefer to call it), in the context of a type of dialectical exchange he would describe as deliberation. And it is clear that deliberation could be an appropriate kind of dialectical framework for the use of the *argumentum ad populum*, not only in legal argumentation of the kind that would sometimes, for example, be evaluated in a criminal trial in court but also as the typical kind of everyday, practical reasoning used in ethics and political argumentation about means and ends.

7. The Shift Away from Dialectic

This distinction between the dialectical type of argument and the demonstrative or knowledge-based type of argument, typical of scientific reasoning, was drawn very clearly by Aristotle in particular. Aristotle recognized both kinds of argument as being legitimate, and he recognized that each kind had its distinctive kinds of argument used in reasoning. The medieval period followed this way of thinking, and Aquinas, most notably, even developed it further. However, since the Enlightenment, the demonstrative or scientific model of argument has been so dominant that concern with the dialectical type of argument in the logic textbooks, and in academic disciplines generally, has fallen away, and this dialectical type of argument has been given little if any recognition as a genuine kind of argument that is worth serious consideration.

The historical explanation of the one-sided view of the *argumentum ad populum* found in the modern treatment of this argument in the logic textbooks is to be found in a paradigm shift that took place at the Enlightenment period. During this period, the scientific conception of argument based on the model of Euclidean geometry—what Aristotle called the demonstration—came to be the dominant conception put forward by philosophers as the only route to finding the truth of a matter. The subsequent dramatic successes of scientific research validated this conception more and more strongly as time went by until, in the early twentieth century, philosophy had opted exclusively for it. Aristotle's dialectical concept of argument was now almost completely forgotten, and was presumed to be of no importance or value beside the concept of argument as a scientific inquiry based on premises known and established as true, based on scientific research.

According to the new paradigm, dialectic is not a useful way of discovering the truth of a matter, or of proving that a proposition is true or false. Dialectic is now dismissed as "subjective," and scientific reasoning—the model being Euclidean geometry with its axioms and deductively derived theorems—taken as the only way of discovering the truth, or proving that something is true. This paradigm has lasted from the seventeenth century right up to the beginning of the second half of the twentieth century, when it began to be eroded by a new relativism.

George Kennedy sees a parallel between this shift away from dialectic and rhetoric in the seventeenth century and the criticisms of the sophistic rhetoric raised by Plato and Aristotle in the ancient world (1980, 222). In both instances, there was a shift from a method of argument that was perceived as subjective and open to erroneous or sophistic reasoning toward a method that was seen as objective and reliable, as based on truth and leading to truth in a guaranteed line of reasoning.

The starting point of this shift was Descartes' *Discourse on Method*, with its explicit adoption of the geometric model for philosophical reasoning, starting from "indubitable" axiom-like premises and using careful deductive reasoning to derive conclusions only from these bedrock axioms.[6] According to Kennedy (1980, 22), the most specific manifestation of this shift to the new thinking was the *Port-Royal Logic* of 1662 (see Arnauld 1964). This observation is highly significant because it was in this logic textbook that we find the *argumentum ad populum* first mentioned as a distinctive type of argument, in a place where it was likely to be taken note of by subsequent writers of logic textbooks.

Another work that Kennedy mentions (1980, 222) as highly influential in starting this paradigm shift is the book *De L'Esprit Geometrique* by Pascal, also (significantly) known as *L'Art de Persuader*. Pascal, because of his literary gifts, was an important figure in popularizing new ideas. His best known success in this direction was his destruction of casuistry by the popular success of his satirical work *Lettres Provinciales*, the effects of which are well described in Jonsen and Toulmin (1988). But his less known work, *De L'Esprit Geometrique* expressed the Enlightenment viewpoint that scientific, technical and factual information and reasoning is the only kind of knowledge worth having.

In *De L'Esprit Geometrique* (see "Reflections on Geometry and the Art of Persuading," trans. Robert W. Gleason, 1966), Pascal writes that what he calls "the art of persuading" should be a methodical "carrying through to their conclusion of a complete set of satisfactory proofs" on the model of geometric reasoning (319). The following set of necessary rules for using geometrical proof in the art of persuading is given.

> *The rules for definition:* 1. Never undertake to define a thing which is in itself so well known that no unambiguous terms are available in which to explain it. 2. Never admit any term in the slightest degree

---

6. It is interesting that Hamblin (1970, 234) calls such axioms "starting points" in his discussion of the concept of argument.

obscure or ambiguous, without proving a definition. 3. Never employ in any definition any but well-known words, or words already explained.

The rules for framing axioms: 1. Never admit any of the requisite principles, without first securing general agreement, however clear and self-evident the principles may be. 2. Never lay down as an axiom anything that is not immediately self-evident.

The rules for demonstration: 1. Never undertake to demonstrate a thing self-evident, and requiring no elucidation by way of proof. 2. Prove every proposition that is in the least obscure, and use for such proof only very obvious axioms, or propositions already agreed upon or demonstrated. 3. Always substitute mentally the definition for the thing defined, so as not to deceive by equivocation in the use of terms having a restricted meaning. (320–21)

Instead of listening to the logicians who have "endeavored to meet sophistry and ambiguity in reasoning by inventing a terminology full of barbarous names which cause dismay in all who hear them" all we need to do to arrive at "unshakable proofs" in our arguments is to follow the method of the geometers (326).

Since the ascendancy of the Enlightenment paradigm, the humanities have receded into a place of less and less importance in the university, and in public opinion generally, on the assumption that only objective scientific knowledge is worth having and paying for. Deductive logic, codified by mathematical logic, came to be thought of as the only serious branch of logic worth teaching. The fallacies took on a place of small importance in the logic textbooks, and the types of argument associated with public deliberation, judgment and practical reasoning were treated as if their only interest to logic was their danger as sophistical deceptions.

The old idea of dialectical reasoning in Aristotle, as an instrument for raising critical questions on controversial issues of public affairs, dropped from sight. Nobody thought of logic in dialectical terms any more, and logic as a subject came to be identified with syllogistic logic—Aristotle's deductive logic—and its modern counterparts, propositional logic and quantifier logic. The Enlightenment transformation of logic into a purely abstract and objective calculus was complete.

8. *Consensus Gentium* Arguments

As dialectic faded away, with the rise of science as the model of what constitutes reasoning based on good evidence, so too the *ad populum*, as a recognizably reasonable type of argument, faded into obscurity. Only in one field was it preserved as an argument of any merit: theology. In modern theology, the *consensus gentium* argument, or argument from general agreement across nations—sometimes also called the "common consent" argument—continued to be deployed to prove the existence of God, despite severe attacks on it by leading modern philosophers.

In an article surveying the history and various forms of the *consensus gentium* argument, Paul Edwards shows how the complicated versions of this argument advanced by philosophers can be conveniently grouped into two types (1967, 148). In the first type of argument, the universality of belief is taken as evidence that the belief is instinctive, or based on longings or needs that are instinctive. The conclusion of this type of argument, then, is that the belief must be true. This version of the argument is called by Edwards the "biological variant."

There is also another type of *consensus gentium* argument Edwards calls the "anti-skeptical dilemma." In this type of argument, the universality of belief is treated as evidence for the truth of the belief in conjunction with the additional premise that the believers "use reason in arriving at their position." According to Edwards, these two types of *consensus gentium* arguments have most frequently been used by philosophers and theologians in the past to argue for either the existence of God or the immortality of the human soul as their conclusions (147).

The biological version of the argument has been attacked more than it has been supported by leading philosophers. Locke, in his essay, *Concerning Human Understanding* (1961) (book 1, section 4), rejected the premise that there has been a universal, instinctive belief in God on two grounds. First, John Locke noted that there had been atheists among the ancients. Second, Locke argued that the universality of an idea or belief does not establish its innateness. Locke argued that the ideas of sun and heat are also universal without being what he called "natural impressions of the mind" (book 1, section 2).

John Stuart Mill, in his *Three Essays on Religion* (1874), rejected the biological version of the argument on the grounds that it is circular. Mill argued that the argument presupposes the belief that the human mind was made by a god who would not deceive his creatures, and then pointed out that this premise presupposes the conclusion to be proved, namely, that God exists. It seems, however, that there are versions of the biological argument which are certainly not open to Mills' objection on grounds of circularity, and may also be defensible against Locke's criticisms. One of these arguments, cited by Edwards (1967, 149), is attributed to Charles Hodge (1872). According to this version of the argument, the biological instinct to believe in God is said to be similar to the function of the eye and the ear. The eye, in its structure, presupposes that there is light to be seen, and, similarly, the ear presupposes, in its structure, the existence of sound. By analogy, then, the conclusion is reached that our religious feelings and aspirations necessitate the existence of God (Hodge 1872, 200).

Case 5.1   The truth is, that all the faculties and feelings of our minds and bodies have their appropriate objects; and the possession of the faculties supposes the existence of those objects. The senses suppose the existence and reality of the objects of sense. The eye, in its very structure, supposes that there is such an element as light; the sense of hearing would be unaccountable and inconceivable without sound; and the sense of touch would be inconceivable were there no tangible objects. The same is true of our social affections; they necessitate the assumption that there are relations suited to their exercises. Our moral nature supposes that the distinction between right and wrong is not chimerical or imaginary. In like manner, our religious feelings, our sense of dependence, our consciousness of responsibility, our aspirations after fellowship with some Being higher than ourselves, and higher than anything which the world or nature contains, necessitates the belief in the existence of God.

The argument Hodge uses is based on the premise that all people have moral and religious feelings, aspirations, and values. The conclusion drawn is that these could only be grounded in a being higher than ourselves, just as the sense of hearing would be "unaccountable and inconceivable" without the existence of sound. The argument seems to be a weak one, that would be challenged by many skeptical philosophers, both ancient and modern. And it is based on a questionable analogy. But still, it is an interesting variant of the *ad populum* argument.

Another variant of this biological version of the argument, cited by Edwards (1967, 149), rests on a premise that each of us has a hunger built into us—a hunger for something greater than we are. But then, the second premise of this version of the argument is that every hunger has a normal gratification. The conclusion is that if our religious hunger did not have a proper gratification, it would be difficult to see how it got into our nature in the first place. In other words, the existence of such a religious longing presupposes the existence of some cause of its being in our nature.

The difficulty for the biological type of *consensus gentium* argument is to get from the premise that a belief in God is instinctive to the conclusion that this instinctiveness provides grounds for indicating that the belief is reasonable or that it is founded on some kind of compelling or reasonable evidence. For even if it can be argued that such a belief is instinctive—and this premise seems to be both psychiatric and yet, partly empirical in nature—even if one can grant this premise, which seems highly debatable, it is even more difficult to get from it to the conclusion that such an instinctive belief is rationally founded and gives a good reason for accepting the conclusion that God exists.

Whether there does, in fact, exist such a religious instinct, and what can be concluded from it, are matters that have come in for considerable discussion by anthropologists. Many of these objections and further discussions are outlined by Edwards (1967, 151–52). As Edwards puts it, because of the empirical nature of these arguments, they have come under fire by anthropologists on the grounds of a number of exceptions that have proved very irritating to the supporters of the biological *consensus gentium* argument. One of the devices used to attempt to defend the biological version of the argument against these irritating criticisms has been the additional premise that the unbelievers are too morally or mentally defective to count as true representatives of human opinion. This move surely seems like a questionable way of getting around the various objections.

The premise of the *consensus gentium* argument is no longer as persuasive as it once was. Nowadays, the trend is more and more toward a loss of belief in religion, and toward a consensus that God does not exist. To counter this erosion of the plausibility of the premise, the argument needs to be bolstered up by additional assumptions that those who believe in God do so on the basis of some special insight, knowledge, or instinctive feeling of a kind that is based on their being in a special position to know about religious truth. But such arguments have not appeared to be very plausible to modern audiences. It is one thing to have a longing or instinctive feeling that God exists, but the step from linking this feeling to the conclusion that God really exists, apart from this perception or feeling, is not one that is acceptable to post-Enlightenment thinkers as a warranted inference. Far from it. Such a logical leap is just the sort of argument that appears highly dubious to modern secular skeptics who advocate scientific rationality as their standard of reasonable argument.

9. The Antiskeptical Dilemma and Pascal's Wager

The biological variant of the *consensus gentium* argument has not seemed plausible to modern audiences. Neither has another variant, called the antiskeptical dilemma. But the reasons for their failure are highly instructive. It is also interesting to see why its modern replacement, Pascal's Wager argument, has been successful in relation to conventional modern views.

A carefully developed version of the antiskeptical dilemma argument can be found in Joyce (1923, 179).

Case 5.2 [This argument] rests simply on the principle that man's intellect is fundamentally trustworthy: that, though frequently misled in this or that particular case through accidental causes, yet the instrument itself is sound: that, of its own nature, it leads, not to error, but to truth. It follows from this, that if the human race, taken as a whole, agrees in regarding a given conclusion as certain, it is impossible to suppose that that conclusion is false. Could a general conviction of this kind be mistaken, it would argue that something is amiss with the faculty itself: that it is idle for man to search for truth, since the very organ of truth is fallacious. Pure skepticism would be the whole logical attitude. In point of fact, man cannot use his intellect without recognizing its trustworthiness. It is its own sufficient guarantee. When we judge, we do not judge blindly: we *see* that our judgment is true. This being premised, we urge that there is a veritable consensus among men that God exists. All races, civilized and uncivilized alike, are at one in holding that the facts of nature and the voice of conscience compel us to affirm this as certain truth.

This argument is presumptive in nature. It states that human conviction must generally be reliable, even though it can lead to error in some cases. Hence a general conviction, based on what everyone or nearly everyone believes, is likely to be trustworthy. The "veritable consensus" among human beings that

God exists, is a premise that leads to the plausible conclusion that God does exist in fact. From this premise, along with the foregoing assumptions, it follows that the only acceptable alternative is belief in the existence of God.

This version of the common consent argument for the existence of God is a species of *reductio ad absurdum* argument. The second component of the argument, especially, is based on the assumption that everyone believes in God because it is rational to do so, that is, because the belief is based on some kind of presumption or reasoned assumption. What is this reasonable basis of this assumption? As the second part of the argument specifies, it is a negative, conditional proposition to the effect that, if the population of believers are mistaken in accepting the existence of God, it would somehow follow that human intellect and our search for the truth is irrational or untrustworthy. This last assumption does not seem to be reasonably acceptable, for it would seem to be possible to argue that assuming its opposite leads to an untenable situation of pure skepticism. The ultimate conclusion of the argument, then, is that we must trust the reasoning of those in the past who have always accepted the existence of God since reason is fundamentally trustworthy.

As Edwards notes, Joyce's version of the antiskeptical dilemma argument has been rejected on two grounds (1967, 150). The first objection is the rejection of the claim that belief in God is universal in the human race. The second objection centers on the presupposition that these believers arrive at their belief in God by means of reason or on the basis of some evidence based on the trustworthiness of the intellect. As Edwards notes, it seems extremely doubtful whether the majority of people, in fact, do use reason or have used reason in arriving at their conclusion that God exists. A third objection is that the argument postulates a false or dubious dichotomy when it states that pure skepticism is the only alternative to accepting the belief of the whole of mankind in the existence of God as reasonable. This argument is a not very credible use of disjunctive reasoning, and, in fact, it seems easy to criticize it on the basis that it is a simplistic dichotomy. There seems to be no good reason to think that pure skepticism is the only alternative to the belief in the existence of God as accepted supposedly in popular opinion.

In his evaluation of the antiskeptical dilemma, Edwards breaks this argument down into three substages. The premise of the first substage, as in the biological version, is the proposition that all human beings believe in God. However, the basis for supporting this premise is not that there is an innate tendency in people to believe in God. Instead, the support for this premise is sought in the contention that it is based on reason. This aspect of the antiskeptical dilemma type of argument seems to make it a subspecies of position to know reasoning. That is, the presumption behind the argument is that the people who believe in God do so because it would be unreasonable to believe otherwise. The basis for this contention is made clear in the second stage of the argument, which states that, if the whole of mankind were mistaken in this belief, it would follow that "it is idle for men to search for truth." The argument, here, seems to be a form of disjunctive reasoning that postulates two dichotomous alternatives. The one alternative is that the popular belief in the existence of God is true. The other alternative, that this belief is false, would allegedly have the consequence that it would lead to skepticism of a sort which would be incompatible with human rationality. The third stage of the argument cited by Edwards (1967, 50), in his analysis of it, is the contention that, since reason is fundamentally trustworthy, universal skepticism is not an acceptable alternative.

The reason that the antiskeptical dilemma fails to persuade the modern audience is not hard to discern. People no longer believe in the kind of human rationality that Yankelovich identified with the process of coming to judgment in public deliberation (see Chapter 4, section 9). They no longer see dialectical argument as a standard of rationality that can stand up to scientific rationality, and exist alongside it. Skepticism about this sort of dialectical rationality is not something that is unacceptable to the modern thinker. Far from it, such skepticism is exactly the viewpoint on rationality he or she accepts.

An argument that is, by comparison with the *consensus gentium* argument, highly convincing to the modern mind, has however been furnished to fill in for these older, no longer convincing *ad populum* arguments. Who came up with this argument? Not surprisingly, it was Pascal. It is interesting to contrast the logic of the antiskeptical dilemma with a very different type of argument for accepting the proposition that God exists put forward by Pascal in his *Pensées* (1670)—the famous wager argument. Pascal put his argument in the form of a bet, based on a calculation of the probability of winning or losing, and the numerical value of the two outcomes. This way of calculating the costs and benefits by a numerical probability measure is highly characteristic of the modern point of view, whereby decision making is reduced to a scientific and numerical calculation.

Pascal's first premise is that God is infinite, whereas we, as human beings are finite.

> We know, therefore, the existence and the nature of the finite, because, we ourselves are also finite and have extension in space.

> We know the existence of the infinite, but we do not know its nature because, although like ourselves it has extension, unlike ourselves it has no limits. (Gleason ed. 1966, 90)

He concludes from this premise that we, as finite human beings, cannot know anything about the nature of God. On this basis, he asks us to consider a bet: Does God exist or not?

> Well, let us take your point, and let us begin by saying: "Either God is, or He is not." But which way shall we lean? Here, reason can decide nothing. A vast gulf separates us, and across this infinite void a game is being played that depends upon the toss of a coin. What is your wager, heads or tails? According to reason, you cannot bet on either, because (also strictly in conformity with reason) neither probability can be ruled out. (90–91)

Not only that, Pascal adds, but we *must* wager, because we are already "embarked upon it."

> The prudent thing is not to wager. Certainly. But in this case you *must* wager: you have no option, you have embarked upon it (and you cannot now withdraw from the game). Which will you take, then?

Then Pascal calculates the outcomes of the two sides of the bet.

> Let us estimate the gain and the loss if we call, "Heads!" and wager "That God is." Compare the two chances: if you win, you win everything; if you lose, you lose nothing. Don't hesitate, then. Make a bet that God exists. (91)

If you bet on the hypothesis that God exists, and you are right, then you win everything, infinity, eternal bliss. By comparison, if you lose, it does not matter much by comparison. According to Pascal, "The chance of winning or losing is fifty-fifty" (91). But the value of winning is infinitely great.

> But here is a game in which the prize actually is eternal life and eternal happiness, with one chance of winning against a finite number of chances of losing, and our stake is also finite. That

removes the element of chance, and settles the matter: wherever there is an infinite opportunity, and where there is no infinity of chances of losing against the one chance of winning, there is no need for hesitation. You can and you must stake all. (91–92)

Pascal concludes that the rational course of conduct for anyone who recognizes the logic of the wager argument is to "follow the people who know the road," and to behave as though you believe. Your course of action should be to take holy water, go to mass, and follow the accepted rituals of those who already believe. He writes, "This will lead you naturally toward belief and will calm you . . . drive the beast out of you." (93).

The beauty of Pascal's argument is that it no longer depends on dialectical notions like the *ad populum* argument. Nor does it even seem to rely on presumptive reasoning, or on deliberation using practical reasoning to arrive at a prudent decision on a course of action, of the kind Aristotle and Aquinas cited. It appeals instead to the kind of reasoning used in modern science—or at least advocated by Enlightenment thinkers as the kind of reasoning that should be used in science—reasoning based on a numerical calculation of probabilities. As the basis of the calculation, the concept of infinity is incorporated into the argument. This is another notion that is acceptable to the Enlightenment model of reasoning, and that was adopted by Newton and Leibniz as an essential component of scientific argumentation and methodology.

Thus Pascal's argument is the perfectly modern argument for the existence of God, made to order for the new Enlightenment thinking of the era of expanding scientific rationality. It enables us to unload all of that old unpersuasive baggage of the appeal to popular opinion, and other outdated dialectical notions needed by the *consensus gentium* argument.

Or does it? Well, not entirely. Pascal refutes the reply that one can opt out by failing to take the wager on the grounds that one has already "embarked" on it. In other words, as a living being, you are "involved" in life, and you must make practical decisions on what to do (or what not to do) every day. Here he seems to appeal to the notions of presumptive reasoning and deliberation that are so central to dialectical argument. According to Pascal, to get from acceptance to belief, the prudent course of action is to do what religious believers do.

Once one starts to base this line of reasoning on human, practical deliberations on what to do, the Enlightenment method of qualifying the outcomes based on numerical calculations of probabilities becomes somewhat questionable, however. Does it make sense to claim that the afterlife postulated by the religious viewpoint can be assigned the value of infinity? To modern thinkers who have adopted the Enlightenment standard of scientific rationality—and would reject dialectical argument as a serious or significant standard of rationality to be used in arguments—the answer is that such an assignment is perfectly acceptable and one they can be comfortable with. Moreover, they would be predisposed to deny or doubt that the Pascal's Wager argument has any need to rest on dialectical notions such as presumptive reasoning in practical deliberation.

10. Toward a New Dialectic

What is most striking about Aristotelian dialectic is that it is based on premises that are generally accepted opinions, as opposed to what Aristotle called demonstrative reasoning, which is based on premises that are "primary and true." Such an account means that *ad populum* arguments, while they are out of place in demonstrative reasoning, have a legitimate, and indeed an essential and very important place, in dialectical reasoning.

But how is a premise based on appeal to popular opinion meant to be used in Aristotelian dialectical argumentation? It seems that dialectic for Aristotle represents a framework of argument in which there is a genuine conflict of opinions on some controversial issue. It could be a conflict between two current views in popular opinion, say on politics, or it could be a conflict of opinions between the many and the wise. But at any rate, dialectical argument presupposes a conflict between two opposed theses or propositions, where one proposition is opposed to the other. The strongest type of opposition is the kind of case where the one proposition is the opposite (negation) of the other.

Post-Enlightenment Pascalian thinking does not allow dialectical argumentation as representing a kind of reasoning that has any command on rationality. The only kind of rationality is scientific thinking, which has one of two forms. It can be the kind of argument Aristotle called demonstrative, which Pascal thought of as deductive reasoning along the lines of axiomatic Euclidean geometry. Or it can be based on probability. No room is left for argumentation based on conflicts and opposed theses, because this kind of argumentation is not scientific.

Dialectical questions, in Aristotelian dialectic, are concerned with matters about which there is difficulty, controversy or dispute. Endoxic propositions can function as presumptively acceptable promises, when used in dialectical arguments, because, at least comparatively, there is not the same kind of controversial quality to them. They can be used as common starting points to help a dialogue go forward. They are accepted, not universally perhaps, but generally accepted by the broad majority at a given time. For dialectical purposes, to help a discussion to throw light on a controversial conflict of opinions or dispute, endoxic premises can be useful. That does not mean they are beyond challenge, of course. It only means they have a certain usefulness as helpful presumptions.

As Aquinas showed, endoxic premises can also be useful to assist deliberation where, like Aristotelian dialectic, the dialogue is concerned to determine which argument is stronger, where a choice needs to be made between mutually exclusive alternatives or opposed propositions. In a deliberation, the argument is set in the context of a balance of considerations, and the sequence of argumentation is directed toward judging the most prudent course of action, from the available opposed alternatives. Here, too, a premise can be a proposition that is generally accepted, a presumption that tentatively represents the best intelligence available, even if it is not conclusively known to be true.

Aristotelian dialectic, as a framework for the use of reasoned argumentation, appears to be similar to the type of conversational exchange called the persuasion dialogue in Chapter 4. Deliberation appears to be a different type of dialogue that is concerned with trying to confer together to find a prudent course of action in a given set of circumstances. Generally, as observed in Chapter 4, premises based on popular opinion can function as common starting points, in a dialogue exchange where two parties have a central conflict of opinions. But within this framework, it seems that Aristotelian dialectic could allow for different uses of a premise based on popular opinion. One party in a dialectical dispute could use such a premise to try to persuade the other party to come to accept her (the first party's) thesis. This type of argument would be a positive use of appeal to popular opinion. But an arguer could also use an appeal to popular opinion premise to derive a contradiction or falsehood, by a sequence of inferences from this premise. Such an argument would show that the original premise, expressing a popular belief, must be false. This negative use of argument from popular opinion could be a way of challenging commonly held views. And we know from the platonic dialogue that this type of argument was commonly used by Socrates in his elenchtic questioning sequences.

If the *ad populum* argument can have different uses, the key to evaluating it should perhaps be sought not exclusively in the argument itself (or its argumentation scheme), but in the conversational framework or type of dialogue in which it is used. Aristotle distinguished between various types or uses of arguments—demonstrative, dialectical, didactic, examination and contentious. But perhaps it would be better to say that these categories represent types of dialogue, or forms of conversational exchange, in which arguments are used for varying purposes, depending on the context of use. Aquinas added the deliberation as another type of dialogue that, in addition to the five categories explicitly mentioned by Aristotle, could be considered a framework of dialogue or "conferring" in which arguments are used.

These considerations suggest that the *ad populum* appeal can best be understood and evaluated as an argument that has different uses in different types of dialogue. It suggests a return to the ancient dialectical viewpoint for evaluating argumentation, but in a modern form.

Chapter Six

THE NEW DIALECTIC

What is needed as a framework to properly evaluate *ad populum* arguments is a modern counterpart to Aristotelian dialectic that can account for premise adequacy of common starting points as presumptions used to move a dialogue, such as a persuasion dialogue or a deliberation, forward toward fulfilling its goal. The new dialectic needs to be seen as the study of how different types of talk exchanges or dialogues function as normative structures in which arguments can be evaluated in relation to how they are used in a talk exchange.

The survey in Chapter 4 of how some different components of these dialectical frameworks relate to our understanding of the *ad populum* as a type of argument that can be reasonable in some instances has already started us toward the need for a new dialectic. What is provided in Chapter 6 is a systematic account of this new and developing framework as it relates to *ad populum* arguments.

1. Types of Dialogue

The new dialectic evaluates an argument not just as an inference, or as reasoning made up of a chain of inferences, but also in relation to how that reasoning is used for some purpose in a context of dialogue. A dialectical evaluation of an argument judges how the argument has been used in a conversational exchange, following Grice's Cooperative Principle (CP): "Make your conversational contribution such as is required, at the stage at which it occurs, by the accepted purpose or direction of the talk exchange in which you are engaged" (1975, 67). However, there can be several different types of dialogue (talk exchanges) that are important as contexts in which *ad populum* arguments are used.

The account of the ten types of dialogue given in Table 6.1 is adapted from the listing of twelve types of dialogue given in Walton (1992a, 95). Of these various types of dialogue, some are more fundamental in their structure as normative models of argument than others. The debate can be analyzed as a mixed type of dialogue that contains elements of the persuasion dialogue and elements of the quarrel. The expert consultation dialogue is a subspecies of information-seeking dialogue. And the pedagogical dialogue is a subspecies of information-seeking dialogue that contains elements of the persuasion dialogue. Another subspecies of information-seeking dialogue is the interview.

In Walton and Krabbe (1995), the critical-discussion dialogue is treated as being equivalent to the persuasion type. However, in Walton (1995), the critical discussion is classified as a special subtype of persuasion dialogue. According to this classification, persuasion dialogue is treated as the general or generic type of dialogue under which the critical discussion falls. Also, in Walton and Krabbe, the quarrel is treated as a specific type of dialogue that falls under the general heading of eristic dialogue.

A systematic classification of six basic dialogue types is given in Walton and Krabbe (1995, 80), reprinted here as Figure 6.1. The four other types of dialogue listed in Table 6.1 can all be analyzed as mixed types of dialogue that are compounds of two or more of the basic subtypes in Figure 6.1, or are special subspecies of one of these types.

There are many different conventionalized types of dialogue that represent conversational contexts in which arguments are used in everyday argumentation exchanges. No claim is made that the list of ten in Table 6.1 is complete. However, for the purpose of identifying, analyzing, and evaluating arguments associated with informal fallacies, these ten types appear to be the most generally useful. And the six basic types identified in Figure 6.1 appear to be the most fundamental and most necessary for any method of studying fallacies.

In this chapter, the persuasion dialogue and the deliberation are emphasized as key to understanding and evaluating *ad populum* arguments. However, in subsequent evaluations of cases of *ad populum* arguments in later chapters, the other types of dialogue will come to be important as well.

Table 6.1 Ten types of dialogue

Type of dialogue	Initial situation	Individual goals of participants	Collective goal of dialogue	Benefits
Persuasion	Difference of opinion	Persuade other party	Resolve difference of opinion	Understand positions
Debate	Adversarial contest	Persuade third party	Air strongest agruments for both sides	Spread information
Inquiry	Ignorance	Contribute findings	Prove or disprove conjecture	Obtain knowledge
Negotiation	Conflict of interest	Maximize gains (self-interest)	Settlement (without undue inequity)	Harmony
Quarrel	Personal conflict	Verbally hit out at and humiliate opponent	Reveal deeper conflict	Vent emotions
Information-seeking	One party lacks information	Obtain information	Transfer of knowledge	Help in goal activity
Interview	Curiosity about position	Develop subject's position	Express interesting position to wider audience	Spread information
Expert consultation	Need for expert advice	Giving advice: decision for action	Informed basis for action	Second-hand knowledge
Deliberation	Contemplation of future consequences	Promote personal goals	Act on a thoughtful basis	Formulate personal priorities
Pedagogical	Ignorance of one party	Teaching and learning	Transfer of knowledge	Reverse transfer

2. Persuasion Dialogue

The *persuasion dialogue*, and its prominent subtype, the *critical discussion*, were introduced in Chapter 4, section 5. As explained there, each party in a persuasion dialogue has the goal of proving his or her thesis, using arguments based on premises that are commitments of the other party.

Fig. 6.1 Systematic survey of dialogue types

Initial Situation / Main Goal	Conflict	Open Problem	Unsatisfactory Spread of Information
Stable Agreement/Resolution	Persuasion	Inquiry	Information Seeking
Practical Settlement/ Decision (Not) to Act	Negotiation	Deliberation	
Reaching a (Provisional) Accommodation	Eristic		

The goal of the critical-discussion type of dialogue is to resolve a conflict of opinions (van Eemeren and Grootendorst, 1984; 1992) by means of rational arguments so that the opinion advocated by one side is seen to be demonstrably better supported by evidence than the thesis of the other side. In a critical discussion, one side has a proposition that she is arguing for which is called her "thesis" and her pro attitude toward this, along with the proposition that constitutes the thesis itself is called the *point of view* of that participant (1984, 5).

There are two basic types of critical discussion. In the one type, there are two participants and each participant has a thesis, and a thesis of the one is the opposite or negation of the thesis of the other. In this type of case, there is a *strong opposition* between the two parties in the sense that, for the one to prove her thesis, she must refute the other party's thesis. The other type of conflict characteristic of a critical discussion is the type where the one party, as before, has a proposition to be proved called the thesis and the other party, instead of having a positive proposition to be proved, merely doubts or has critical questions about the thesis of the other side. So, in this type of case, there is what could be called *weak opposition* between the two parties, defined by the following type of situation. The one party has a positive burden of proof in order to be successful in the critical discussion. She has to prove her thesis according to the standards of evidence appropriate for the dialogue, while, for the other party, in order to succeed, it is necessary for him only that he casts sufficient doubt upon the argument of the other side that she is unable to prove her thesis successfully.[1]

---

[1]. This account represents a description of the critical discussion in our own terms. Van Eemeren and Grootendorst (1984; 1992) use somewhat different terms. A useful brief account of the characteristics and rules of the critical discussion is given in van Eemeren and Grootendorst (1987).

The critical discussion is a subspecies of a more general type of dialogue called "persuasion dialogue" (Walton 1995, 100). In a persuasion dialogue the purpose of the dialogue is to have a revealing and informative discussion of a particular topic even if the original conflict of opinions that began the discussion is not conclusively resolved one way or the other. In a persuasion dialogue, each participant has the goal of persuading the other party that her thesis is true or at least acceptable on a balance of considerations.

The characteristic type of argumentation used by both parties in a persuasion dialogue is commitment-based in nature. The concept of commitment is fundamental to the idea of persuasion dialogue (Hamblin 1970; 1971). The basic idea of commitment advocated by Hamblin is that, ideally, in an argument exchange, both parties should keep track of all the propositions that they have committed themselves to over the course of the discussion. Of course, in real life, commitments are often lost track of or forgotten and participants frequently dispute about whether such and such a proposition really is a commitment of the other side or not. But in Hamblin's idealized model of dialogue, participants would have some kind of device like a tape recorder or a blackboard on which they would keep a log of all the propositions that both parties have become committed to during the course of an argument. Commitment, according to Hamblin's idea, is not a psychological concept but a normative one (see also Eemeren and Grootendorst 1984, 6–7; and Walton and Krabbe 1995, 5–10). An individual's commitments will be inserted into what Hamblin calls your commitment set, in virtue of the kinds of moves you have made in a particular type of dialogue.

For example, if you and I are having a persuasion dialogue on some subject and I make an assertion, then the proposition that is the content of that assertion would go into my commitment store in virtue of the kind of move that I have made by making an assertion at some particular point in the dialogue. What is characteristic of the argumentation in a persuasion dialogue is that each participant has the goal of trying to persuade the other party by using arguments that have premises that are commitments of the other party or, at least, that represent propositions that the other party could become committed to. But the way for a participant to accomplish this successfully is to advance valid or structurally correct arguments that have the other party's commitments as premises and one's own thesis as a conclusion. Hence, commitment-based reasoning is a very distinctive and fundamental type of argumentation in a persuasion dialogue.

A critical discussion, or persuasion type of dialogue generally, will begin with a confrontation stage where the conflict of opinions is explicitly stated. In other words, it must be clear at the outset what the point of view of each party is. For example, if the discussion is on the subject of abortion, one side may argue for the proposition that abortion ought generally to be allowed while the other side may take the opposite proposition and argue that abortion ought not to be generally allowed. This originating conflict of opinions is the most important factor in determining whether an argument will or will not be relevant at some subsequent stage of the dispute. Basically, an argument is relevant in a persuasion dialogue if it can be used by the participant to provide support, that is the proper kind of evidence, for her own thesis or if it can be used to cast doubt upon the contention of the other side or even to refute the thesis of the other side.[2] In general, this type of relevance is called *probative relevance*, meaning that it pertains to how a proposition is proved or disproved in a dialogue. Probative relevance has to do with the use of an argument to support or prove a proposition according to the kinds of evidence recognized as appropriate and legitimate in a given type of dialogue.

Another type of relevance contrasted with probative relevance is *topical relevance* (Epstein 1979 and 1995; Walton 1982). Topical relevance has to do with overlap of subject matters. Consider the two propositions. For example, abortion is a woman's right and Bob is against abortion. These two propositions share common subject matters. They both contain the topic of abortion but they are not probatively relevant to each other, at least in the absence of any further context of the previous argument. They are not probatively relevant because one, as it stands, is of no use in proving or disproving the other proposition.

Generally, in a persuasion dialogue, there will be certain types of arguments recognized as appropriate to resolve the conflict of opinions. Various types of arguments commonly used for this purpose are represented by the argumentation schemes outlined in Walton (1995, chap. 5). However, in a particular case of a critical discussion, there will also be certain types of evidence that will be agreed upon by both parties at the opening stage of the discussion as appropriate. Van Eemeren and Grootendorst (1984) refer to this aspect of the critical discussion as the intersubjective testing procedure (ITP), that is, in a critical discussion, the two parties might agree beforehand that certain sources of opinion might be accepted by both of them as definitive or acceptable evidence with respect to the subject they are discussing.[3]

---

2. See also the qualifications with respect to this example discussed in section 9 of this chapter.
3. For a fuller account of the function of an ITP in persuasion dialogue, see chapter 4, section 5.

For example, both participants might have access to an encyclopedia and agree that any proposition found in the encyclopedia will constitute acceptable evidence for the purposes of their discussion. Another source of evidence might be an expert in a scientific field, for example, who is available for a consultation. For example, on the abortion dispute, some of the questions may concern biology, so that the two participants may agree to consult a biologist and also agree that any proposition vouched for by the biologist as being part of his scientific field will be accepted by both of the primary participants in the critical discussion as acceptable evidence, and both of them will agree not to dispute that evidence or, at least, to tentatively accept it as a basis for constructing premises for arguments.[4] So, in a critical discussion, there will be two sources for premises. One will be the commitments of the other party, which are essentially propositions that have been, in effect, granted by that other party during the course of the previous discussion. And the other source of premises will be the propositions that have been agreed upon by both participants as fulfilling the requirements of what they regard as acceptable evidence.[5]

It should be emphasized that an important aspect of all persuasion dialogue is the commitment-based nature of the argumentation it contains. The sum total of a participant's commitment set at any stage in the dialogue, along with the initial thesis that the participant is supposed to be arguing for, define the arguer's position in the dialogue. The arguer's position represents her point of view at any given stage in the dialogue, as revealed not only by the thesis she has chosen to argue for but also by the argumentation she has used in the dialogue to defend that thesis up to a given point.

3. The Inquiry

A second type of dialogue is called the *inquiry* (Walton 1995, 106–9), which has the goal of uncovering all available evidence on some issue and using this evidence to definitely prove that a proposition is either true or false. In a situation where even after all this work of collecting evidence has been done it is not possible to definitely prove either that the proposition is true or that the proposition is false, a satisfactory outcome of an inquiry could be the third possibility—it cannot be proved that the proposition is true or false. This third outcome could be an important finding, as well.

---

4. See the discussion of common starting points in Chapter 4.
5. As will be indicated in section 5, an introduction of evidence of this sort involves a joining of an expert consultation type of dialogue to the critical discussion.

It is important to recognize that standards of proof in an inquiry are meant to be quite high. Proved, in this sense, is taken to mean that a proposition is definitely established on the basis of premises that are known to be true so that there will be no need to revise or retract this proposition once more information comes to be known in the future. Hence, a key characteristic of argumentation in the inquiry is cumulativeness. To say that an argument is cumulative means that it moves forward in a sequence so that any particular conclusion in that sequence is proved only by premises that are established at prior points in the sequence as definitely true. The purpose of having cumulative argumentation is that there should be no need to have to circle back to a previous point in the sequence of argumentation to retract one's previous commitments. Such a circular sequence of argument with retractions would disturb the whole structure on which cumulative argumentation is based. So, a cumulative argument has the intent of building a line of argument on solid foundations so that the argument is essentially linear or, at any rate, never needs to circle back to previous points (Walton 1991a).

The traditional model of cumulative argumentation is Euclidean geometry where axioms are established at the outset that are intuitively true (Mackenzie 1980). At least, these axioms are propositions of a sort that seem obviously true that there would never be any need to doubt or question them once an argument built on them as premises proceeds. So, in Euclidean geometry, the axioms are numbered and then any conclusion in the subsequent sequence of argumentation always has a lower number than any of the axioms or any of the previous conclusions which have been drawn from those axioms. The whole cumulative structure will have a linear or branching sequence. It will contain no circles, that is, it will contain no cases where a lower-numbered proposition has to be based on an argument containing any higher-numbered propositions as premises.

Aristotle identified a type of argument called *demonstrative argument* where conclusions are only based on better-known premises (Chapter 5, section 2). This notion of the argument's only being good to the extent that it is based on premises which are better established is called the *property of evidential priority* in Walton (1995, 108). Another philosopher who is frequently identified with advocating the model of argument called the *inquiry* is Descartes. Descartes argued that philosophical argumentation should only be based ultimately on premises that are known to be indubitably true (Descartes 1960). The idea seemed to be that these premises are firmly established so that there would never been any need to have to go back to question them, thus disrupting the sequence of argumentation in the inquiry. Pascal was another enthusiast of the inquiry (see Chapter 5, section 7).

Of course, the question of whether scientific argumentation, for example in scientific research, really does take the form of an inquiry has been hotly disputed in the philosophy of science in recent years. Often, scientists, in their rhetoric, particularly when they are teaching students or talking about the aims and methods of science to outsiders, that is, to nonscientists, adopt a rhetorical stance that science should ideally be a form of inquiry. These scientists may stress that science has very high standards for evidence and is very careful to use experimental protocols and only to use reproducible and verifiable evidence in such a way that science can be built on an edifice of propositions that are very well established by hard evidence and so forth. However, in recent years, many philosophers of science question this model of scientific argumentation and would compare scientific argumentation more to the model of argument represented by persuasion dialogue.

According to this interpretation, scientists have clashes of points of view on so-called fundamental paradigms and then argue out these conflicts by attacking the other party and by using techniques that would be characteristic of persuasion dialogue. Probably neither of these models is characteristic of all scientific reasoning at all points at certain stages of scientific reasoning. For example, at a discovery stage, the argumentation does tend to be more of the second type. By contrast, where a science has become very well-established and has highly developed mathematical theories and very well-developed methods that have been articulated in very precise ways, then perhaps it could be said that here the model scientific argumentation does approximate more to that of the inquiry.

Another example of the inquiry is the *public inquiry* into some question of concern such as that of an air disaster. It is very important for the public to try to find out what the cause of the air crash was or, at least, to assemble all the available evidence to see if the problem is one that can be rectified so that a comparable disaster in the future may be prevented. In such a case, then, routinely we have an inquiry set into place and various experts who may have examined the crash site and be familiar with such matters are brought in to testify and give evidence to try to determine what was the cause of the crash. When the data have been collected and various theories are put forth by the parties involved in the inquiry, there tends to be argumentation back and forth between the various parties or groups. And then, after this argumentation stage, there will be a stage of the inquiry where all the parties in the inquiry, or some designated subgroup of them, will get together to write up a report that represents the outcome of the inquiry. And then, at a later stage, this report will be communicated to the general public and the findings of the inquiry will be given.

The key difference between the inquiry and the persuasion type of dialogue concerns the problem of retraction. In general, the critical discussion needs to be an open type of dialogue where retraction is frequently permitted. In a persuasion dialogue, retraction cannot always be permitted. Participants must stick to their commitments generally, but in some circumstances participants must be prepared to alter those commitments or even to retract them entirely.[6] This openness to retraction is a very important aspect of the critical discussion and is essential to its success. The critical discussion needs to be an open and fluid type of dialogue where a party can retract commitment to a proposition if the other party shows that there is adequate evidence to refute that proposition. However, the inquiry is quite different in that its whole purpose is to build up a structure or development of propositions where there is no need for retraction. Thus generally, in the inquiry, retraction of propositions will not be allowed or will only be allowed under very restrictive circumstances, and retraction of any kind will generally go against the attempt of the inquiry to construct a cumulative sequence of argumentation to prove a conclusion. So, we can see, in general, then that the inquiry is quite different in its goals and its methods from the persuasion type of dialogue.

Both the inquiry and persuasion dialogue are aimed toward trying to get to (or toward) the truth of a matter, by using arguments based on evidence to support the truth or falsity of propositions. Arguments in the next two types of dialogue are not really used to try to get to the truth of a matter.

4. Negotiations and Quarrels

A third type of dialogue called the *negotiation dialogue* has a different purpose from either the critical discussion or the inquiry. In negotiation dialogue, the goal of the participant is to make a deal concerning some goods or resources that have economic value that are a source of conflict between the two participants. A participant in negotiation dialogue makes offers to the other party, and also concessions to the other party, in order to divide up these goods in a way that will allow one to maximize one's own gains with respect to those goods that are chiefly important, while making enough concessions to the other party so that that other party will not feel hard done by. Thus, the goal is to make a

---

6. See Walton and Krabbe (1995) for an extensive statement of the exact conditions under which retraction should be permitted in persuasion dialogue.

good deal without losing face, so to speak. The goal is to make a deal or divide the goods in a way that both parties can live with and where both parties can feel that they traded off what was not such a high priority to them in order to get what was of a high priority from their point of view. The optimum outcome of a good negotiation is a win-win situation where both parties feel they got most of what they thought was most important to them, even though they had to take some losses or make some concessions to the other side.

The negotiation dialogue is quite different from critical discussion because the aim of a critical discussion is to move toward the truth of a matter or, at least, get some understanding of the basis of a disagreement that would be helpful, ultimately, in clarifying the disagreement so that the truth of the matter might subsequently come out. So, the critical-discussion dialogue is somewhat directed or oriented toward trying to find the real truth of the matter. Negotiation is less so, however. If you enter into a negotiation dialogue with a view that you are trying to conduct some sort of critical discussion or prove something or find the truth of the matter, then you will fare very badly in the negotiations. While such matters of finding the truth do have some place in a negotiation, it is quite a different and smaller place than in a critical discussion. What matters most in a negotiation is not really what is true, but what the other party will accept. So, again, in negotiation, as in persuasion dialogue, matters of empathy and entering into the position of the other party, and in particular, trying to judge what the other party thinks is important is a key skill in the dialogue.

In *distributive bargaining*, the simplest type of negotiation, the issue is some kind of goods or services which have economic value and the goals of the two parties in wanting to have ownership or use of these goods are in sharp conflict with each other. However, in other kinds of negotiation, for example, in the type called *attitudinal structuring* (R. E. Walton and McKersie 1965, 5), the issue has to do with the personalities of the participants and, in particular, attitudes like friendliness, hostility, or trust, that have less directly to do with money or overtly economic considerations. The concept of commitment is also very important in negotiation dialogue. Walton and McKersie define commitment as the act of "pledging oneself to a course of action" (50). The important thing about negotiation to recognize here, is that it is a legitimate context of dialogue in its own right, which has goals and methods of argumentation that are distinctively different from those of the persuasion dialogue and the inquiry.

A fourth type of dialogue is the *eristic* type of dialogue from the Greek word *eris* or strife. In eristic dialogue, the goal is not to get at the truth of the matter.

Instead, it is to attack the other party and to generally make the other party look bad. Hence, eristic dialogue is a highly adversarial type of dialogue.

The most commonly familiar subtype of eristic dialogue is the *quarrel.* In a quarrel, each party has certain personal harms or grievances that have not been expressed to the other party in an overt way, and the beginning of the quarrel occurs where one party opens up one of these grievances using it to attack the other party as being guilty of causing the problem. The quarrel is accompanied by a highly emotional state. In normal conversations, it is necessary for people to get along and do things together, for example, in business, so that small differences or disagreements need to be put aside or not stated in polite conversation. However, in a lasting relationship, these unstated grievances will tend to build up between the two parties that are involved in the relationship, in the simplest kind of case anyway, and at some point these hidden grievances will burst to the surface, and the one party will start to talk in an emotionally heightened way that is not characteristic of normal polite conversation. This type of exchange, for example, may be accompanied by profanity or by loud shouting, so when the quarrel arrives, it typically does so in a kind of outburst or interruption that involves a changeover from a polite conversation to this different type of dialogue we called the quarrel. Generally, in a quarrel, one party will attack the other party as being a bad person who has caused all kinds of problems for the first party, and then the other party will respond by so-called counterblaming where equivalent grievances will be raised that are said to have been caused by the first party who originally made the complaints.

Ad hominem arguments or personal attacks are characteristic of the quarrel. Typically, the one party will attack the character of the other party, saying that the other person is morally a bad person or has committed some ethical lapse or is a liar or is a thoughtless or insensitive person, something of that sort. The quarrel is often taken to be a highly negative type of exchange, and language theorists generally tend to condemn it. The old saying is that the quarrel generates more heat than light, and it has been perceived that the quarrel is no friend of logic. However, Walton notes that the quarrel can have the good outcome of making the continuation of a personal relationship possible by the revealing and explicit acknowledgment of these grievances (1995, 108). Thus, the benefit of a quarrel cited here is the cathartic effect whereby hidden conflicts or antagonisms can be openly acknowledged by both parties.

According to this normative model of eristic dialogue, the quarrel can have good qualities. In a good or productive quarrel, the closing stage can be a cementing of the relationship between the two parties where one party might say to the other that she did not realize that this thing that had offended them was so important to him, and that she will make a serious attempt in the future not to engage in this kind of behavior any more when he is around. So, the closing stage of the quarrel, where the quarrel has been successful or is of the good kind, can be described by the expression "making up." The two parties acknowledge the importance to the other of this expressed grievance, and indicate to the other party that they will be more sensitive about this in the future.

It does seem a little strange at first to think of the quarrel as a normative model of dialogue in which argumentation can be evaluated as correct or incorrect, for, as noted above, it has generally been assumed in the past that the quarrel is inherently bad or is a deterioration of the dialogue exchange. And in fact, it is true that from a logical point of view of getting at the truth of the matter, the quarrel is of very little use. Nevertheless, it is important in argumentation to understand the nature of the quarrel as a type of dialogue exchange in which argumentation occurs because it is quite a frequent occurrence with types of argument associated with the fallacies that there is a shift from one type of dialogue, such as a critical discussion, to a quarrel or eristic type of dialogue. Understanding how such a shift works in a particular case, is in fact frequently very important in understanding or evaluating a claim that a fallacy has been committed in the argumentation in that case.

Both Plato and Aristotle recognized eristic dialogue as a very important framework of argument and, in fact, both of these philosophers were very worried about the possibility that dialectical reasoning or logical argument directed toward finding the truth of the matter could deteriorate into eristic dialogue. In Plato's dialogue *Euthydemus*, clever Sophists are portrayed who attack each other with tricky arguments and clever traps. Clearly, Plato was worried about this possibility as a degeneration or deterioration of the type of dialectical argument that he was recommending as the method for philosophy.

Aristotle, in his book on fallacies (*On Sophistical Refutations* [1928], 171b24–171b30), compared eristic argumentation to cheating in sports where a participant in an athletic contest is bent on victory at all costs. Both Plato and Aristotle tended to condemn the sophists, a class of practitioners who taught students to improve their argumentation skills by calling the sophists eristic arguers who took lectures for their fees and taught people how to win a dispute with no regard for the truth of a matter. Whether these allegations were historically fair or not, and there are reasons to think they were not (Kerferd 1981), we can see that both Plato and Aristotle were very worried about the kinds of arguments they advocated as appropriate for philosophy, generating into a quarrelsome type of argument.

5. Information-Seeking Dialogue

A fifth type of dialogue is the *information-seeking* type of dialogue where one party wants to get some information that the other party presumably has. So, the role of the one party is to get this information and the role of the other party is to give or transmit this information to the first party. In this respect then, the information-seeking dialogue is asymmetrical in the sense that the role of the one party is quite different from that of the other. The goal of information-seeking dialogue, then, is the transfer of information from one party to the other. The one party lacks some designated information and the other party presumably has this information, so the goal is to redress this distribution of information. An example of information-seeking dialogue would be a recruiting interview by a representative of a company. The recruiter wants to find out whether this person would be a suitable employee and, therefore, wants to get some idea of this person's skills and abilities.

Another type of information-seeking dialogue is the *media interview*, for example, the televised interview where a celebrity is questioned by a media interviewer who tries to get some information about the celebrity's personal life or about some situation which the public is interested in that the celebrity has been involved in. Another situation where argumentation is involved—and it would be appropriate to say that the structure is that of information-seeking dialogue—would be the kind of case where a researcher is searching through a computer database in order to find some information on a topic. The researcher then types questions into the database in the computer or inserts key words that will enable the database to seek out certain items, satisfying the researcher's questions. So the questions or key words put into the computer by the researcher represent attempts to seek out items of information that the researcher needs or wants to find out about. The computer then, following its program, searches through large databases and selects out items that contain the key words inserted by the researcher. In this case, the exchange is one between a human being and a machine or a computer program, but, nevertheless, this can be modeled quite usefully as an instance of an information-seeking dialogue.

A special subtype of the information-seeking dialogue is the *expert-consultation dialogue*. An example would be a kind of case where you need information and advice on financial matters and you consult with a trained financial adviser. Another familiar example would be a case where you are worried about some matter relating to your health, and you consult a physician for information and advice. A common type of argument used in such cases is the appeal to expert opinion, represented by the argumentation scheme (Walton 1996b) identified in Chapter 2, section 10.

Argument from expert opinion is a special type of a more generic kind of argumentation referred to as the argument from position to know. A typical example of this type of reasoning is used when a tourist who is lost in an unfamiliar city asks a passerby where a certain street is located. The passerby, in such a case, does not have to be an expert on city streets, like an engineer or cartographer. But the questioner presumes that this person is in a position to know about the location of the street queried. The argumentation scheme for the argument from position to know is the following, where a is an individual, and A is a proposition (1996b, 61).

(*Pos. Know*) a is in a position to know whether A is true (false).
a asserts that A is true (false).
Therefore, a is true (false).

The critical questions matching this argumentation scheme are the following:

1. Is a in a position to know whether A is true (false)?
2. Is a an honest (trustworthy, reliable) source?
3. Did a assert that A is true (false)?

Position to know reasoning is a presumptive type of argumentation that can be challenged, in a given case where it has been used, by asking one or more of three critical questions above.

Information-seeking dialogue can be functionally joined to another type of dialogue such as a critical discussion or deliberation, in order to make an argument in the critical discussion or the deliberation more intelligent, because it is based on better information. For example, if you are deliberating on what to do with respect to a health problem, it may be helpful to consult with a physician. Such an expert consultation dialogue may then improve the quality of the argumentation used in your deliberation to arrive at a conclusion on a prudent course of action to take.

6. Deliberation

The sixth type of dialogue is called *deliberation* (Walton 1995, 116–18). Deliberation arises out of a need to either take action or at least to consider possible courses of action or inaction in a situation where some kind of action appears to be called for. Typically, in a deliberation, there is a conflict between the two parties on two opposed courses of action that are possible in a given situation, and the one party thinks that the one course of action would be the right or the reasonable thing to do whereas the other party either doubts this or thinks that the other course of action would be the best thing to do in the circumstances. The kind of argumentation that is typically used in deliberation is goal-directed practical reasoning that concludes in an imperative to action. In a practical inference, one premise is a goal premise while the other premise is a means premise that presents some way in a given situation of bringing about that goal based on the agent's knowledge of the particular situation. Then, the conclusion proposes a practical or prudent course of action for the agent to take, based on the information in the two premises. So, the goal of deliberation then, is to reach a decision on how to carry out a practical course of action in a given situation where more than one course of action is possible.

Aristotle described the main characteristics of deliberation quite well in the *Nicomachean Ethics* (1112a30–1112b1), where he wrote that we deliberate about the things that are in our power and can be done. He meant, there, that we deliberate about changeable things in the real world where some possible course of action we can take will change the course of events. Hence, Aristotle contrasted the model of argument he called *demonstration*, which is characteristic of what he called the exact and self-contained sciences, with the model of argument we are calling *deliberation*, which is characteristic of situations where real circumstances are in a process of change. Aristotle did not necessarily think of deliberation as a normative model of dialogue in the way we are here, and he considered deliberation in his *Ethics* rather than in his works on logic and fallacies. However, Aquinas introduced the idea that deliberation is a distinctive framework of the dialogue in its own right (see Chapter 5, section 6). According to both Aristotle (*Nicomachean Ethics*, 1141b11) and Aquinas (1970, Question 14), people do not deliberate about things that are unchangeable; therefore, both Aristotle and Aquinas conclude that practical reasoning is concerned with particular events that are subject to change.

It is clear, however, that Aristotle does think of deliberation as a framework of reasoning in our sense, for he describes it in the *Nicomachean Ethics* as a kind of correctness of thinking (1142b15), suggesting that it involves reasoning as well as calculating. It seems strange to some people, at first, to think of deliberation as a type of dialogue implying an exchange between at least two parties, because much of the ordinary deliberation we are familiar with appears to be solitary in nature, even though Aquinas (see Chapter 5), sees deliberation as a conferring together.

For example, if I am deliberating about a problem of what lecture to give tomorrow, this appears to be a solitary process because I may sit here in my study thinking about the options, and what would be the best topic and what would be the best way to explain that topic to the class, and so forth. But, in many cases, it is possible to reveal interesting aspects of the reasoning used in deliberation, and also to evaluate the argumentation in deliberation by thinking of it as a kind of dialogue exchange where two points of view are represented. For example, if I am thinking about giving this lecture, I might be worried about presenting a topic that's too difficult for the class and thinking of skipping that topic, but yet, there might be another point of view where I am thinking that it is important that we cover this topic because we will need to understand it for something else we need to cover later in the year, or that the students may need to understand this topic because of some other courses that they might take later. So, in such a case, even though I am sitting there alone in my study, there are two points of view being represented.

There are two possible courses of action I can take, and, as I deliberate on this, I may consider the pros and cons on both sides. I may list the advantages and disadvantages of the one possible course of action as compared with the advantages and disadvantages of the other possible course of action. So, in this sense, I would be deliberating and, also, there is a sense in which I am reasoning and arguing with myself, so to speak, by looking at the pros and cons of two points of view represented by the two possible courses of action and the arguments on both sides. So here, even though deliberation is solitary, we can represent it very nicely as a kind of dialogue structure in which argumentation can be evaluated.

In other instances, however, it is clear that several parties are involved. For example, many people may deliberate together in a town hall meeting that has been called together because some particular problem has come up—whether to spend a certain amount of money on a new sewer system at this point or not. Here, the argument can be reduced to two sides: those who are advocating spending the money now for the new sewer system and those who are advocating not spending this money in the budget. So, in this type of deliberation process, there could be a group of people arguing one side, and also an opposed group arguing on the other side, and there may be a third group of people whose minds are not made up and who are listening to the two parties in the other groups and trying to make up their minds which way to vote.

Here we have the other problem, if we have a multiplicity of different people, and it seems difficult to reduce this kind of case, perhaps, to a two-sided dialogue. However, in theory, for purposes of normative modeling of the argumentation in such a dialogue, it is useful to reduce the dialectical structure of the arguments to the two sides: the pro and the con. So, when we say that deliberation is a normative model of dialogue where there are two sides, and the one side is opposed to that of the other, we do not mean literally that there has to be exactly two people involved, or anything of that sort. We use the notion of a participant here in the normative sense, where a "participant" represents a point of view of the one side, so that the participant in the dialogue does not need to be identical with any actual person, or group of persons.

One of the most interesting subtypes of deliberation (with respect to the *ad populum* argument) is the public deliberation of the type identified by Yankelovich. In Chapter 4, section 9, it was shown how Yankelovich thinks of the sequence of reasoning in a public deliberation as going through seven stages, the final outcome in the seventh stage being a public judgment.

7. Dialectical Relevance

Now that the six basic types of dialogue have been outlined, the new dialectic will evaluate an argument in a given case in light of how that argument was used in the given context of dialogue for that case. If, in a given case, the dialogue the participants are supposed to be engaged in is a persuasion dialogue, for example, then the argument used in that case should be judged to be relevant if it has a legitimate place in the persuasion dialogue. Dialectical relevance, in other words, should be evaluated relative to the conversational exchange a given argument is part of. It follows that an argument may be relevant in one type of dialogue exchange, but not relevant if the conversation is supposed to be another type of dialogue.

In Walton (1995, chap. 6), a dialectical concept of relevance is put forward that is meant to be applicable to informal fallacies. This concept of relevance is pragmatic in nature in the sense that it is meant to be applied to particular cases where a charge has been made by one party that another party to a discussion or dialogue has committed a fallacy of relevance. This concept of relevance is also normative in nature in the sense that it is meant to be applied to an individual case, and then an argument in that case is to be determined as relevant or irrelevant on the basis of an assessment of what type of dialogue or conversation the participants were supposed to be engaged in. Accordingly, this normative and pragmatic notion of relevance is also dialectical. Any argument, or other move in argumentation, is to be judged as relevant to the extent that it fits into a general type of dialogue or a conversation of a conventional kind as a useful move or argument at some stage of the dialogue that contributes to the goal of the dialogue as a whole.

According to the definition given in Walton (1995, 163), a move in a dialogue is said to be *dialectically relevant* if it performs a legitimate function in the argumentation at some stage of a dialogue the move is part of. In particular, an argument will be judged to be relevant or irrelevant in a given context where it is an instance of an argumentation scheme that is used in that type of dialogue. So, dialectical relevance of an argument in a given case depends on the stage of the dialogue we are in when that argument is used, the type of dialogue that is involved, the goal of this type of dialogue and the argumentation scheme corresponding to the argument used. Evaluating dialectical relevance in a case will also depend on what is known about the prior sequence of argumentation in the given case and, in some cases, it will depend very much on the institutional setting or special framework of a given case.

Generally speaking, an argument is relevant if it is the type of move in a dialogue that is made in an appropriate place and that corresponds in an appropriate way to the proper goal for that dialogue. As Grice (1975) showed, in his discussion of relevance, participants in a collaborative conversational exchange will tend to presume that any remark by one's speech partner is relevant, or even try to make it relevant by interpreting it in a way that makes it come out as a relevant contribution to the conversation.

A phenomenon that is very important in evaluating relevance in argumentation is the *dialectical shift*, or transition from one dialogue to another during a sequence of argumentation (Walton 1995, 118–22; Walton and Krabbe 1995, 100–107). Dialectical shifts can be licit or illicit. An example of a licit shift would be a case where two parties are having a critical discussion on an issue, and they both agree to refer to a third-party source or ITP to get information or knowledge that would be helpful in clarifying some factual matter important to their discussion on some point of the issue (see Chapter 4, section 5). In such a case, there has been a licit shift from a persuasion dialogue to an information-seeking (or perhaps an expert consultation) type of dialogue. An example of an illicit shift would be a case where two parties are supposed to be having a critical discussion of an issue, and the one party continually engages in aggressive *ad hominem* attacks against the other party in a quarrelsome dialogue. To the extent that these quarrelsome attacks do not contribute to the critical discussion of the issue the two participants are supposed to be talking about, they can be judged to be dialectically irrelevant. Of course, the *ad hominem* attacks could be relevant in some sense. They could be part of an eristic dialogue exchange which would express the feelings of the one party. But if the dialogue is supposed to be a critical discussion of a particular issue, then the *ad hominem* arguments could be evaluated as dialectically irrelevant from the point of view of that discussion. Cases of this sort of use of *ad hominem* argumentation can be found in Walton (1995, 36–38).

8. Relevance of *Ad Populum* Arguments

Appeals to popular opinion to support an argument are generally out of place in the inquiry type of dialogue, although they could be relevant in some isolated cases. Appeals to popular opinion could more generally be relevant, however, in many cases of the negotiation and eristic types of dialogue, especially where one party is trying to exert pressure on the other to go along with what is regarded as group popular opinion. However, it is the persuasion and deliberation types of dialogue that seemed to be most central in the cases of *ad populum* arguments featured in Chapters 3 and 4. Therefore in addressing the question of how to evaluate relevance of *ad populum* arguments, it is best to begin with a consideration of these two types of dialogue.

Ad populum arguments are most easily seen to be relevant in deliberation because reasoned arguments in deliberations frequently involve taking into account normal and accepted practices relative to a group or to a population. For example, political deliberations involve public policies that affect many people. And even many individual deliberations about how to proceed in a particular situation involve public policies and perceptions. In such cases, *ad populum* arguments would be relevant, even if (as noted in Chapter 4) they are generally weak arguments of a presumptive type that play a small part in shifting a balance of considerations one way or another in a dialogue. In persuasion dialogue, it is less evident why and how *ad populum* arguments can be relevant. But we need to recall, from Chapter 4, that arguments in this type of dialogue are supposed to be based on premises accepted by the person or audience to whom the argument is addressed.

Since persuasion dialogue is commitment-based (see section 2, above), it will clearly be very important in order for an arguer, to mount successful arguments for purposes of persuasion, to understand the position of the other side. In fact, the characteristic called *empathy*—that is, the ability to imaginatively enter into the position of the other side and to appreciate the chief considerations that the other party might likely to be adduced both for and against that position—is very important. Empathy is important to gaining an understanding of the requirements of premise adequacy in a persuasion dialogue.

A critical discussion has a strongly adversarial aspect because both parties are trying to advocate their own point of view, and indeed, to raise critical questions about, or even refute, the point of view of the other side. But, nevertheless, the critical discussion also has several strongly collaborative aspects as well. One of these collaborative aspects is that a participant must be able to get beyond his own partisan view enough to at least appreciate the point of view of the other side. This empathetic identification with the position of the other side is quite necessary in a critical discussion, in order for a participant to mount arguments that will be persuasive because, of course, the key identifying feature of such a persuasive argument is that it is based on the commitments of the other party. It is this factor of being able to identify premises that do, in fact, represent the position of the other party, that is critical to a participant's success in any persuasion dialogue.

The implications of the concept of empathy become apparent when we ask the question of whether a speaker who is trying to convince a mass audience to accept some particular proposition or to act in a certain way, could be said to be engaged in a critical discussion with that audience. Even though the speaker and the audience may not be taking turns in arguing with each other in a way that would be normal in a critical discussion, still, this kind of situation could be seen as a kind of persuasion dialogue, or looked at from the point of view of the model of a persuasion dialogue, in that the speaker is trying to get the audience to accept some conclusion that presumably they are doubtful about by using premises that are commitments of the audience. At least this aspect of using the commitments of the audience as premises would be characteristic of persuasion dialogue. Now, of course, writers on rhetoric have often noticed that, when a speaker is trying to persuade a mass audience to accept some proposition or take a particular course of action, an important skill is the ability of the speaker to enter into the mindset of the audience. The speaker must be aware of the different attitudes and values of the audience and use this as the basis for his argument.

Kennedy cites this aspect of awareness of the audience's attitudes as being characteristic of the successful rhetorician (1963, 92). In ancient theories of rhetoric, for example, Kennedy notes that a rhetorical quality which was of interest to Aristotle was the character of the audience to which the speaker must suit his language and argument (*Rhetoric* 1365b22ff. and 1388b31ff.). Kennedy also notes that a similar psychological approach to rhetoric is characteristic of the theory of *kairos* (the opportune moment) in Gorgias' theory of rhetoric. According to Aristotle, the successful rhetorician will have to base his argumentation not only on the knowledge of the character of his audience but also on the states of mind or emotions known as *pathos* of the audience. So, if Aristotle's theory is correct, appealing to mass emotions of a crowd is not inherently fallacious as an argument. The question of evaluating the *ad populum* argument as fallacious or not raises another question. This secondary question is whether or not such emotional appeals to the values and feelings of the audience should be considered relevant in a given case. But note that if the speaker is trying to persuade the audience based on the audience commitments along the lines of the model of persuasion dialogue, then there could be grounds, in some cases, for saying that the speaker's empathetic use of the position of the audience in his arguments could be dialectically relevant.

But one must take care to examine each case individually in making any such sweeping judgments about the relevance of *ad populum* appeals in rhetoric addressed to a mass audience. Evidently, Mark Antony, in Case 2.7, was not attempting to engage in a critical discussion, or any other type of persuasion dialogue, with the audience at Caesar's funeral. Nor was the occasion one where a critical discussion would have been expected, or particularly appropriate. He was, it seems, trying to provoke the crowd into action, and if anything, his speech had an inflammatory eristic quality. The problem with using Case 2.7 as a textbook illustration of the *ad populum* fallacy was, in fact, the difficulty of trying to determine, from the facts given in Fearnside and Holther's account of the case, what type of dialogue Antony was supposed to be engaged in.

The debate is a mixed type of dialogue that has elements of the persuasion dialogue, but also has elements of eristic dialogue. Mass rhetoric, particularly in cases of political debate, in election campaigns and the like, can therefore be problematic to generally classify. Political debate also typically contains elements of deliberation and negotiation dialogue. In cases where one type of dialogue is systematically mixed with another, the best one may be able to do in determining whether an argument is relevant or not is to make a conditional evaluation. That is, one can evaluate the case by ruling that the given argument is relevant (or is not relevant), on the assumption that the argument is supposed to be part of a particular dialogue—for example, a critical discussion of a particular issue. One can then leave open the question of whether the argument, as used in that case, was really supposed to be used to contribute to the goal of the critical discussion, or not. And one could also assess the given textual evidence for and against this assumption. Such conditional evaluations of relevance, while hypothetical in nature, are often very useful and informative in helping a critic to assess whether an argument is fallacious or not, as used in a given case.

At any rate, there are cases where (arguably) more than one type of dialogue is involved contextually in assessing the argument in the case.

9. Persuasion Dialogue and Public Policy

Relevance of *ad populum* arguments needs to be evaluated on a different basis in deliberation than in a persuasion dialogue. But in evaluating actual cases, it may require some care to clearly distinguish between these two types of dialogue. For example, the dialogue on tipping is used in Walton (1992a, 7–11) as an illustration of a persuasion dialogue. But clearly the dialogue in this case also relates to matters of public policy, i.e., whether tipping is generally a good practice as a policy or accepted procedure for rewarding service. The presence of this element of public policy even suggests elements of deliberation in the case.

A closer look at the kinds of critical discussion that are typical of everyday argumentation, especially in disputations on ethical subjects, reveals that elements of deliberation are very often tangentially involved in the structure of the persuasion dialogue. Take a hypothetical case of a critical discussion on the abortion issue as an illustrative example. Suppose the conflict of opinions in the dialogue is that one party is for abortion—the so-called "pro-choice" viewpoint—and the other is against abortion—the so-called "pro-life," or "anti-choice" viewpoint. Each side has a thesis, and one thesis is the opposite (negation) of the other. Thus it seems appropriate to view the dialogue as a critical discussion that has the purpose of resolving this conflict of opinions. So far, one might think, the dialogue seems to be a straightforward case of a critical discussion.

A look under the surface will reveal, however, that there are elements of the deliberation involved. For right at the outset, there is an ambiguity in the issue that needs to be clarified. Are the two participants arguing about whether abortion is an act that he or she would personally undergo, or would accept in the case of an unwanted pregnancy in his or her personal case (or in his or her family)? Or are they arguing, in the abstract, whether or not abortion is a good thing? Or are they arguing about whether or not abortion should be allowed generally, as a matter of social policy (or, if regulated, a matter of law)?

In the first and third instances, deliberation is clearly involved, and the second instance may well reduce to the third. Deliberation is most clearly involved in the first instance, where an action that is a personal choice is being discussed. But not only is deliberation involved in the third type of dialogue as well, but we can also see that the *ad populum* argument is relevant in this kind of deliberation, which is about public policy. Clearly on the issue of whether abortion should be allowed or not, as a matter of social policy, the question of public opinion on the abortion issue is relevant. For if everyone is for (or against) abortion, as a matter of public opinion, then this general opinion must strongly influence the question of whether or not a proposed policy for or against abortion is feasible, or even appropriate.

Of course, if the dispute is really about the second issue—of whether abortion is or is not a good thing, in the abstract—then popular opinion is less relevant, and arguably, not even relevant at all. Looking at the issue of this discussion this way brings us to what Damer called the "is-ought fallacy" (1987, 57–59). Abortion could be wrong (or right) in the abstract, as a moral question, even if everyone actually believes that it is right (wrong).

In the case of any discussion on an ethical issue such as abortion then, we need to be very careful to clarify what issue (exactly) the dispute is supposed to be about. It is possible to have a purely critical discussion (the second type of dialogue above) that contains no admixture of deliberation dialogue. But in fact, most dialogues on the abortion issue in everyday conversational disputes tend to be the third type of discussion: about what public policy should be. And in many instances, there are shifts from one type of discussion to the other. In many cases, there is a failure to clearly distinguish between these kinds of dialogue, and it is easy for participants to slip from one type of discussion to the other without perceiving any difference in how they are arguing or what they are arguing about.

This mixing of deliberation with the critical discussion type of dialogue is characteristic of much political debate—for example, in a town hall meeting or a parliamentary debate. The initial purpose of the meeting may have been to deliberate on what to do in relation to a practical problem that requires action. But as the sides form up, and positions are set in place by two opposed viewpoints, the dialogue may often take the form of a critical discussion.

Thus care is needed in evaluating the relevance of *ad populum* arguments of the kind frequently cited as examples in the logic textbooks. These cases often are based on controversial issues of public policy in political rhetoric or debate, of a kind that may combine elements of both deliberation and persuasion dialogue. To evaluate such cases using the methods of the new dialectic, therefore, one must be careful to sort out the various levels and types of dialogue involved.

10. The New Perspective on Evaluation

The new dialectic represents a new way of evaluating an argument as correct or incorrect, strong or weak, reasonable or fallacious, in relation to how that argument has been used in a given case within a context of dialogue. This approach seems new and radical because the dialectical point of view has been neglected for so long, and dismissed as unimportant and purely subjective by post-Enlightenment thinkers. But dialectic only seems radical because of this one-sided modern perspective on logical evaluation of arguments that has been dominant for so long. In fact, the new dialectic can easily be seen as a development and refinement of the old dialectic that was familiar to the ancients, and thought by them to be fundamentally important for evaluating arguments, and for conducting the affairs of one's life generally.[7]

The dominant modern, post-Enlightenment view sees an argument as a set of propositions, some of which are designated as premises, where one proposition is singled out as the conclusion. The argument is then evaluated by judging whether the conclusion follows from the premises by a valid inference (where validity is determined by the logical form of the argument).[8]

In contrast, the dialectical view sees an argument as a move (or speech act: a question or reply, or other verbal action) made by one party in a dialogue exchange with another party where the two parties are reasoning together for some collaborative purpose. The dialectical evaluation of an argument cannot just go by the logical form of the argument, to test this form to see if it represents a valid inference. The dialectical evaluation must take into account how the argument has been used to make some point to a respondent (audience), insofar as the contextual evidence that can be reconstructed from the text or discourse in the given case reveals what this point was supposed to be.

---

7. It is emphatically different from Hegelian-Marxist dialectic, however, which uses this term to apply the so-called dialectical triad of thesis, antithesis, and synthesis to historical events and economic matters. It is time the historical meaning of this term is rescued from this corruption of it to mean something altogether different from what Aristotle had in mind.

8. The *ad populum* as a type of inference is the subject of Chapter 8.

The problem with *ad populum* arguments was that from the modern, post-Enlightenment point of view, they did not seem to make any sense at all as rational arguments. They clearly were not deductively valid, and there seemed to be no existing standard in logic against which they could be seen as having some point or use. Hence it was easy to take a negative attitude toward them, and categorically dismiss them as fallacious.

But from the point of view of the new dialectic, the problem is no longer such a simple one, or one that can be peremptorily resolved by declaring *ad populum* arguments irrelevant, on a blanket basis. From a dialectical point of view, we are required to look at each case individually, and judge the *ad populum* argument in relation to the particulars of the case, insofar as these are known.

The job of evaluating *ad populum* arguments by this new method is not finished yet, however. In fact, it has now just started, and we have taken the first step of moving to the new dialectical point of view. But before any further progress can be made in applying it, a next step needs to be taken.

Chapter Seven

AD POPULUM SUBTYPES

One thing that is evident from this survey of the standard treatment of the *ad populum* is the lack of consistency in the textbooks on how this type of argument should be defined. A related problem is that so many of the texts define this type of argument as inherently fallacious, thereby failing to separate two questions. One is the question of defining the *ad populum* as a distinctive type of argument. The other is the problem of evaluating this type of argument as fallacious or not.

As Michael Wreen has noted in criticizing Copi's treatment of the *ad populum* fallacy (1993, 62), this way of combining the definition and the evaluation of the *ad populum* is problematic because it requires that the evaluative work done before or at the same time is the work of identifying the argument. Clearly, it would be better before tackling the evaluation problem to try to arrive at some consensus or clear definition on what the *ad populum* argument is.

In fact, the cases studied so far indicate there are many distinctively different subtypes of *ad populum* arguments. The function of Chapter 7 is to distinguish and identify these subtypes. Moreover, a serious attempt is made to identify the argumentation scheme of each subtype, to the extent such a representation is possible. Where a practically useful modeling of the argumentation scheme is directly not feasible, an analysis and identification of the subtype by other means is attempted. In section 10, a summary of all the eleven subtypes that have been identified is presented.

1. The Mob-Appeal Subtype

The most prominent subtype of *ad populum* featured by the textbooks, the mob-appeal subtype, occurs where a speaker whips up the emotions and enthusiasms of a mass audience, as described in Chapters 3 and 4. Hurley describes this type of "appeal to the people" (*argumentum ad populum*) as the arousal of a "mob mentality."

> The *direct approach* occurs when an arguer, addressing a large group of people, excites the emotions and enthusiasm of the crowd to win acceptance for his conclusion. The objective is to arouse a kind of mob mentality. This is the strategy used by nearly every propagandist and demagogue. Adolf Hitler was a master of the technique, but it is also used with some measure of success by speechmakers at Democratic and Republican national conventions. Waving flags and blaring music add to the overall effect. Because the individuals in the audience want to share in the camaraderie, the euphoria, and the excitement, they find themselves accepting any number of conclusions with ever-increasing fervor. (1994, 118–19)

The distinguishing characteristic of this subtype is the exploitation by a speaker of the group dynamic of the crowd. Jevons defined *argumentum ad populum* as a "weapon of rhetoricians and demagogues" used to "excite the feelings" of a "body of people" (1878, 179). This early account set the standard for many textbooks over the following hundred years, as shown in Chapter 3.

As noted in Chapter 4, section 1, what probably influenced the textbooks after World War II to use the term "demagogue" so widely in describing the mob-appeal type of *ad populum* fallacy was, in fact, the case of Hitler, cited by Hurley. The mass public meetings of the Nazi era, so carefully staged as settings for the delivery of propaganda, provide the kind of setting characteristic for this type of argument. Mob rhetoric of this type has been shown to be very dangerous, and well worth studying, so we can be aware of its misuse as an instrument of political agitation and propaganda. But the question of how such propaganda is based on some underlying, identifiable type of *ad populum* argument (called the mob-appeal argument) has by no means been answered by the textbook accounts.

As Wreen observed, many textbooks confuse the evaluation and the identification problem by defining the mob-appeal type of *ad populum* argument in negative or condemnatory terms—in effect defining it as fallacious without really identifying it. Werkmeister writes that an emotional speech to "the gallery" might be an appeal to the "passions and prejudices of the populace" instead of "presenting empirical evidence and logical argument" (1948, 57). Engel treats the title "fallacy of mob appeal" as equivalent to the Latin phrase *argumentum ad populum.* He defines it as "appeal to the masses," a fallacy that "invites people's unthinking acceptance of ideas that are presented in a strong theatrical manner" (1976, 113). Using the example of Nazi mass meetings, it is easy to condemn the mob-appeal type of *ad populum* argument as inherently fallacious. But until the type of argument is identified, the device of declaring it fallacious because it was used by evil people, with dangerous and destructive consequences, is too easy a method of dismissal.

What if the example of the use of the same kind of mob appeal was a case of a union leader appealing to the emotions of an assembled crowd of coal miners to get them to fight for workplace safety rules that are badly needed in the mine? Or, what if the orator is a feminist leader who uses an emotional appeal to a mass audience of women to try to get them to fight for the noble cause of equal rights? Would we be so quick to immediately condemn such cases of the use of powerful and emotional crowd rhetoric as "mob-appeal" *ad populum* fallacies?

What then is the so-called mob-appeal type of *ad populum* argument, if it should not be defined negatively (and prejudicially, it might be added) as the speaker's appeal to "prejudices" or "unthinking passions" that an audience accepts uncritically? So far, the closest we have gotten to answering this question is the standard treatment of the *ad populum*, which posits the mob-appeal type of *ad populum* argument and the bandwagon type. The bandwagon type is characterized in the textbook accounts by the form of argument "Everybody believes *A*; therefore *A* is true." In the mob-appeal type of case, the speaker is not claiming as his premise that everybody (in general) believes a particular proposition, or accepts it as true. Instead, he appeals to the beliefs or—as the standard treatment has it—the unthinking prejudices and passions of this particular audience or group, even if other people or groups are against these opinions. This mob-appeal concept is highly contextual, in that it presumes that the respondent of the argument is located in a group who are all subjected to a theatrical presentation of the argument in a setting with certain accoutrements, e.g., waving flags, blaring music, and so forth. As a type of argument, it appears to be defined by this special type of situation or rhetorical context, as much as by anything else.

Another characteristic is the appeal to enthusiasm and excitement, or even "euphoria." Perhaps then the defining characteristic is the emotional feeling of excitement produced by the group, or by the speaker who appeals to this feeling in a group—a certain type of group with common feelings that bond them together. The mob-appeal argument is directed to this group, whereas the bandwagon argument has a different focus.

In the bandwagon type of *ad populum* argument, the speaker tries to get the audience to accept a proposition A by arguing that "Everyone (generally) accepts A, and that therefore you (in this audience) should accept A." Here "everyone" refers generally to a group of people outside this particular audience. Presumably, the particular audience being addressed does *not* accept A. Arguing "Everyone else accepts A" is a way of trying to get this audience to accept A, using the bandwagon argument.

The dialectical structure of the mob-appeal type of argument is inherently different. The strategy of the mob-appeal *ad populum* is to home in on the beliefs (sometimes called the "prejudices" or "passions") of the particular audience being addressed. Instead of appealing to what anyone else (some external group, or the general population) believes, the mob-appeal *ad populum* arguer appeals internally to the deeply held views or commitments of the mob being addressed. The mob-appeal orator tries to get the audience he addresses to accept some conclusion he wants to persuade them of, or he tries to get them to undertake some course of action, by using premises that are propositions already accepted by them—propositions that everyone in the audience already enthusiastically accepts, or can be brought to accept, by appealing to their values or commitments as a group.

So, the question is, What is the relationship, if there is one, between the mob-appeal argument and the bandwagon argument? Many of the textbooks assume, as shown in Chapter 3, that the mob-appeal argument is a subspecies or special case of the bandwagon type of *ad populum* argument. But it appears that this is not necessarily the case because the dialectical structures of the two types of argument are inherently different. Moreover, the mob-appeal type of *ad populum* argument is so deeply rhetorical in nature, requiring a crowd ambiance, passionate enthusiasms of the mob, and so forth, that it seems highly dubious that it could be reduced to the bandwagon type of argument.

2. The Pop Scheme

What is the form of the bandwagon argument? There appear to be some differences of opinion in the various accounts given in the textbooks. Almost all the textbook accounts surveyed in Chapter 3 express the form of the bandwagon argument in terms of beliefs. But some do not.

In Walton (1989, 89), it is postulated that two basic forms of argument are implicit in an *ad populum* appeal.

> (*P1*) Everybody accepts that *A* is true.
> Therefore, *A* is true.
> (*P2*) Nobody accepts that *A* is true.
> Therefore, *A* is false.

(*P1*) and (*P2*) are called the two basic forms of the *argument from popularity*.

Freeman calls the kind of argument that has the form of (*P1*) *bandwagon appeal*, and the kind that has the form of (*P2*) the *abandon-ship fallacy* (1988, 70). Many other textbooks have used the expression "bandwagon argument" (or a comparable phrase) to describe the *ad populum* argument, and used forms of inference comparable to (*P1*) and (*P2*) to describe this type of argumentation.

Vernon and Nissen cite the following form of what they call the *bandwagon fallacy*, where *p* is a proposition and *x* an action (1968, 148).

> (*V1*) The majority believes *p* (or does *x*).
> ──────────────────────
> *p* is true (or *x* should be done).

Johnson and Blair postulate two comparable forms in which, they write, "The fallacy of *popularity* occurs whenever an argument proceeds from the popularity of a view to its truth" (1977, 159).

> (*F1*) Everyone believes *A*.
> Therefore *A* is true.
> (*F2*) No one believes *A*.
> Therefore *A* is false.

Johnson and Blair qualify these forms by claiming that they represent the fallacy of popularity only as it occurs "in its purest and most blatant (and rarest) form" (159). This account suggests that (F_1) and (F_2) represent only the underlying form of the fallacy of popularity, so that in most cases where the *ad populum* argument is present, additional factors would be involved.

But do any of the examples of the *ad populum* argument presented in Chapters 2 and 3 really have this form? It seems that the vast majority of them do not have exactly this form, but instead have a form where the "everyone" is some designated group of persons. This observation would suggest that a better representation of the common form underlying *ad populum* arguments is offered by the following pair of argumentation schemes.

This new proposed pair of schemes for the underlying form of the *ad populum* argument make reference to a particular group by the use of a variable, G.

(S_1) Everybody (in a particular reference group, G) accepts A.
Therefore, A is true (or you should accept A).

A secondary scheme is also applicable in some instances.

(S_2) Everybody (in a particular reference group, G) rejects A.
Therefore, A is false (or you should reject A).

But it is the primary scheme (S_1) that is applicable to most cases of *ad populum* arguments. (S_2) is the negative variant, used to dissuade, while (S_1) is the fundamental form of *ad populum* argument, used to persuade. In light of the importance of (S_1) in our subsequent discussions of the *ad populum* argument, let us call it the *pop scheme*. More specifically, (S_1) will be called the *positive pop scheme*, and (S_2) will be called the *negative pop scheme*. But where the differentiation is not important to the discussion, we refer to the pop scheme generally, primarily having (S_1) in mind.

The pop scheme is defined as an argumentation scheme used in a framework of conversation (dialogue) where one party (the proponent) is using the argument for some purpose in relation to a respondent (audience).[1] In the pop scheme, the pronoun "you" in the conclusion refers to the respondent. Generally speaking, in the use of the pop scheme, the respondent does not need to be a member of the group G. However, in the mob-appeal type of *ad populum*

---

1. The meaning is that of Chapter 6, that is, the argument is dialectical in nature.

argument, it seems generally that the respondent is presumed to be a member of G.

Whether the pop scheme represents a strong or weak type of argument in a particular case clearly depends (possibly among other variables) on what particular group G is referred to in the scheme. As noted in our case studies, *ad populum* arguments are in many cases quite weak at best. However, if the group G referred to is a group of experts in a domain of knowledge, or is otherwise in a privileged epistemic position, the argument could be considerably strengthened.

3. Position to Know

Another variant of the *ad populum* argument is the use of appeal to accepted opinion of a group that is in a special position to know about the proposition in question. Often there is an appeal to what the experts believe or accept, as in the claim "This proposition is accepted by everyone in the scientific community." This subtype represents an overlap between the appeal to expert opinion, based on (G7) (see Chapter 2, section 10) and the pop scheme. The group G in the pop scheme is a group of experts in a domain D. Hence (G7) is applicable. In this subtype of *ad populum* argument, the pop scheme, a weak form of argument is reinforced by the implicit support of (G7) making the resulting argument much stronger. For example, in Case 3.7, the historian supports his thesis by claiming, "Every historian of the period knows it was common practice. . . ." However, in most of the cases studied so far, the *ad populum* argument is not based on appeal to the opinion of an expert in a domain of knowledge or academic field, but is a weaker claim.

Attempting to seek out the logical basis of the bandwagon type of argument in its being a knowledge claim of some sort does not seem to be a very promising approach. For one thing, the *ad populum* argument of the bandwagon type is generally a weak and defeasible type of argument, as I have noted, and this characteristic is inconsistent with an argument based on a knowledge claim. Moreover, as we saw in Chapter 3, the standard textbook treatments of the *ad populum* argument are unanimous in their portrayal of this type of argument as being based on belief, not on knowledge. In the standard textbook treatments, the bandwagon argument is portrayed as having a premise of the form "Everybody believes that this particular proposition is true." None of the textbooks postulate this premise as a knowledge claim of the form "Everybody knows that this particular proposition is true." However, a modification of the claim that the *ad populum* should be based on a knowledge justification is possible.

In Walton (1992b, 77), an example of the *ad populum* argument from Johnson and Blair (1983, 157) is analyzed as a type of argument based on the concept of position to know. To say that someone is in a position to know that a particular proposition is true is not to say that this person actually knows that this proposition is true or even that this person has expert or scientific knowledge of this proposition. It is only to say that such person is in a position such that, if this proposition were true, they would have access to the kind of evidence that would normally be required to show that it is true or to support its being true.

Johnson and Blair discuss an example where a stranger is visiting a community, and is making a decision about going fishing in a local lake (1983, 158). He finds that everyone in that community believes that the fish in this lake are contaminated. Johnson and Blair conclude that this finding might be "some reason" for this person to believe that the fish are contaminated. The type of argument involved in Johnson and Blair's case is analyzed in Walton (1992b, 77) as having the following form.

> Everybody (or everyone in some group) accepts proposition A as true.
> These people are in a position to know that A is true or, at any rate, presumably have some reason for accepting A as true.
> Therefore, A may be accepted as true.

Quite clearly then, this argument has the form of the argument from position to know, that is, the argumentation scheme (*Pos. Know*) in Chapter 6, section 5.

As another illustration of this form of argument, Walton (1992b, 94) considers the case of someone who is getting off the train in the central station of a foreign city, and sees the crowd moving off in one direction that he presumes to be the direction of the exit, and therefore, follows along with the crowd in the hope of getting to the exit. What would be a reasonable basis for this person, acting on such a presumption, of following the crowd? Well, one basis could be position to know. His presumption is that these people are likely to be familiar with this station, and probably, or presumably, would know the right direction to go toward the exit. Though, in such a case, the person is not necessarily presuming that these people have scientific knowledge of the train station or that they are experts on train stations generally, or this particular train station. He is only presuming that, since these look like local people, they are probably familiar with this train station, and are therefore likely to be in a position to know which way to go to get toward the exit.

Wreen also thinks that *ad populum* arguments of the bandwagon sort are based on a position to know justification. Wreen gives the example of somebody who wants to know the quickest way to get to City Hall from Veterans' Stadium in south Philadelphia. Wreen then cites the premise "Everybody who lives in south Philadelphia believes that if the SEPTA trains are running, the quickest way to get to City Hall from Veterans' Stadium is to take the Broad Street subway." Using this example as a case in point, Wreen cites three conditions as requirements for an *ad populum* argument of the bandwagon type to be a "strong good argument" (1993, 70).

1. The group in question is in a good position to know the truth or falsity of the proposition in question.
2. Disagreement within the group about the proposition and/or matters related to it is not significant or widespread.
3. As far as sharing their belief with others is concerned, members of the group have no vested interest in being anything but honest, and are not known to be liars about such matters.

Using these three criteria to evaluate *ad populum* arguments of the bandwagon type, Wreen sees this type of argument, generally, as being similar to argumentation from testimony; that is, Wreen makes the claim that the logic of the evaluation of testimony is similar to the logic of the evaluation of *ad populum* arguments of the sort typified by his case about getting from City Hall to Veterans' Stadium.

It should be noted that there is a certain similarity between this type of *ad populum* case and the kind of case where a witness testifies in court where the witness is not giving expert testimony, but say, for example, eyewitness testimony relating to some incident that supposedly took place and figures in a trial. The reason such a witness is called to the stand is that, presumably, the witness was in a position to know about the incident in question. That is, if the witness was a bystander, for example, and had a good view of the scene, and the question is whether the defendant fired a shot from a revolver, then the reason for bringing the witness forward in court is that he was presumably in a position to know whether the alleged act occurred or not and would also be in a position to provide details of what happened. In a legal case, calling a witness to testify in this kind of situation would not necessarily imply that the witness was an expert, or that the witness was giving scientific testimony of some sort. Thus, in such a case, we could make a distinction between expert testimony and a case of witness testimony where the witness is not an expert, but is, let us say, simply an eyewitness of some situation or fact that allegedly occurred. In such a case, then, it would be appropriate to say that the witness was in a position to know whether a particular proposition as alleged is true or not.

So conceived, then, a position-to-know claim would not necessarily be a knowledge claim. It would only mean that the person who is in a position to know has or had access to the kind of evidence that would be needed to justify a particular claim. So, despite the occurrence of the word "know" in the expression "position to know," the position to know type of claim is not, at least necessarily, a knowledge claim. Rather, it is a belief or acceptance claim, but a reasonable belief or acceptance claim based on access to some kind of evidence that would be appropriate for a case in point.

Eyewitness testimony is notoriously fallible, as has been shown by recent social science studies (Loftus 1979). But, nevertheless, it is widely accepted, both in law and in everyday argumentation, as a reasonable basis for accepting or at least adjudicating a claim. As a basis for presumptive reasoning, it does have a certain claim to acceptance which could be justified as a form of evidence appropriate for some types of dialogue. However, eyewitness testimony is not a kind of knowledge claim, and is, in general, different from scientific evidence or appeal to expert opinion as a type of basis for an argument, because eyewitness testimony is essentially a single-person testimony where what one person says is taken as a presumptive basis for accepting a proposition as true, provided we have some reason to think that this person was in a position to know, and is also giving reliable testimony.

But there is a difference between this argument from single-person testimony and the *ad populum* argument. The difference is that, in the case of eyewitness testimony, it is the first-person testimony of a single individual. In the case of the bandwagon type of *ad populum* argument, the premise is that everybody accepts or believes that a particular proposition is true. Though, in the case of the bandwagon *ad populum* argument, one ancillary justification for this type of argument as having some presumptive reasonableness is that it is or could be based on a position to know claim. But, on the other hand, there is also an additional element, and that is, with the bandwagon type of *ad populum* argument, a whole group of people are involved, and presumably, they are unanimous or all agree that proposition A is true. So there is an additional element involved in the bandwagon type of *ad populum* argument, involving the consent or agreement of a presumably large group of people. Not only are they in a position to know, but they all agree that this is the accepted way to do something or that this particular proposition is taken as true. In the train station case, for example, it is not just one single person who is presumably in a position to know, and perceived as walking toward the exit. Rather, in this case, the situation is that a large crowd of people—that is, all the people who are getting off the train—are moving in the same direction.

The position-to-know subtype of *ad populum* argument can be represented as having the following form.

> (*PKA*) Everybody in this group *G* accepts *A*.
> This group is in a special position to know that *A* is true.
> Therefore *A* is (plausibly) true.

This position to know type of *ad populum* argument is a supplemented version of the basic pop scheme, because the second premise of (*PKA*) above has been added. The assumption is that the people in the group have access to some information or evidence that you (the respondent) lack. On this assumption, it may make sense for you to do what they are doing, or to accept what they say as likely being true.

4. Informed Deliberation

Many of the cases cited in Chapter 2 contained *ad populum* arguments where it could not rightly be said that the group in question was in a special position to know that the proposition in question was true. Instead, in these cases, the basis of the *ad populum* argument was that the group cited had engaged in some process of intelligent discussion or informed deliberation, and that therefore their acceptance of the proposition *A* provided some grounds for supporting the conclusion that *A* might (plausibly) be true, or might be acceptable, or might represent a prudent course of action for us (the respondents), in a similar situation.

For example, in Case 2.2 the assumption supporting the *ad populum* argument was that the favoring of one verdict by the jury was the outcome of a long process of deliberation. Since it is presumed that this deliberation took the form of an intelligent and informed discussion, based on the facts of the case, the *ad populum* argument that the majority of the jurors agree on this verdict puts pressure on the dissenter to go along with their decision. Here the basis of the *ad populum* argument is that of an intelligent discussion or informed deliberation by a group. But it does not seem to be implied or required that this group had to be in a special position to know about the guilt or innocence of the accused.

Hence, this type of *ad populum* argument is not based on an appeal to expert opinion, or on a position-to-know basis. It is based on a decision to follow a group of other persons who, one has some reason to think, know the way, or know the right way to do something, because they have thought about it. In the absence of hard information, or better available evidence, this type of *ad populum* argument can sometimes be a presumptively reasonable, if tentative and defeasible, line of reasoning, even though it is even weaker than the position-to-know subtype.

The following argumentation scheme represents the general form of this deliberation-based type of ad populum argument.

> (*PDA*) Group G has deliberated intelligently and extensively on whether to accept proposition A or not.
> Everybody in G accepts A.
> Therefore A is (plausibly) true.

(*PDA*) could be described as a weaker form of position to know type of *ad populum* argument, based not on knowledge or (purely factual) information, but on deliberation of the kind that has successfully arrived at a reasoned judgment or policy.

It is useful to give names for these various subtypes of *ad populum* arguments. Arguments having the form of (*PKA*) could be called *position-to-know* ad populum *arguments*. The special subtype where the group G are experts could be called *expert-opinion* ad populum *arguments*. And the *ad populum* arguments taking the form (*PDA*) could be called *deliberation* ad populum *arguments*. Note that this last type of argument need not only be used in a deliberation type of dialogue, as will become clear in Chapter 8.

Some cases appear to combine the position-to-know type of *ad populum* argument and the deliberation-based type.

Case 7.1   In a sailboat race where there were a lot of markers that had to be passed, and where it was very easy for the participants to get disoriented and become lost, the competitors made elaborate charts before the race, and during the race, spent a lot of time using a compass to try to figure out the route. The captain of one sailboat was asked what strategy he used. His reply: "Well, we try to prepare carefully by making good charts. But if you really are getting lost, you often just follow some other fellow who seems to be very successful."

Here, following the others instead of following the chart could be an error. But if the chart becomes too confusing, and the evidence it provides is uncertain, following the pack might be a "good bet," or a good guess.

Other examples of the use of this kind of *ad populum* reasoning are stock market decisions where an investor acts quickly to follow other investors, thinking they might have information that you have not heard yet.

In Case 7.1, the basis of the captain's reasoning in following the other sailboats could be supported in either of two ways. Since the boats he is following are farther ahead in the race, they can see the markers or buoys before he can. So they are in a better position to know. But, in addition, the other factor is that the captain presumes that these other competitors have thought out the route more carefully, based on elaborate deliberations with maps, compasses, and other methods of calculation used to try to figure out the route.

The same two kinds of supporting considerations apply to the case of stock market "stampedes." Perhaps the other investors are in a position to know, although they are not supposed to have "insider information." But then again perhaps they have just engaged in intelligent deliberation.

5. Moral Justification

The *ad populum* argument in Case 2.4 was based on the premise that all the countries in Europe and North America that do not have the death penalty are countries that have good qualities with respect to human rights. The argument in this case is based on the following argumentation scheme.

> (MJA) Everybody who is good, or who represents a group *G* with good qualities, accepts policy *P*.
> Your goal is (or should be) to be a good person, or a member of a group with good qualities.
> Therefore, you should accept *P*.

Added to Case 2.4 was a negative argument to the effect that if we decide to have a policy of capital punishment, we will be "joining countries like Africa [*sic*] and Turkey that are not models of democratic civilization and human rights." This argument could partly be an appeal to intelligent deliberation as a basis for the *ad populum* appeal. But more is involved in it. The appeal is to the moral values credited to the policies of the countries cited. In this case, the *ad populum* argument is reinforced and supported by an appeal to the (supposedly good) moral values of the group or groups cited.

This moral justification type of *ad populum* argument can be used in different ways. In Case 2.4, it is used to argue for an action or policy by using the premise "Everybody (who is good) is doing it." In other cases, the *ad populum* argument is used as an excuse. When somebody is accused of doing something bad, their reply is, "Well, everybody else is doing it, so it couldn't be so bad after all—or at least it is excusable." In such cases, the response to an allegation by a speaker that the respondent is engaging in some morally culpable action is to simply say, "Everybody's doing it." This was exactly the reply given by looters in Los Angeles after the Rodney King verdict was announced (reported on CBS Evening News, April 29, 1992).[2] A bystander who objected to this line of argument asked rhetorically, "If everyone was jumping off a cliff, would you do it?" (*20/20*, May 1, 1992). The argument being objected to is clearly a form of *argumentum ad populum* used to offer moral justification for an action.

One issue with this subtype of *ad populum* inference is whether it is really an explanation or an action (or has elements of both). While it does have elements of explanation, one interpretation of it that is very plausible is as a species of *ad populum* argument used to morally justify a speaker's conduct in the face of implied or overt criticism.

The implication of this type of *ad populum* is that if everyone in a group G is doing something, then doing that thing must be an acceptable norm of conduct for that group. The moral justification subtype of *ad populum* argument has the following form.

> (MJE) Everybody in group G does x (or accepts proposition A as a policy).
> Doing x (or accepting A) shows that x (or policy A) is an acceptable norm of conduct for G.
> I (the speaker) am a member of G.
> Therefore, my doing x (or accepting A) is morally justified as an acceptable action (or policy).

Both (MJA) and (MJE) fit under the general heading of moral justification *ad populum* arguments, but the two subtypes have distinctly different argumentation schemes, and are used in two different ways in dialogue.

---

2. See "Riot Wasn't Based on Rodney King," *USA Today*, May 5, 1992, 1A and 2A.

A variant on the kind of *ad populum* argument based on the premise "Everybody else is doing it." is the defense used in the following case.

Case 7.2   A physician is accused of malpractice on the grounds that the medical treatment he applied to a patient turned out badly. The physician defends himself by arguing that this type of treatment is the normal and accepted procedure for the condition of this patient. In other words, he argues that all the other physicians are using this same type of treatment.

This type of *ad populum* argument is a defense against medical malpractice that is generally accepted in law as a reasonable line of argument. In medical ethics, a physician can answer that he applied a wrong treatment by using the argument "This form of treatment is the standard treatment accepted by everyone in the medical profession, in these circumstances, and for this problem."[3] However, this use of the *ad populum* argument is also based partly on expertise, and is hence partly a species of position to know argument.

This type of *ad populum* argument is based on position to know reasoning, because the physician is appealing to accepted expert opinion in a domain of knowledge, as based on standard practices. But it also combines elements of a moral use of *ad populum* put forward to reply to a criticism that the arguer has done something unethical in the past. He is replying to the charge of malpractice by arguing, "Everybody else (in the profession) is doing it; therefore it is acceptable." Hence, the argument is comparable, in this respect, to the argument in the looters case, which was also used as a kind of excuse, or defense against a criticism that the person had acted in an unethical way.

The difference with the physician case above is that it is also based on expert opinion, and therefore it combines the moral argument with the position-to-know (appeal to expert opinion) type of argument.

6. Popular Sentiments

One very important type of *ad populum* argument in everyday argumentation is something close to the bandwagon type of argument. But the bandwagon form does not precisely capture the thrust of this type of argument. The circumstance

---

3. According to Ficarra (1968, 59), a physician may be held liable for an injury due to medical malpractice on four grounds: (1) lack of learning and skill of an average doctor; (2) failure to exercise reasonable care; (3) failure to use best judgment; or (4) departure from approved methods in general use.

on which this type of argument is based is the constantly changing nature of public opinion from one era and social situation to another.

For example, during the era of World War II, in North America, public discourse of all kinds was definitely slanted toward the point of view that our enemies, the Germans and the Japanese, were bad people, and that our attempts to defeat them was a noble struggle against evil forces. Any argument based on a premise expressing this general point of view could be assured to have a weight of presumption in its favor. And, conversely, any argument based on the assumption that the Germans or the Japanese were nice people, or that their efforts in the war were positive, would have a very strong weight of presumption against it. These presumptions were evident even in the language used in the media to report on developments in the war during this period. The enemy efforts would be expressed in highly negative language, and the allied efforts would be described in highly positive language.

This sort of bias is normal in everyday argumentation, and even though it is more strongly evident in a wartime situation, it is not in itself fallacious or logically incorrect. However, it does indicate a certain spin or bias that can be appealed to in an argument. In these particular circumstances, there will be a certain popular sentiment or horizon of opinion that will definitely favor a particular point of view. Appealing to this popular sentiment, in the right circumstances, with the right sort of argument, and at the opportune moment, can considerably strengthen one's argument.

In context, an argument based on a current presumption of this sort generally seems to be a positive argument, or one that would not be likely to be questioned. But out of context, the same argument can appear less persuasive, because the slant in it is much more evident. For example, if someone who is eighteen years old in 1995 reads a North American newspaper that was written in 1943, the strong slant toward supporting the war effort evident in the language and arguments used in reporting events of the period would be evident. It might even seem quaint, and sometimes even amusing, that the reporting of the period would show such a consistent and prevalent bias and intensity in expressing a viewpoint.

The fact that both an arguer and her audience or readership are in a particular era and set of social circumstances tends to make these popular biases less evident, and it is for that reason that it can be easy to exploit such preconceptions and attitudes without anyone noticing or paying much attention. This closeness to the situation is what makes *ad populum* arguments based on these preconceptions and attitudes rhetorically deceptive and easy to exploit. On the other hand, the fact that such biases change so rapidly in a different set of circumstances is what makes the *ad populum* argument of this type so untrustworthy. For someone removed from the situation, it is easy to see how the argument rests on a bias or point of view, but for someone in that situation, the bias would not be noticeable, because it is a normal aspect of all arguments used in that situation.

Some of the textbooks describe this type of *ad populum* argument as the appeal to "popular sentiments," where "the feelings or attitudes of a group of people are appealed to to win acceptance" (Michalos 1969, 372). The idea of this way of distinguishing the *ad populum* seems to rest on drawing a line between emotion or feeling, on the one hand, and cognition, on the other. Michalos defines the argument as "tugging at the emotional heartstrings" of the audience. One might ask here, What is wrong with appealing to a respondent's emotions in an argument? The answer of Michalos is that it is fallacious "in the absence of a plausible argument for some view" (372). But could an appeal to emotion or feelings not be a plausible argument for a conclusion in some cases? According to Hamblin, we should not be too quick to rule this possibility out (1970, 44).

This way of describing the *ad populum* makes it somewhat different from mob appeal, because the latter is a more narrow appeal to the particular instincts of the massed crowd (by demagogues and the like). Presumably, appeal to popular sentiments is a more inclusive category.

Quite a few of the textbooks use the word "prejudices" when defining what appears to be this subtype (e.g., Fearnside 1980, 14). The fault here would be the direction of the argument to the specific commitments or views of the target audience. But is it a fallacy to direct your efforts at rational persuasion to using premises that your audience or respondent is committed to, or is prepared to accept? In general, it would seem not to be, for the purpose of persuasion dialogue generally is so to argue (as indicated in Chapter 6). However, a fallacy could be involved if the audience accepts propositions that could be fairly called "prejudices." But to define or evaluate this type of argumentation we would have to have a theory of prejudice. This is a tall order (see Walton 1991b) and so it is better perhaps not to try to define a special subtype of *ad populum* fallacy by simply saying it is a kind of argumentation that appeals to prejudice.

Perhaps what could be meant by the appeal to popular sentiments or pieties is the kind of argument that appeals to what is sometimes called conventional wisdom, meaning that audiences' opinions change, but at certain times they tend to favor trends that are popular at a given time. For example, at the present moment in North America, we could expect a popular audience to enthusiastically condemn any proposition that a female was not equal to a male in a certain respect. Such a presumption could carry great weight in an argument, in the current climate of opinion.

People seem to be generally aware that one's argument is made very powerful if one has a popular presumption on her side. Also, that argument will be very weak and difficult to defend if one appears to contravene such a popular presumption. Perhaps, then, this concept of conventional wisdom or popular presumption is what is meant by the popular sentiment notion. If so, it does represent a distinct and important subspecies of *ad populum* argument.

If the appeal to popular sentiments has an argumentation scheme, it seems to be closely related to the scheme *argument from commitment*, defined in Walton (1996b, 56) as an appeal to a respondent to accept proposition *A* in virtue of her being committed to *A*, e.g., as indicated by prior actions or pronouncements. But appeal to popular sentiments seems to be a special kind of instance or use of argument from commitment where a speaker uses as a premise a proposition that his particular audience of the moment is committed to temporarily, but where this proposition is of such a type that commitment to it is highly retractable and unstable. The idea seems to be that things could go rapidly one way or the other, depending on the sentiments of the audience at a given time. So, such an argument from commitment should not be viewed as inherently fallacious, but it should be viewed as generally weak and unstable in nature.[4]

7. Common Folks, Snobbery, and Vanity

The characteristic of the common-folks (or plain-folks) subtype of *ad populum* argument is that the speaker tries to identify with some values of a group of people attached to being an ordinary member of the group, that are common to his audience. Politicians, for example, try for an "average person" or "ordinary guy" *persona*, to suggest that they have the common touch. The handlers of George Bush publicized his liking for pork rinds as a snack, evidently as a strategy to portray him as a man who had common, folksy tastes.

Kilgore (1968, 49) distinguishes a special subtype of *ad populum* he calls the "common-folks appeal," contrasted with two other subtypes, called "the bandwagon fallacy" and "appeal to the gallery."

---

4. Note the contrast between mass opinion and public judgment cited by Yankelovich (see Chapter 4, section 9).

THE COMMON-FOLKS APPEAL. The fallacy of the common-folks appeal attempts to secure acceptance of a conclusion by the speaker's identification with the everyday concerns and feelings of an audience rather than on the basis of adequate evidence. For example: "I'm sure you will recognize that I am more competent than my opponent. When I was in high school I had to get up at four-thirty every morning to deliver papers. In college I was barely able to make C's and had to do janitorial work in order to make ends meet to put myself through school. Therefore, I would make a better congressman."

An experienced public speaker interested in persuading an audience often seeks to identify himself with their concerns, interests, and way of life. The "common-folks" appeal becomes a fallacy when such techniques of identification are used as a substitute for relevant evidence in an argument.

The fallacy, according to Kilgore's evaluation, is a failure of relevance. However, the common-folks appeal is such a regularly used tactic of political rhetoric that it would seem inappropriate to judge it as always fallacious. Clearly, however, it is a type of argument that can be used with powerful rhetorical effect.

Hitler was a master of the common-folks type of *ad populum* appeal in his rhetoric. According to Duncan, Hitler's book *Mein Kampf* was written as a dramatic struggle in language very familiar to the common people of the time in Germany (1962, 242). Ernst Hanfstaengl was a literate member of Hitler's inner circle who later escaped to Switzerland and eventually took up residence in the United States. A careful observer, Hanfstaengl, in his book *Unheard Witness*, described how Hitler's vocabulary reflected the language of the common people.

> I had by this time heard a number of his public speeches and was beginning to understand the pattern of their appeal. The first secret lay in his choice of words. Every generation develops its own vocabulary of catchwords and phrases, and these date thoughts and utterances. My own father talked like a contemporary of Bismarck, the people of my own age bore the stamp of Wilhelm II, but Hitler had caught the casual camaraderie of the trenches, and without stooping to slang, except for special effects, managed to talk like a member of his audience. In describing the difficulties of the housewife without enough money to buy the food her family needed in the Viktualien Market he would produce just the phrases she would

have used herself to describe her difficulties, if she had been able to formulate them. Where other national orators gave the painful impression of talking down to their audience, he had this priceless gift of expressing exactly their own thoughts. (1957, 70–71)

So the threat of the demagogue, so emphasized in the textbook treatments of the mob-appeal type of *ad populum*, may be partly based on the common-folks type of argument, where the "man of the people" uses common-folks-based rhetoric.

The plain-folks appeal, as described by the textbook accounts, does not seem to exactly fit the mold of either of the pop schemes, ($S1$) or ($S2$). Instead, what it seems to express is the argument scheme below.

> (*PF1*) I (the speaker) am an ordinary person, i.e., I share a common background with you (the audience).
> Therefore, you ought to take what I say as being more credible or acceptable.

On the other hand, you could interpret the plain-folks appeal as being a species of pop scheme argumentation, as represented below.

> (*PF2*) I (the speaker) am an ordinary person, i.e., I share a common background with all the members of this audience (group G).
> You (the respondent) are a member of this audience (group G).
> Therefore, you should accept what I say.

However you construe it, the plain-folks appeal is a distinctive subtype of *ad populum* argument whereby the speaker attempts to portray herself as a certain sort of person who is similar to the persons in an audience.

The common-folks subtype appears to be the direct opposite of another subtype called the appeal to snobbery. Instead of trying to pose as a member of the common folk, the arguer tries to get the respondent to identify with an elite group whose members are admired because they are not common.

Hurley gives the following example of a subspecies of *ad populum* argument he calls *appeal to snobbery* (1994, 119; reprinted from Chapter 3):

Case 3.19: A Rolls Royce is not for everyone. If you qualify as one of the select few, this distinguished classic may be seen and driven at British Motor Cars, Ltd. (by appointment only, please).

What appears to be distinctive of this type of appeal is the exploitation of the wish to belong to an elite social group. The implication of the argument is that by taking the recommended action, you (the respondent of the argument) can belong to this elite group, or at least be so perceived.

Rescher writes that an *ad populum* argument substitutes "snob appeal" for "mob appeal" when it appeals to the attitudes of *our crowd*, as opposed to the attitudes of *the crowd* (1964, 80).

The appeal to snobbery, as a subtype of *argumentum ad populum*, can be modeled as having the following structure.

(*AS1*) Everybody in this group G accepts A (or has some property, or possesses some object).
This group G is elite, i.e., everyone who belongs to it has prestige.
Prestige is an important goal for you (the respondent).
If you accept A (acquire property P or buy object O), then you will be a member of the group G.
Therefore you ought to accept A, etc.

Case 3.2, where an advertisement cites Stovepipe hats as "widely used by the nobility and gentry" is a good example of the appeal-to-snobbery subtype of *ad populum*. Many of the cases cited by the textbooks as appeal to snobbery subtypes of *ad populum* arguments are commercial advertisements.

In fact, many of the examples of the *ad populum* fallacy generally cited by the textbooks—not just the appeal to snobbery ones—are advertisements of one kind or another. However, in many of these cases, the type of appeal is not exactly the same as the appeal to snobbery defined above. To deal with this broader category, a new subtype is introduced, called the appeal to vanity. The two categories are closely related, however, and in some cases it might be hard to fit an example into one category to the exclusion of the other. For example, Case 3.1, where the salesman describes the customer as "a man of your high standing in the community" seems like an appeal to vanity, but it could also be an appeal to snobbery. The difference is generally that the appeal to vanity directly flatters the respondent, as in Case 3.14 from Weddle (1978), reprinted below, whereas the appeal to snobbery refers to a group that has status.

Case 3.14: You were probably born with a bigger share of intelligence than most of your fellow men and women . . . and taught how to use it.

And you appreciate the difference. You aren't ashamed of having brains. You enjoy using them. That's why *The Hundred Greatest Classics* belong in your home.

In this case, there is something of an appeal to snobbery, because the respondent is said to be more intelligent than fellow men and women. But the main appeal is to vanity.

Hurley defined the *appeal to vanity* as a subspecies of *ad populum* argument where a product is associated with a celebrity, the implication being that if you use this product, you will be "admired and pursued" (1994, 119). Case 3.18 from Hurley is reprinted below.

Case 3.18: Only the ultimate in fashion could complement the face of Christie Brinkley. Spectrum sunglasses—for the beautiful people of the jet set.

The first appeal in this case is to vanity, but snobbery comes in when the jet set group is cited. Many of the textbooks are particularly hard on advertisers for using this type of appeal. Copi has a particularly memorable critique of advertisers who "glamorize" their products by selling "delusions of grandeur" (1972, 79–80). As we recall from the passage from Copi quoted in Chapter 3, section 2, where the twentieth-century advertisers are described as "hucksters" and "ballyhoo artists" that use attractive models to arouse the approval and admiration of viewers.

We certainly recognize the *ad populum* appeal used in ads as a characteristic type of appeal to vanity that has its irrational aspect. However, ads are a form of commercial or advocacy speech, used to sell a product, as everyone should be aware. Hence to criticize them for a failure to present evidence, or to present an unbiased evaluation of the product (as one would expect, for example, in an evaluation by *Consumer Reports*) is somewhat naive.

At any rate, we can represent the appeal to vanity as having the following form of argument.

(AV1) Everybody in this group of admired (popular) people G accepts A (possesses A, etc.).
If you carry out action x, then you will belong to this group G.
Therefore, you should carry out action x.

So represented, arguments of the type (AV1) are special instances of the pop scheme (S1).

Evaluating these arguments depends on the context of dialogue. The purpose of advertising (a species of commercial speech) may not be so much designed to persuade the respondent to accept a proposition as true, based on evidence. It may be more like a negotiation type of dialogue where the purpose is to "make a deal," or to get the respondent to buy something.

8. The Rhetoric of Belonging

One kind of appeal that can be identified as a species of *ad populum* argument is the division of the world into "believers" and "nonbelievers," excluding everyone who does not embrace the speaker's point of view from the valued class of true believers. A good example is the speech of the union leader Walter Reuther that describes leadership in the "American movement" as a "sacred trust," excluding those who "want to use the labor movement to make a fast buck" (Bailey 1983, 134; quoted in Walton 1992b, 100–101).

Case 7.3: I think we can all agree that the overwhelming majority of the leadership of the American movement is composed of decent, honest, dedicated people who have made a great contribution involving great personal sacrifice, helping to build a decent American labor movement. . . . We happen to believe that leadership in the American movement is a sacred trust. We happen to believe that this is no place for people who want to use the labor movement to make a fast buck.

Bailey calls this speech strategy the *rhetoric of belonging*. This type of argumentation has some elements of the subtype of *ad populum* argument usually called mob appeal, but the two types of appeals are inherently distinct. Mob appeal is characterized by a whipping up of enthusiasms in a mass audience, whereas the rhetoric-of-belonging argument tends to be quite subtle and trades not so much on enthusiasm as on a negative tactic of discouraging disagreement by implying an exclusion from a group. Of course, the feeling of belonging to a group could very well be an important part of the mass enthusiasm characteristic of the mob-appeal argument, but it is by no means the whole thing, or the essential defining characteristic of the mob-appeal subtype of *ad populum* argument.

The rhetoric-of-belonging argument can also be used in combination with the moral justification type of *ad populum* argument, by defining the group in question as being good, or as standing for the good, as opposed to "enemies" of the group, who are on the side of evil. This dividing of the universe into "us" and "them" is characteristic of the rhetoric of belonging. But the adding of the ethical dimension, which is often imported by presumption into the language of a speech, is not an essential or defining characteristic of the rhetoric-of-belonging subtype of *ad populum* argument.

It should be added here, as well, that trying to establish group solidarity or using arguments to promote common group values in a speech is not an inherently fallacious kind of argumentation. The epideictic, or as Perelman and Olbrechts-Tyteca call it, the "epidictic" genre, is a type of ceremonial speech used to embellish and enhance group values.

> Unlike the demonstration of a geometrical theorem, which establishes once and for all a logical connection between speculative truths, the argumentation in epidictic discourse sets out to increase the intensity of adherence to certain values, which might not be contested when considered on their own but may nevertheless not prevail against other values that might come into conflict with them. The speaker tries to establish a sense of communion centered around particular values recognized by the audience, and to this end he uses the whole range of means available to the rhetorician for purposes of amplification and enhancement. (1969, 51)

Thus there is nothing inherently fallacious about making a speech to increase the intensity of adherence to certain group values. What is distinctive about the rhetoric-of-belonging argument is its appeal to the respondent's insecurity or fear of being excluded.

The type of argument characteristic of the rhetoric of belonging can be represented by adding supplementary premises to the pop scheme, as follows.

(*RB1*) Everybody in this group G accepts A.
Being a member of this group G is highly valued for you (the respondent).
If you do not accept A, you will be out of this group G.
Therefore, you should accept A.

In (*RB1*), the scheme for the rhetoric-of-belonging subtype, the third premise has a negative function, and takes the form of an argument from negative consequences, by attaching a penalty (a loss or negative value) to nonacceptance. Perhaps the rhetoric-of-belonging argument can explain part of the idea of mob appeal. But it seems that the mob-appeal subtype, as conceived by the textbook accounts, is a distinct type of *ad populum* argument in its own right. At any rate, defining the rhetoric-of-belonging subtype of *ad populum* argument seems less difficult than defining the mob-appeal subtype.

The rhetoric-of-belonging type of *ad populum* argument can be used in different ways to function as a component in other arguments. In the most straightforward type of case, a speaker uses this argument in addressing a group, exploiting the fear or insecurity of the individuals in the group being addressed. However, in another type of case, the arguer can address someone outside the group, and cite peer pressure of the group on her (the arguer).

The classic case of the *peer pressure* type of *ad populum* argument is the teenager who appeals to her parents to buy an expensive pair of running shoes by arguing, "Everyone at the school has these shoes except me." The implication is that it is normal for all the other teenagers to have these sneakers, and that this is a good reason why she should have them, too (despite their expense).

This is quite a complex type of argument that is difficult to classify as a distinctive subtype. The argument seems to use the rhetoric-of-belonging type of argumentation, but uses it to suggest that if the teenager is excluded from the group (because of not having this brand of running shoes) there will be bad consequences for her. It uses the excluding or negative premise of the rhetoric-of-belonging argument, but in a different way than it is described above. Instead, it uses it as joined to the use of argumentation from consequences, so the upshot is that the parent may appear to be at fault for causing these negative consequences. Here the *ad populum* is used in a different way than it normally is, and the argument is not just a straightforward use of the *ad populum*. But there is definitely an *ad populum* element in it.

The usual setup of the *ad populum* argument is that of a speaker saying to a respondent audience, "Everybody in group G accepts A, so you should accept A." But in this case the speaker is saying, "Everybody in group G has object O, and since it is important for me to belong to G, and it is necessary for me to have O in order to belong to G, then you had better provide me with O, for otherwise I will suffer negative consequences by being excluded from group G." This is a more complex type of argument than other *ad populum* arguments we have examined, for it combines other types of argumentation with the *ad populum*.

In the simplest kind of case, the rhetoric-of-belonging subtype functions as a negative *ad populum* argument threatening the respondent with exclusion from "us"—the valued or fashionable group. This negative or exclusionary aspect was evident in Case 3.3, where the respondent was warned, "You ought to learn the bugaloo, as everyone bugaloos, and you will be left out if you don't."

9. Structure of the Mob-Appeal Subtype

With most of the subtypes of the *ad populum* recognized so far, the argumentation scheme is a composite of the pop scheme and some other type of argument. In each of these *ad populum* arguments, a premise or a set of premises is added to the pop scheme, to generate a form of argument characteristic of each of the *ad populum* subtypes. The main exception is the mob-appeal subtype of *ad populum*, which, as noted in section 1, has a dialectical structure that is inherently different from the bandwagon type of argument.

It seems then that the most difficult subspecies to classify, using the pop scheme as its basis, is the mob-appeal type. This type seems to depend heavily on the psychological dynamics of crowd behavior. It does not seem appropriate to add a premise such as "I (the speaker) am appealing to mob enthusiasm." Generally, it seems hard to know what to make of this category as having a distinctive form of *ad populum* argument.

Perhaps this difficulty arises because the mob-appeal subtype is heavily contextual in nature, and depends for its identification on defining its distinctive theatrical presentation as a mode of speech. In fact, it seems dubious that the mob-appeal type of argument is really based on the pop scheme, in any way that can easily be codified or defined as a distinctive form of argument. The problem is that the mob-appeal type of *ad populum* is so heavily psychological in nature, and so particularized to a specific audience, occasion, setting, mood, and so forth. This rhetorical nature of the mob-appeal type of *ad populum* suggests that it is not possible to define it as a distinctive type of *ad populum* argument using an argumentation scheme. Instead, it seems that the structure of the mob-appeal subtype is to be sought in the dialectical context of its use as an argument.

A leading characteristic of the mob-appeal subtype is the speaker's tactic of getting the group to look to its own interests and enthusiasms as an identifiable group, and to place these interests before any considerations of the evidence on the question being debated, or taking into account fairly the arguments on both sides of the issue. This factor is a leading characteristic that separates eristic dialogue from persuasion dialogue. In the quarrel, there is an appearance of paying attention to a logical assessment of the issue by weighing the arguments on both sides (as if the dialogue were, say, a critical discussion). But this appearance is a sham. Really, in the quarrel, only one's own side is given any real weight, and the viewpoint of the other side is treated merely as a target of attack. This characteristic of the argumentation in the eristic type of dialogue could be called *closed-mindedness*, meaning that one's point of view is never given up, even in the face of overwhelming evidence to refute it.

This lack of openness to defeat, characteristic of the closed-minded attitude, is the very thing that the speaker in the mob-appeal type of *ad populum* argument strives to create and utilize in his arguments. And generally, it does seem to be a characteristic of the mob-appeal subtype of *ad populum* argument, as the textbooks conceive of this type of argument, and as our survey of it would indicate. For example, in Mark Antony's speech, he appeals to the enthusiasm of the crowd to avenge Caesar by stressing that Caesar was an "ordinary guy," was one of them, had left money in his will to them, and so forth. As Fearnside and Holther pointed out (1959), considering the evidence, on whether Brutus was guilty or not, is not important to the rhetorical success of the speech. What is important is that the group must see itself as a group that enthusiastically identifies itself as such, and moves quickly to take action against anyone who is perceived to be opposed to the group. It is this characteristic that is central to mob appeal as a way of arguing in a speech.

But there are also three other characteristics that serve to help identify the mob-appeal type of *ad populum* argument. One is the use of the rhetoric of belonging to establish group solidarity through the negative tactic of discouraging possible disagreement, by implying exclusion from the group. Thus not only is anyone who is opposed to the group seen as a hostile outsider or enemy—if you are not with us you are against us—but the argument suggested is that if anyone disagrees, they could be classified as belonging to the "outsiders." The rhetoric of belonging, as stressed in section 8, is not just appeal to group enthusiasm, but use of a particular negative tactic used to discourage disagreement. In the mob-appeal type of *ad populum* argument, this negative tactic is a method of bolstering closed-mindedness by indicating that there is a penalty for open-mindedness.

The second characteristic of the mob-appeal subtype of *ad populum* argument is that it is directed very much to the commitments of the audience, and uses these commitments as its premises. Moreover, it doesn't matter whether these commitments can be rationally justified, as in a critical discussion, where this justificatory aspect would be important. Nor does it matter whether these commitments are the outcome of a reasoned deliberation, a coming to public judgment. All that matters is that the audience accepts them, if possible enthusiastically, and holds them dearly as group values. These commitments do not have to be "prejudices" or wholly irrational beliefs. But they do represent popular sentiments based on a slant or bias toward the interests and commitments of the particular group being addressed. Hence, the mob-appeal subtype does incorporate, as one of its characteristics, an appeal to popular sentiments type of argument of the kind defined in section 6 above.

The third characteristic of the mob-appeal subtype is its incorporation of the common-folks type of *ad populum* argument as one of its components. This characteristic is perhaps less essential than the first two, but it is generally an important aspect of how the mob-appeal argument works by building on a consolidation of group values, commitments and interests. Generally, the speaker portrays himself as an ordinary member of the group. By identifying himself with each of the ordinary members of the massed group, he can portray himself as a "fighter" for the group—the implication being that all the members of the group are supposed to display a solidarity and massed collectivity in promoting the interests of the group.

To sum up then, the mob-appeal type of *ad populum* argument is a composite of three other subtypes: the rhetoric of belonging subtype, the appeal-to-popular-sentiments subtype, and the common-folks-appeal subtype. Each of these three argument types is an important component of the type of argument used in the mob-appeal *ad populum*. But these three subtypes are not sufficient to define the mob-appeal subtype as represented by the general target conception of this type of argument described by the standard treatment of it in the textbook accounts. The fourth component is dialectical in nature—it is the characteristic of closed-mindedness that the speaker utilizes and tries to reinforce in the mob-appeal type of *ad populum* argument.

It might be noted here briefly that the incorporation of the characteristic of closed-mindedness does not necessarily make the mob-appeal type of *ad populum* fallacious in all cases where it is used, according to the normative standards of the new dialectic.[5] For, as defined in Chapter 6, eristic dialogue is a legitimate type of dialogue in its own right as a context for the use of arguments.

---

5. Despite the rather negative-sounding connotations, "mob appeal" is a term that can be retained, if used with care. Perhaps "massed crowd appeal" would be an alternative name that does not seem so negative.

Only if there has been an illicit shift in an *ad populum* argument from another type of dialogue the participants were supposed to be engaged in, to the eristic type of dialogue, would the *ad populum* argument used in that first type of dialogue be dialectically irrelevant or fallacious. However, the question of how to evaluate *ad populum* arguments will be taken up in Chapter 8. For now, this point on evaluation is only mentioned in order to forestall the reader's possible tendency to think that, according to our way of defining the mob-appeal subtype above, it has to be a type of *ad populum* argument that is inherently fallacious.

10. Summary of Subtypes

When all the subtypes are presented below, it becomes evident how the *ad populum* argument works generally, as a species of plausible argument. It is generally a weak type of argument that gets most of its plausibility from being bolstered up through support from other arguments it is combined with in practice. This hypothesis could be called the bolster thesis. This bolster thesis about how the *ad populum* works will ultimately become the key to its evaluation as a type of argument (in Chapter 8).

To begin with, there is the argument from popularity, in its two forms, which represents the basic type of argument underlying the *ad populum*.

Argument from Popularity

(P_1) Everybody accepts that A is true.
Therefore, A is true.
(P_2) Nobody accepts that A is true.
Therefore, A is false.

As expressed above, the "everybody" means literally every person, but in practice, this premise tends to have a less absolute form. According to the probabilistic variant of the argument from popularity, the premise would be based on a statistical poll, or other form of inductive claim, to the effect that the majority, or such-and-such percent of people, accept A as true. According to the (generally even weaker) presumptive variant of the argument from popularity, the premise is expressed as a plausibilistic generalization of the form "People generally (but subject to exceptions) tend to accept A as true." This presumptive generalization would refer to what would normally be expected, and is subject to defeat in particular cases.

Although ($P1$) and ($P2$) represent the general, underlying form of the appeal to popular opinion as a type of argument, in fact, usually a specific group of people is referred to in cases of the kind surveyed in Chapters 2 and 3. The following two forms represent the pop scheme.

Pop Scheme

($S1$) Everybody (in a particular reference group, G) accepts A.
Therefore, A is true (or you should accept A).

($S2$) Everybody (in a particular reference group, G) rejects A.
Therefore, A is false (or you should reject A).

The argument from popularity is a very weak form of argument, and *ad populum* arguments only become very strong or plausible when expressed in the form of the pop scheme, where (a) a particular group is put in for the variable G, and/or (b) supplementary premises are added to the pop scheme. These configurations result in a number of subtypes of *ad populum* arguments, as listed below.

Position-to-Know Ad Populum *Argument*

(PKA) Everybody in this group G accepts A.
This group is in a special position to know that A is true.
Therefore A is (plausibly) true.

Expert-Opinion Ad Populum *Argument*

(EOA) Everybody in this group G accepts A.
G is a group of experts in a domain of knowledge.
Therefore A is true.

Deliberation Ad Populum *Argument*

(PDA) Group G has deliberated intelligently and extensively on whether to accept proposition A or not.
Everybody in G accepts A.
Therefore A is (plausibly) true.

Moral-Justification Ad Populum *Argument*

(MJA) Everybody who is good, or who represents a group G with good qualities, accepts policy P.

Your goal is (or should be) to be a good person, or a member of a group with good qualities.
Therefore, you should accept *P*.

Moral-Justification (Excuse Subtype) Ad Populum *Argument*

(*MJE*) Everybody in group *G* does *x* (or accepts proposition *A* as a policy).
Doing *x* (or accepting *A*) shows that *x* (or policy *A*) is an acceptable norm of conduct for *G*.
I (the speaker) am a member of *G*.
Therefore, my doing *x* (or accepting *A*) is morally justified as an acceptable action (or policy).

Snob-Appeal Ad Populum *Argument*

(*AS1*) Everybody in this group *G* accepts *A* (or has some property, or possesses some object).
This group *G* is elite, i.e., everyone who belongs to it has prestige.
Prestige is an important goal for you (the respondent).
If you accept *A* (acquire property *P* or buy object *O*), then you will be a member of the group *G*.
Therefore, you ought to accept *A*, etc.

Appeal-to-Vanity Ad Populum *Argument*

(*AV1*) Everybody in this group of admired (popular) people *G* accepts *A* (possesses *A*, etc.).
If you carry out action *x*, then you will belong to this group *G*.
Therefore, you should carry out action *x*.

Rhetoric-of-Belonging Ad Populum *Argument*

(*RB1*) Everybody in this group *G* accepts *A*.
Being a member of this group *G* is highly valued for you (the respondent).
If you do not accept *A*, you will be out of this group *G*.
Therefore, you should accept *A*.

All eight subtypes listed above are based on the pop scheme format. All eight of these subtypes can be described as hybrids. They are based on the pop scheme but they are reinforced by the addition of other arguments, such as argument from position to know, for example, to the pop scheme. The pop scheme only represents the structure of the very weak argument from popularity, and *ad populum* arguments, as used in practice, gain what strength they have by being reinforced by these other backing arguments (according to the bolster thesis).

The plain-folks, or common-folks appeal type of *ad populum*, can take two basic forms represented by the argumentation schemes (*PF1*) and (*PF2*) below. The difference between the two is that in (*PF2*), there is a specific group identified, where (*PF1*) is a more straightforward argument from commitment directed to an audience not necessarily composed of an identifiable group.

Common-Folks Ad Populum *Argument*

(*PF1*) I (the speaker) am an ordinary person, i.e., I share a common background with you (the audience).
Therefore, you ought to take what I say as being more credible or acceptable.

Common-Folks *(Group Subtype)* Ad Populum

(*PF2*) I (the speaker) am an ordinary person, i.e., I share a common background with all the members of this audience (group G).
You (the respondent) are a member of this audience (group G).
Therefore, you should accept what I say.

For example, in Case 3.5, no specific group was identified in the common-folks appeal. The speaker remarked that when he was in high school he had to get up at four-thirty every morning to deliver papers. In countries favoring free enterprise, or possibly in any country, this kind of appeal makes the speaker seem like an ordinary person, and will generally gain some support with an audience. In other uses of the common-folks argument, however, the appeal is made to a group that is more specifically identified. For example, in Case 3.6, a speaker describes the opposition he claims to be against as "big business" or "vested interests." As a positive type of example, a speaker at a feminist rally may make continual references to herself as being female, stress the importance of being a woman, and relate personal experiences of the difficulties she had in her life because of her being a woman.

Finally, the mob-appeal subtype, as analyzed in section 9 above, is based on three of the other subtypes: the rhetoric of belonging, the appeal to popular sentiments, and the common-folks subtypes.

To sum up then, two generic argumentation schemes for the *ad populum* type of appeal have been identified: the argument from popularity and the pop scheme. The following eleven subtypes have been identified, using these generic schemes as a basis:

1. The position-to-know *ad populum* argument
2. The expert-opinion *ad populum* argument
3. The deliberation *ad populum* argument
4. The moral-justification *ad populum* argument
5. The excuse subtype of the moral-justification type
6. The snob-appeal *ad populum* argument
7. The appeal-to-vanity *ad populum* argument
8. The rhetoric-of-belonging *ad populum* argument
9. The common-folks *ad populum* argument
10. The group subtype of the common-folks type
11. The mob-appeal *ad populum* argument

Chapter Eight

A NEW BASIS FOR EVALUATION

The new method of evaluating *ad populum* arguments set out in Chapters 8 and 9 will show that many of the examples cited by the textbooks as fallacious instances, when more properly analyzed, are revealed to be arguments that are weak and open to critical questioning, but are not in such bad shape (as far as the evidence indicates) that they should properly be called fallacious. The question of when and why such arguments should be evaluated as fallacious is reserved for Chapter 9. The assumption is that the charge that an argument is fallacious is a more serious and severe criticism than the allegation that the argument is open to critical questioning, or has not been sufficiently supported.

Before we get to the task of evaluating fallaciousness, in Chapter 9, it is necessary to lay out, in Chapter 8, the general method of evaluating *ad populum* arguments, and the assumptions and principles behind the use of this method. The steps required in the method are summarized in sections 9 and 10. In the past, the logical basis for justifying or criticizing *ad populum* arguments has not at all been understood, in any comprehensive or systematic way. It is necessary to extend Gricean conversation theory into largely uncharted territory to get some grasp of the real basis of support of *ad populum* arguments.

1. Evaluation as Contextual

The first point to be noted about evaluating *ad populum* arguments is that such an argument needs to be evaluated in the dialectical context in which the argument was (supposedly) used in a given case. The new dialectic implies a relativity of evaluation to a context of use. This relativity of different normative standards is very hard for some people—those who presume that there should only be one standard of rational argument—to get used to. An *ad populum* argument—the very same argument, with the same premises and the same conclusion—could be used reasonably in the context of one type of dialogue, and could be correctly judged to be a fallacy, as used in the context of another type of dialogue.

In the context of a persuasion dialogue, *ad populum* arguments can be relevant, as noted in Chapter 4, particularly when they are used as common starting points in a discussion. But they are irrelevant in many cases, as well. And even when they are relevant, they are typically quite weak arguments, and best seen as presumptive arguments that need to be evaluated in relation to the larger body of evidence in a given case. But it still remains something of a mystery exactly why *ad populum* arguments are useful and relevant in persuasion dialogue. A solution to this mystery is offered in sections 4 and 5 below.

Ad populum arguments can be relevant as a basis for accepting a proposal in negotiation dialogue, where group negotiations are involved, especially those affecting or depending on public policies and practices. However in the inquiry, *ad populum* arguments are generally not relevant, and can be (almost) automatically excluded as having no real value or use. In eristic dialogues, *ad populum* arguments can be used, and do seem to have a place, but arguments used in quarrels do not represent a kind of reasoning that is of much importance in logic, except as something to be wary of (in case of a shift from another type of dialogue to a quarrel).

The deliberation type of dialogue is more central, for many of the cases of *ad populum* arguments studied in Chapters 2 and 3 appeared to be used in deliberations, and in many instances were identifiable as the subtype of *ad populum* argument classified as deliberation-based in Chapter 7. *Ad populum* arguments used in political deliberations are often relevant, because in a democratic system, popular opinion may be very important to take into account, particularly in advocating policies that everyone, or some group, may be obliged to follow (or to approve). As noted in the case of the traveler arriving at the train station in a foreign city (Chapter 4, section 2), an *ad populum* argument can be a presumptively weak argument that is reasonable (nonfallacious) when used in a deliberation, in the absence of relevant, more conclusive evidence, or in relation to other evidence that is available in a case.

In evaluating *ad populum* arguments used in deliberation, much depends on the stage the deliberation is in. If the prior deliberation has been informed and thoughtful, taking into account and weighing all the relevant evidence on the various alternatives, then the conclusion representing the outcome of that deliberation can carry a good deal of weight in subsequent deliberations on the same, or a comparable issue. But the problem with many arguments based on appeals to popular opinion is that public deliberation on the issue may be at a very early stage, or may not have even begun.

The problem with so many media reports of public opinion issues, according to Yankelovich, is that these reports are very good at arousing a sense of issue in relation to the first two stages of public deliberation, but are often very sketchy in reporting the subsequent stages which concern the resolution of the issue (1992, 24–25). In this sense, the media does not serve the resolution and consensus processes of public deliberation in a democratic society very well. According to Yankelovich, the media often does very well in the initial phases of information distribution, but does a poor job at examining the dialectical conflicts in the various points of view expressed as solutions to the problem. For Yankelovich then, whether an appeal to popular opinion using a poll in a particular case should be correctly described as a mass opinion argument, as opposed to a public judgment argument, depends on the phase at which the poll is used during this extended sequence of deliberations: "If it catches people's views in earlier stages, it's very poor quality and not accurate" (25). At this stage it could be called mass opinion (see Chapter 4, section 9).

On this basis, Yankelovich presents three criteria for evaluating an appeal to public opinion which is of poor quality, as opposed to one which is of good quality (23–24). The first criterion of poor quality is volatility, meaning that people change their minds every time you ask the same question in a slightly different way, or if you ask the same question at a different time. The second criterion is inconsistency, meaning that people hold different views in different compartments of their mind without putting the two views together. An example Yankelovich gives here is that people might be for protectionism, when you ask them if they are for it or against it, but in another context, if they have the issue of protecting American jobs in a compartment of their mind, then if you ask them if they are for or against protectionism, they'll be against it. So, here we have an inconsistency. The third criterion is consciousness of costs, trade-offs and consequences generally of the opinion held.

Public opinion polls are useful in all kinds of deliberations, especially in a democratically governed free market economy. But, of course, such polls are also frequently misused, or erroneous conclusions are drawn from them, as indicated in Chapter 1. In Chapter 9, various fallacies associated with the use of public opinion polls are surveyed.

Now some advice has been given on how to evaluate appeals to popular opinion in five of the six types of dialogue studied in Chapter 6. But what about persuasion dialogue? Finding the basis for evaluating *ad populum* arguments in persuasion dialogue is a more elusive and subtle undertaking, reserved for sections 4 and 5, below. Before embarking on this quest for understanding, some more general comments on the method of evaluating *ad populum* arguments dialectically are in order.

2. Evaluation as Dependent on Identification

Although the evaluation of an *ad populum* is dialectical in nature, and requires taking the context of use of the argument into account, the more traditional logical task of identifying the form of the argument must be an integral part of the evaluation. Indeed, the first goal in assessing any *ad populum* argument used in a given case should always be to aim to identify the subtype. This process requires a matching up of the given *ad populum* argument to one of the argumentation schemes set out in Chapter 7.

The step of identification is vital to the evaluation of an *ad populum* argument, because the different subtypes are, in many instances, quite distinctively different kinds of arguments, with different premises that need to be supported in different ways. Some subtypes require a quite different kind of supporting evidence from others. Some of the subtypes even seem to run counter to each other.

Some of the *ad populum* arguments cited above are based on a kind of appeal to trendiness that seems to suggest that a particular action or product is better because it is new, and represents the cutting edge of what is supposedly an emerging trend. Other *ad populum* arguments seem to go in the other direction, suggesting that a policy or action is better because it is based on some tradition, or precedent that has been followed by many persons, groups, countries or civilizations in the past (see Chapters 2 and 3). Here, the idea is that it has worked in the past, or was found to be a good policy by many people who have adopted it in the past, and is therefore a good idea now. The different *ad populum* subtypes can be based on different bases of support, and these differences are vitally important to recognize, before attempting to evaluate an *ad populum* argument as weak or strong in a given case.

The first step in evaluating an *ad populum* argument is to identify the premises and conclusion of the argument in a given case as specifically as possible, but this step frequently requires analysis of the text of discourse in the case. For as we saw in so many of the cases cited in Chapters 1 and 2, the additional premises (expressing position to know, etc.) may not be stated explicitly. The next stage is to evaluate the argument, once the premises and conclusion of the argument have been located, in the given case. The first important point at the evaluation stage is to carefully distinguish between judging (1) whether or not the premises are true, or have been supported adequately in the given case, and (2) whether the *ad populum* meets the requirements of the argumentation scheme, so that it can be judged to be structurally correct as an inference. The second aspect is conditional, meaning that in a structurally correct inference, *if* the premises are true (or adequately supported) then some weight of presumption is shifted toward the conclusion (by those premises), in a dialogue.

In making such an evaluation, the old standard treatment idea that *ad populum* arguments can be routinely or even automatically evaluated as fallacious must be given up. Instead, now we must look at an argument, once identified as a particular *ad populum* subtype in a given case, and ask critical questions about (a) the premises of the argument, and whether they are true, or can be supported adequately, (b) the dialectical relevance of the argument, and (c) the larger body of evidence in the given case in which the strength or weakness of the *ad populum* argument is to be evaluated. The new dialectical approach to evaluating *ad populum* arguments is based on the recognition that although these arguments are generally weak and presumptive in nature, making them open to critical questioning, they can still frequently be useful arguments in shifting a burden of proof on a balance of considerations. In such cases, the *ad populum* argument should be judged as correct, or reasonable (as used in a context).

There are many reasonable uses of *ad populum* arguments in political cases, in business and advertising, and in legal argumentation. One of these proper uses of public opinion research findings, cited by Davis and Abbott, is its use in cases involving trademark infringements and unfair competition (1989, 22). According to Davis and Abbott, these cases often require research into the consuming public's mind to assess the impact of trademarks, logos and advertising on the general public. Another legal kind of case they cited, where public opinion arguments are appropriately used, is in obscenity cases (22–23). Obscenity laws are frequently too general for a jury to determine because they are expressed in terms of prevailing community standards. In order to determine what the prevailing community standard may reasonably be taken to be in a particular locale and at any particular time, a public opinion survey can be used. So, it is clear here that, just as in political argumentation, there are legitimate uses for *ad populum* arguments based on public opinion research findings in legal cases. It should not be said that *ad populum* arguments, in these cases, are inherently fallacious. Such arguments do have their uses, and can be reasonable, provided care is taken not to commit the various fallacies cited in Chapter 9, and provided the proper conclusion is drawn with care and circumspection from the data about public opinion collected by the researcher.

Even in cases of individual deliberation, as we saw in the case of the person getting off the train in a foreign country, *ad populum* arguments can be reasonable. And as is true in this case, *ad populum* arguments can be especially strong when they are reinforced by a position to know type of premise. Also, in this particular case, the person getting off the train did not speak the language, so there was no other source of information or relevant evidence available, and therefore the *ad populum* argument was correctly used as a basis to justify a prudent course of action in the situation.

So, in some cases, *ad populum* arguments can be good (nonfallacious) arguments, even if they are defeasible and presumptive.

3. Bolstering and Critical Questions

Another aspect that has proved to be very important in evaluating *ad populum* arguments is how such arguments are frequently bolstered in strength by being partially based on position to know premises. Such arguments are hybrids. They are *ad populum* arguments of the appeal to popularity type combined with appeals to expert opinion, or other kinds of arguments that have distinct argumentation schemes in their own right. You could say that these are not "true" *ad populum* arguments because they are combined with other types of arguments. But the textbooks classify them under the heading of the *ad populum*, and this classification makes practical sense, because many of the most common types of *ad populum* arguments that have been identified for study, and that are frequently used to mislead arguers, are in fact among these hybrid subtypes (as shown in Chapter 7).

For example, the position-to-know subtype should be evaluated by taking into account that it has another premise, in addition to the premise much stressed in the standard treatment to the effect that everybody believes a particular proposition. In addition, another premise needs to be taken into account to raise the question of whether the group cited in the first premise is really in a position to know whether the proposition cited is true. But this position-to-know factor could also be taken into account by thinking of it as being a critical question asked when the position-to-know type of *ad populum* argument is put forward by a participant in a dialogue. In such a case, the respondent could evaluate the *ad populum* argument by raising the appropriate critical question of what is the proponent's position to know as a basis for asserting the first premise.

Following this approach, it would be fair to make a comparison between the structure of the *ad populum* argument and the structure proposed for the appeal to expert opinion type of argument given in Walton (1989, 192–97). According to the scheme (G7) seen in Chapter 2, section 10, the appeal to expert opinion is a form of knowledge-based argument that has several premises and a conclusion. One premise is that the authority or expert cited is an expert in a particular domain D of knowledge. Another premise is that the expert asserts that a particular proposition A is known to be true. A third premise is that this proposition A falls within the domain D of the expert's field of scientific knowledge. The conclusion of the argument is that A may plausibly be taken to be true. According to the analysis given in Chapter 2, section 10, the appeal to expert opinion should be evaluated as a presumptive type of argument that shifts a weight of evidence based on considerations of burden of proof in a dialogue toward the conclusion if the premises can be supported adequately by the proponent of the argument.

Corresponding to an instance of this type of argument is a set of critical questions that can be asked by the respondent to whom the argument was addressed. One of these critical questions is whether or not the authority cited is a genuine expert in a domain of scientific knowledge. Another critical question is whether the opinion vouched for by this particular expert agrees with the views of other experts in the same field.

For our purposes here in studying the *ad populum* argument, one type of critical question is especially important to notice. In connection with the appeal to expert opinion-based type of *ad populum* argument, one appropriate critical question that needs to be considered is whether the expert can back up his opinion by evidence within his field of scientific expertise if challenged by the proponent to do so. That is, in using the appeal to expert opinion as a presumptively correct form of argument, the assumption is that the expert has based his opinion on objective evidence within his field of scientific knowledge. Thus, it should be appropriate in a context of dialogue for the expert, if questioned, to at least be able to cite this evidence, even if it may be difficult for him to explain it and justify it completely to a layman respondent who is questioning his opinion on this matter. The idea of such a critical question is that it should be possible, in principle, if this opinion is based on scientific knowledge, for the expert to bring forward some kind of evidence or support that acknowledges that the opinion has been based on some kind of scientific findings or research or propositions taken to be true by other experts in the field.

The remaining critical questions for the expert opinion-based type of *ad populum* argument are the same as those for responding to the pop scheme generally. It needs to be asked whether in fact the premise is true that everybody accepts A, whether the appeal to popular opinion made by the premise is dialectically relevant, and what other factors should be taken into account in assessing the evidential worth of the appeal in a balance of considerations.

We now turn to the more difficult problem of how to evaluate cases where the *ad populum* appeal is purely of the appeal to popularity type, and is not one of the subtypes based on position-to-know reinforcement. It has always been more difficult to see how, if at all, these types can be justified.

4. Seeking a Basis for Acceptance in Persuasion Dialogue

One of the most puzzling things about evaluation of *ad populum* arguments is why these arguments have any plausibility at all in a persuasion-type of dialogue, apart from their being bolstered up by supplementary arguments, such as position to know arguments. In a critical discussion, why should an argument of the argument from popularity form "Everybody accepts A, therefore A is true" be accepted as a plausible, if weak reason for (tentatively) agreeing to accept A, for the sake of argument? A clue is to be found in Frans van Eemeren and Rob Grootendorst's concept of common starting points in a critical discussion (1984; 1987; 1992) (see Chapter 4, section 5). But apart from it being justified by an ITP, why should a participant in a critical discussion be led to accept a proposition as a premise simply because the other participant argues "Everybody accepts this proposition"? What kind of basis is this attempt at justifying an argument?

A general problem with evaluating *ad populum* arguments, of the more straightforward kind that have the form of the argument from popularity, is that these arguments are not based on knowledge, or even position to know, or prior deliberation. They are very weak arguments, and one might wonder what claim they have to acceptance in persuasion dialogue. Why should one accept them at all, and in light of the frequent superficiality, changeableness, and proneness to error of popular opinions, should not there be a presumption in favor of their nonacceptance, or even rejection? If there is some general reason for provisionally accepting them in persuasion dialogue, the problem is to identify this basis for justification.

One possible solution to this problem lies in the observation made in Chapter 6 that the critical discussion is a type of dialogue exchange that is partly adversarial and partly cooperative. It is adversarial because a participant's primary aim is to find any convincing arguments that refute the opponent's thesis, and hence the dialogue functions best when both participants are strongly partisan advocates of their opposed views. But, on the other hand, persuasion dialogue, in order to function well and not degenerate into eristic dialogue, must also be cooperative. Participants must use relevant arguments based on commitments of the other side, and generally follow rules of politeness (Gricean maxims) in taking turns in properly addressing and replying to the arguments of the other side (Grice 1975).

This duality requires that a successful persuasion dialogue needs to be balanced—a certain partisanship is good, but it must be a controlled partisanship. If a proposition goes against your thesis, you are obliged to attack it, disagree with it, or at least question it. But if a proposition is perfectly harmless, or does not disagree with your thesis, or is not even relevant to it, as far as you can tell, then there is no obligation on you to prove it is false, or even to question it. And you should perhaps even be generally willing to accept such a proposition for the sake of argument, if you have no argument against it. For without some basis of willingness to accept agreement of this kind, a critical discussion is not likely to be very productive in leading toward a resolution of the conflict of opinions that originated from it.

These principles would seem to suggest that if everyone generally thinks that a proposition is true, and accepting that proposition would pose no argument that would go against your thesis in a persuasion dialogue, then according to the Gricean Cooperative Principle or (CP), you should accept that proposition, for the sake of argument, at least provisionally.

However, if we look around in the Gricean maxims of polite conversation that come under the general heading of the (CP) (Grice 1975, 67–68), no maxim appears to express the principle of acceptance counseled above. In fact, the maxim of quality seems to go in the opposite direction. "Do not say that for which you lack adequate evidence" (67). True, as counseled above, it could be cooperatively valuable to accept a proposition, even if it is based only on an appeal to popular opinion indicating that the proposition is harmless or relatively trivial, in relation to what is being disputed in the given critical discussion. But if you lack evidence for that proposition but accept it, then that acceptance could be costly later on, if the proposition you accepted turns out to be false—or, even worse, if it can be somehow used by your opponent to defeat your thesis, in a way that you could not reasonably have anticipated earlier. So why accept any proposition in a critical discussion, if it cannot be proved beyond reasonable doubt?

Accepting propositions as commitments in a persuasion dialogue can be hazardous, because your opponent may later use them against you. So would not it be better strategy and safer to reply "No commitment" when your opponent asks you to grant anything she cannot definitely prove right away? The answer is "Yes, it would" and this answer poses a general problem for the management of commitments in a persuasion dialogue.

Basically, what is required to make a persuasion dialogue productive to fulfill its goal is some sort of incentive for a respondent to take on commitments, even where the proponent cannot force him to do so, on the grounds that she can prove this proposition right away (according to the standards required for fulfilling burden of proof). It is exactly this general problem of taking on commitments that is confronted and solved in the permissive persuasion dialogues or formalized *PPD* types of dialogue studied in Walton and Krabbe (1995). Generally, there are many dimensions to this problem of commitment management in persuasion dialogue, concerning conditions under which retractions of commitments should be allowed, as well as conditions under which a participant should be required, or at least encouraged, to take on commitments in a dialogue, even ones that have not been strongly proved (or proved beyond doubt).

But now the special problem of taking on commitments posed by the *ad populum* argument needs to be solved. Evidently some Gricean-like maxim is needed that would offer guidance as a basis for evaluating arguments from popularity in persuasion dialogue. But no such Gricean maxim, of the kind we need, exists.

5. The Maxim of Nondisputativeness

There is another Gricean maxim that could also perhaps be brought into play here. According to the maxim of quantity, a participant is told to make her contribution "as informative as is required" for the purposes of a conversational exchange, but not "more informative than is required" (Grice 1975, 67). This maxim would seem most applicable to an information-seeking dialogue. At any rate, it does not appear to be directly applicable to cases of use of an *ad populum* argument in a persuasion dialogue. But could a maxim somewhat like the maxim of quantity be used to set a balance of presumption between the aggressive partisanship and the need for cooperativeness in a persuasion dialogue?

The answer to this question resides in the purpose of a critical discussion, which is to resolve a conflict of opinions. Any persuasion dialogue centers around a controversy that forms the issue to be settled by the dialogue. This issue could be, say, the abortion issue, where the proponent is pro-choice, and the respondent takes the opposed, pro-life point of view. Any proposition closely related to either of the propositions in conflict will itself be controversial is this particular persuasion dialogue. For example, the proposition "The fetus is a person" is relevant to the propositions to be proved on both sides of the issue, and so it is definitely a controversial proposition. But the proposition "Socrates lived in Athens" is not controversial, in relation to the persuasion dialogue on the abortion issue. It could be controversial in the context of another critical discussion, say on Greek philosophy, but it is not controversial (nor would it be likely to be) in the persuasion dialogue on abortion. In general then, some propositions will be controversial in a given critical discussion, and others will not be.

Generally, if a proposition is definitely noncontroversial in a given critical discussion, and if it appears unlikely that it will become controversial at some later stage of the discussion, it could easily be granted by one side, for the sake of argument, even if the other side cannot really prove this proposition, except for giving some weak support for accepting it, based on the premise: this proposition is not controversial—everyone generally accepts it, no matter which side of this critical discussion they are on. Here we have a weak argument for at least tentatively accepting a proposition (until we might run into trouble with it), in order to allow the discussion to go ahead on a provisional basis.

In fact, a pair of maxims relating to noncontroversiality in a conversation have been stated by Atlas and Levinson (1981, 40).

Maxims of Relativity

1. Do not say what you believe to be highly noncontroversial, that is, to be entailed by the presumptions of the common ground.

2. Take what you hear to be lowly noncontroversial, that is, consistent with the presumptions of the common ground.

A comparable maxim of relativity, reformulated in Levinson, propounds the conversational rule "Don't bother to say what is noncontroversial" (1987, 66). Atlas and Levinson see these maxims of relativity as expressing a more general conversational principle that includes the Gricean maxim of informativeness as a special case. Their notion of "the common ground" is similar to what van Eemeren and Grootendorst call "common starting points" in a discussion.

The maxims of relativity do not apply, at least in any direct way, to *ad populum* arguments, but they do suggest that what could be a comparable kind of maxim having to do not with informativeness but with disputativeness. Such a maxim would guide a participant in a critical discussion to be open to accepting a proposition that is noncontroversial, for the sake of argument. The basis for accepting such a proposition in a persuasion dialogue, that is of key importance to evaluation of *ad populum* arguments, is noncontroversiality. If a proposition is noncontroversial, in the sense that everyone (and especially everyone on both sides of the issue of a given controversy) accepts it, then that could be a good reason for a respondent not to dispute it (at a given point in a given dialogue). Such a maxim of noncontroversiality would not require that a participant take on a burden of proof to defend his acceptance of such a proposition, as one he can give sufficient evidence to prove. Rather the maxim would limit disputativeness by giving the option to tentatively accept a proposition, on the negative and tentative basis that one has no reason to dispute it.

What is important with respect to the *ad populum* is that this kind of maxim could be useful in a type of dialogue like a critical discussion as a way of limiting excessive and counterproductive disputativeness. Let us call the following principle *the maxim of disputativeness*: "Don't bother to dispute a premise of the other party's argument if that premise is noncontroversial." More specifically, the maxim of disputativeness can be reformulated as a positive principle: "Only dispute something if it appears to go against the view you are defending, or if it appears to be false, or if you have some reason to think it is false, or could be used to refute the view you are trying to defend." The maxim of nondisputativeness reflects the need for tempering one's partisanship in a critical discussion with some need for cooperativeness. It is too much of a waste of time and energy to question or dispute everything, and therefore it can help the discussion along to only disagree with or argue against those propositions that you have some reason to disagree with or argue against.

The maxim of nondisputativeness is built on a dialectical principle that has generally been ignored in western logic, but has often been emphasized by the Nyaya philosophers of India, according to Chakrabarti.

> As Nyaya logicians are never tired of saying: no enquiry is conducted in an absolute vacuum, but only within the framework of various things which are known or accepted and various other things which are disputed. Even about disputed things something must be known, for otherwise no meaningful inquiry about them could be initiated at all. Indeed, things under inquiry and questioning are such that they are known in general terms, but not in specific terms. Accordingly, evidence is required neither for what is completely known nor for what is completely unknown. Thus it is the presupposition of any rational inquiry that there exists broad consensus over certain matters. (1995, 133)

This summary of the Nyaya philosophy shows that it did postulate something like the principle of nondisputativeness as a basis of support for accepting presumptions on matters in which "there exists broad consensus." In the Nyaya logic, then, there would appear to be an acceptance of something very close to the *argumentum ad populum*, based on a principle very similar to that of the maxim of nondisputativeness.

In light of the theory of presumptive reasoning outlined in Chapter 4, the maxim of nondisputativeness can be put forward as the basis for accepting an appeal to popular opinion based on presumption in a persuasion dialogue. If the proposition is not generally in doubt, because everyone generally accepts it, and if there is no reason to dispute it, in relation to the conflict of opinions at issue, because it is not controversial, then that could be a good enough reason for provisionally accepting it in the dialogue, at least up to any point in the sequence of argumentation where this proposition might come into doubt, by virtue of becoming relevant to the controversy that is at issue. Such acceptance would be regarded as defeasible, meaning that later retraction of it in the dialogue should be possible, if a good reason for rejecting it arises.

6. Dialectical Bias in Argumentation

The textbook treatments frequently categorize *ad populum* arguments as fallacious on the grounds that they appeal to the bias or prejudice of an audience.

But a more careful distinction needs to be made. Although prejudice is generally a harmful kind of thing, which seems to imply faulty reasoning of some kind in an error of "pre-judging," bias is not, in itself, necessarily harmful or bad in all arguments. Blair (1988) distinguishes between "bad bias," or at any rate, bias of a kind that is harmful, or is a problem, from a logical point of view, and "good bias," or bias of a kind that is normal and can be perfectly reasonable in argumentation.

In persuasion dialogue, a participant's aim is to argue as strongly as possible to support her thesis, and to ask critical questions about, or even mount arguments to refute her opponent's thesis. It is therefore natural and normal for a participant in a critical discussion to display in her argumentation a bias toward her own point of view, and bias against her respondent's point of view. This kind of bias can be described as good, productive, normal and harmless, in a persuasion dialogue (and in some other types of dialogue as well).

When then does such a bias become harmful or obstructive? When does it become a problem, from the point of view of the critical evaluation of arguments and fallacies? An answer is given in a new theory of dialectical bias in Walton (1999). According to the new theory, dialectical bias of an argument is best defined pragmatically, as relative to the context of dialogue in which that argument was (supposedly) used. An argument that could be evaluated as containing a harmful or criticizable bias in an inquiry, might be not so criticizable as having a harmful bias when used as part of a persuasion dialogue. Also, we generally expect arguments to be highly biased in eristic dialogue, in a way that should not be regarded as an acceptable bias in a critical discussion.

According to the new dialectical theory of bias, the quarrel is a much more one-sided framework of argumentation than the critical discussion. The critical discussion, in order to be successful in its aim, must be a more balanced kind of dialogue exchange where certain Gricean maxims of polite conversational cooperation are observed by both sides. Each side must base its arguments on premises that are commitments of the other side. Thus reasonable argumentation in a critical discussion requires empathy to discern what the position of the other side really is. Moreover, a participant in a critical discussion must display an attitude of open-mindedness. She must be receptive to conceding, or giving up a commitment, if the other side can show that there is enough evidence against this proposition to warrant giving it up. As shown in Chapter 6, it is this characteristic that is so important in distinguishing between persuasion dialogue and eristic dialogue.

In a persuasion-dialogue framework, a certain bias or favoring one's own point of view is perfectly understandable, normal and acceptable. Indeed, a positive bias in pro-argumentation for a participant's point of view is useful and even necessary to keep the argumentation in a persuasion dialogue moving forward toward it goal.

But such a bias becomes pathological or negative, from a point of view of evaluating the argumentation in a critical discussion, where the argumentation is prematurely closed to contra-argumentation of the other side, or is otherwise not of a kind appropriate for use at a particular stage of the critical discussion. Bias of the harmful kind is often detectable when there has been an illicit or disguised dialectical shift—for example, in a case where an argument is supposed to be part of a critical discussion, but where the arguer is really engaged in negotiation dialogue, e.g., where he has something to gain by taking a particular point of view, and is simply trying to promote his own interests. Several indicators of dialectical bias are set out in Walton (1997b), but two of the most important are closure to opposed argumentation and having something to gain.

Taking bias into account is especially important in the common-folks and mob-appeal subtypes of *ad populum* arguments, where the speaker's strategy of rhetoric is to appeal to some commitment or point of view that is important to the audience, and that binds the audience together as a group. The speaker tries to establish a common bond with the audience, using the group's bias as the basis for his *ad populum* appeal. But just because an *ad populum* argument is biased in this way, it does not follow that it should necessarily be judged to be fallacious.

The so-called mob-appeal subtype, where the sentiments and bias of a mass audience that can be roused to enthusiasm is appealed to by a speaker, needs to be re-evaluated. If the speaker and the audience share a group affiliation, a common bond, a set of shared values, or a bias, it is not necessarily fallacious if the speaker appeals to this bias in an *ad populum* argument addressed to the group.

7. Mob Rhetoric and Mass Enthusiasm

The following case is the account given in the famous book *Popular Delusions and the Madness of Crowds* (Mackay, 1852) of the speech of Pope Urban II given to an assembled crowd at Clermont, in Auvergne, in November 1095. In his speech, Urban called for the forming of a religious army, or crusade, to drive the Turks from an area where they were interrupting pilgrim traffic to Jerusalem, and to recover the Holy Sepulcher in Jerusalem from the Muslims. This speech was an important event in starting what is now called the first crusade, which culminated in the conquest of Jerusalem by an army of crusaders led by Godfrey of Bouillon on July 15, 1099. According to Mackay, on the occasion of Urban's speech at Clermont, the great square before the cathedral church was densely crowded with people who had assembled there (1980, 363). The pope stood on high scarlet-covered scaffolding above the crowd, surrounded by a brilliant array of bishops and cardinals. His oration is described by Mackay as follows (364).

Case 8.1: He began by detailing the miseries endured by their brethren in the Holy Land; how the plains of Palestine were desolated by the outrageous heathen, who with the sword and the firebrand carried wailing into the dwellings and flames into the possessions of the faithful; how Christian wives and daughters were defiled by pagan lust; how the altars of the true God were desecrated, and the relics of the saints trodden under foot. "You," continued the eloquent pontiff (and Urban II. was one of the most eloquent men of the day), "you, who hear me, and who have received the true faith, and been endowed by God with power, and strength, and greatness of soul,—whose ancestors have been the prop of Christendom, and whose kings have put a barrier against the progress of the infidel,—I call upon you to wipe off these impurities from the face of the earth, and lift your oppressed fellow-Christians from the depths into which they have been trampled. The sepulchre of Christ is possessed by the heathen, the sacred places dishonoured by their vileness. Oh, brave knights and faithful people! offspring of invincible fathers! ye will not degenerate from your ancient renown. Ye will not be restrained from embarking in this great cause by the tender ties of wife or little ones, but will remember the words of the Saviour of the world himself, 'Whosoever loves father and mother more than me is not worthy of me. Whosoever shall abandon for my name's sake his house, or his brethren, or his sisters, or his father, or his mother, or his wife, or his children, or his lands, shall receive a hundredfold, and shall inherit eternal life.'"

According to Mackay, "The warmth of the pontiff communicated itself to the crowd," who enthusiastically interrupted the speaker from time to time with loud shouts of "*Dieu le veult!*" (God wills it!) (364). According to Mackay's account, Urban took advantage of these shouts by recommending that '*Dieu le veult*!' be the war-cry in the coming crusade, in which he urged all participants to "bear the cross of the Lord" as the holy emblem of the engagement (365).

The red cross became the symbol of the crusade, and this symbolism was taken up by the people with great enthusiasm, according to the description of the "crowd madness" given by Mackay:

> A singular feature of the popular madness was the enthusiasm of the women. Every where they encouraged their lovers and husbands to forsake all things for the holy war. Many of them burned the sign of the cross upon their breasts and arms, and coloured the wound with a red dye, as a lasting memorial of their zeal. Others, still more zealous, impressed the mark by the same means upon the tender limbs of young children and infants at the breast.
>
> Guibert de Nogent tells of a monk who made a large incision upon his forehead in the form of a cross, which he coloured with some powerful ingredient, telling the people that an angel had done it when he was asleep. This monk appears to have been more of a rogue than a fool, for he contrived to fare more sumptuously than any of this brother pilgrims, upon the strength of his sanctity. The Crusaders every where gave him presents of food and money, and he became quite fat ere he arrived at Jerusalem, notwithstanding the fatigues of the way. If he had acknowledged in the first place that he had made the wound himself, he would not have been thought more holy than his fellows; but the story of the angel was a clincher. (366–67)

The enthusiasm and religious fervor that Urban's speech appealed to was an important factor in its rhetorical success. There arose several armies of crusaders who assembled in Constantinople at intervals between 1096 and 1097, who went on to conquer Antioch, and ultimately, Jerusalem. The first crusade led to a series of seven subsequent crusades over the next two centuries. Ultimately, the crusades resulted in massive destruction and loss of life, with little that could be described as a positive outcome. Probably the main lasting results were the destruction of the Byzantine civilization, and a decline of tolerance on both the Christian and Muslim sides. Thus while the speech was rhetorically successful in provoking a mass audience to take action, it is hard not to see the consequences of the first crusade as more negative than positive.

It is this kind of speech exactly that is portrayed in the standard treatment as a mob-appeal *ad populum* to the enthusiasm of the massed audience. Urban II and his audience were enthusiastic Christians, and he appealed to this commitment in a rousing speech to the "faithful" to take action against the "heathens." Such a fiery emotional appeal to the "prejudices" or bias of the mass, popular audience is exactly the type of argumentation characterized by the standard treatment as the mob-appeal fallacy.

But from the viewpoint of the new dialectic, the argumentation advanced in this case needs to be evaluated in light of the dialogue exchange that was supposed to be taking place between Pope Urban II and his audience. If this dialogue was supposed to be a balanced deliberation on whether the policy of embarking on a crusade was a prudent course of action, or if it was supposed to be a critical discussion on the pros and cons of whether crusading is generally a good or bad practice, it could be judged a dismal failure. Far from examining the merits of the arguments on both sides of the issue, Urban enthusiastically pushed for one side, demonstrating a strong bias. The opposition were described in the most negative terms as "outrageous heathens," who are "vile," and the argument is one-sidedly in favor of "the great cause." Hence, from a logical perspective, it seems easy to condemn this speech. But was it really supposed to be a balanced deliberation or a critical discussion? And if not, is it fair or reasonable to condemn it on the grounds that it fell short of the normative requirements for one or the other of these types of dialogue?

Pope Urban's speech is typical of many such speeches that encourage the audience to see themselves as victims of some other group (described in negative terms in the speech). As victims, the audience is told they need to bond together in solidarity, and take action enthusiastically to demand, and even to seize, what is rightfully theirs. Such a speech reaches out to the audience as an advocacy group (nowadays called an "action group"), promising them rewards, remuneration, or advancement of their interests of some kind, if they stand together and take unified action against the opposed interests (the "oppressors").

When this kind of speech is made in a certain setting, in front of a mass audience, or on a ceremonial occasion, we do not expect the kind of argumentation required in a balanced deliberation or a critical discussion. And in fact, if you criticize the speaker, or the adherents of the group, to their faces, for not discussing the issue in a balanced, more objective way, they will probably reply: "That is not important. What is important is that people are dying, or their rights are being violated, and lives, and vital interests are at stake!" What such a response suggests is that the conversation is not supposed to be that of the balanced deliberation or critical-discussion type. Instead, enthusiastic group solidarity is claimed to be relevant, justified, and important, because the situation is one of a fight—a noble struggle or "crusade" against "oppressors," or hostile interests that are "taking away our rights."

The problem then, for a dialectical evaluation of the argumentation in this kind of case, is to determine what kind of dialogue the speech in the given case was supposed to be part of in the first place. Before confronting the question of whether or why such a mob-appeal case should be judged to be an instance of the *ad populum* fallacy or not (in Chapter 9), we need to be more carefully aware of what it means to say that an *ad populum* of this sort is an appeal to the bias or prejudice of the audience.

8. Appeal to Snobbery and Vanity

The appeal-to-snobbery and appeal-to-vanity subtypes of *ad populum* certainly sound like bad or fallacious arguments, because of the highly negative connotations of the words "snobbery" and "vanity" in the name of the argument. But as with all the subtypes of *ad populum* arguments, care is needed to evaluate the context of dialogue in which this type of argument is supposedly being used, before condemning the argument as fallacious in a sweeping declaration.

Judging from the cases of appeals to snobbery and vanity cited in Chapter 3, it seems that the focus of the textbook treatment of these kinds of *ad populum* arguments is on commercial speech, and advertisements for products—especially the ubiquitous ads sponsored by manufacturers, and found in popular magazines and on television. The famous passage from Copi (1972, 79–80) quoted in Chapter 3, section 4, characterizes the twentieth-century advertiser as a "huckster" and "ballyhoo artist" who has elevated the status of the *ad populum* "almost" to a "fine art." These advertisers according to Copi are selling us "daydreams" and "delusions of grandeur" to get us to buy their products.

Particularly in North America, we are all very familiar on a daily basis with this constant barrage of commercials directed at us from all sides, and so it is easy to be sympathetic to Copi's condemnation of these ads. But what really is the basis of these condemnations? What is it about these ads that would justify the claim that they are somehow illogical or critically deficient as arguments because they are instances of the *ad populum* fallacy?

The basis of this condemnation would appear to be that the ads are logically defective and deceptive, because they do not prove what they assert. They claim that the products are good, or are a good buy, but instead of supporting this claim with relevant evidence, they make all kinds of *ad populum* appeals based on vanity, snobbery, and "delusions of grandeur." Hence, according to the standard treatments, these ads commit the *ad populum* fallacy.

To evaluate this condemnation of these ads, we have to (at least, according to the new dialectical method) ask first of all, what type of dialogue are the arguments in this type of commercial message supposed to be part of. An advertisement is a kind of "one-shot" dialogue exchange where the manufacturer of the product produces a message that is designed to reach a large number of viewers. The purpose is, presumably, to get the viewer, or respondents in the audience, to buy the product. The viewer's response (to the extent that he or she visibly has one) is to buy the product or not.

This framework can be described as a sort of dialogue exchange where one party is putting forward an argument, but it is extremely dubious that it is a critical-discussion, or persuasion-type of dialogue. In fact, people (even very small children) are very adept at recognizing a commercial message for what it is, and realizing that it is different from other types of dialogue, such as a critical discussion, that look at the relevant arguments on both sides of a controversial issue, or a deliberation, such as a *Consumer Reports* article that examines the pros and cons of various alternatives and recommends a "best buy," or an information-seeking type of dialogue like a news report. When commercial products are pitched in school within the format of a news report or a factual lesson, even very small children will recognize the beginning of the part where the product pitch begins, saying, "Hey! It's a commercial."[1] Commercial speech in an ad can be recognized as a distinct type of message, and we all realize that the purpose of such a message is to advocate and sell a product in a straightforwardly one-sided way that offers no pretense of being a balanced and open discussion, like that of a persuasion dialogue. In fact, the dialogue framework of an ad is much more eristic in nature—it is clear to everyone that the ad is making a pitch for one side, and that the object is to get you to buy the product, by any means that is legally and ethically acceptable to an audience.

Hence, to criticize *ad populum* arguments used in commercial ads on the grounds that such arguments do not prove what they assert, is an indication of a somewhat naive and unrealistic viewpoint on what kind of dialogue exchange the ads are supposed to represent. To claim that the *ad populum* arguments in these ads are fallacious because they do not present relevant evidence to support

---

1. See *CBS News* (1993, 19). When a video on the Alaska oil spill, produced by Exxon, claiming that Exxon had cleaned up the mess, was shown to a seventh grade class, one twelve-year-old student commented, "We've just seen a commercial."

their conclusions is to operate on the naive presumption that the purpose of the ad is to convince viewers rationally to come to accept or believe some claim or thesis proposed in the ad, as the outcome of a critical discussion or reasoned deliberation. The advertising firms who make up these ads would find such an attribution of the purpose of the message in an ad quite funny. Judging from the ads themselves, the producers of them are under no illusion that the purpose of the ad is to rationally convince the viewer that some thesis is true, based on relevant evidence. Nor are the viewers of the ads under any illusion that this is supposed to be the purpose of the ads.

In short, it is one thing to warn readers of logic textbooks that *ad populum* arguments as used in commercial ads are powerful and rhetorically effective arguments to pitch a product. It is quite another thing to declare that such uses of *ad populum* arguments are fallacious because they are irrelevant, or fail to present legitimate evidence to prove their claims. Much more thought needs to be put into studying the dialectical context in which these *ad populum* arguments are used, before any rush to hasty or simplistic evaluations could be warranted.

9. Identification and Analysis

In approaching any *ad populum* argument given in a particular case, the very first step is to identify the type of argument. That is, one must determine which one of the various argumentation schemes in Chapter 7 best represents the form of the *ad populum* used in this particular case. However, even though these identification schemes have been clearly defined in Chapter 7, the step of matching the scheme to the particulars of an *ad populum* argument used in a given case is not a trivial job. The main reason is that some of the supporting premises used as part of an *ad populum* argument tend not to be explicitly stated in particular cases.

Consequently, it is necessary, at least very frequently, in order to carry out the task of identification in a given case, to do a certain amount of analysis of the given text of discourse to search out premises that have not been explicitly stated as part of the *ad populum* argument. For example, frequently in studying cases, it has been found crucial to recognize that certain groups who have been cited in *ad populum* arguments are groups that are generally presumed to be in a position to know, or to have expertise in some domain of knowledge relevant to the claim made in the *ad populum* argument. When such premises are important to the argument, but have not been explicitly stated in the given text of discourse of a case, a task of analysis of the case is clearly necessary to be carried out before the argument can be properly evaluated.

One of the most important (and neglected) tasks in analyzing an *ad populum* argument in a given case is to determine what type of conversational exchange the argument is supposed to be part of. If it is a persuasion dialogue, the mob-appeal type of rhetoric can straightforwardly be evaluated as an inappropriate argument on several grounds: on the grounds that such an appeal is irrelevant and fails to present evidence of the kind required in a persuasion dialogue, or that such an appeal to the bias of the audience is made in a closed-minded way that may be appropriate for negotiation or eristic dialogue but is out of place in persuasion dialogue.

But if there is no evidence that the argumentation in the case is supposed to be a contribution to a persuasion dialogue, it might be naive and hasty to condemn the *ad populum* argument as fallacious on the grounds that it is irrelevant in a persuasion dialogue. The best one can do, in such a case, is to conditionally evaluate the argument by saying that it is irrelevant if it is supposed to be a contribution to a persuasion dialogue.

The problem with the standard treatment, of course, is that it is not based on any applicable theory of argument, like the new dialectical theory, so the need for careful analysis of the text and context of discourse in a given case is not apparent, and has generally been overlooked. Very short one-liner cases, with no indication where the argument came from, or how it is supposedly to be used for some purpose in a context of dialogue, are typical of the standard treatment.

With the advent of the new dialectical theory, however, it is possible to appreciate the need for careful analysis of a case prior to evaluation of the *ad populum* argument in it.

10. The Four Steps of an Evaluation

The first step to take in evaluating an *ad populum* argument, and the key to all evaluation, is to distinguish between two questions. Are the premises true (or can they be justified)? And is the structure of the inference such that it reasonably warrants acceptance of the conclusion, given that the premises are true (or can be justified)? The first question is about the acceptability of the premises. The second question is about the inference from the premises to the conclusion. As the cases studied in Chapters 1 and 2 made clear, it is vital to distinguish between these two questions in evaluating *ad populum* arguments.

Even prior to this first step of evaluation, the type of *ad populum* argument needs to be identified. This identification of type is very important to assist in locating the premises of an *ad populum* argument in a given case. It is also essential in order to judge which argumentation scheme is appropriate to be used to evaluate the structure of the *ad populum* argument.

The second step of evaluation is to judge the dialectical relevance of the *ad populum* argument. What is required here is to identify the type of dialogue the *ad populum* argument is supposedly a part of. So one has to ask the question, What type of dialogue are the participants supposed to be engaging in, with reference to the given case, as far as the text and context of discourse furnish enough evidence to determine?

The third step is to evaluate how strong the *ad populum* argument should be taken to be, in the given case. The problem here is that *ad populum* arguments are often very weak, properly evaluated in a context of dialogue. Some are stronger than others, depending on the argumentation scheme of the *ad populum* argument used in a given case, and the type and stage of dialogue in which the argument was used. But typically an *ad populum* argument just shifts a small weight of presumption toward acceptance of its conclusion, as part of a larger body of evidence in which a balance of many considerations needs to be weighed. A common mistake of evaluating an *ad populum* argument is to judge it in isolation from this larger body of evidence of which it is just one small part. Hence, at this third step, it is important to ask: what other evidence is relevant in the case, that needs to be weighed in conjunction with the *ad populum* argument?

At this third step of evaluation, it is important to recognize that an *ad populum* argument can be relevant, but it could still be fallacious, or otherwise open to criticism, if other evidence is available in a case, and should be taken into account, but is ignored. In this kind of case, the fallacy is that of jumping too hastily to a conclusion on the basis of an *ad populum* argument.

The fourth step of evaluation is to judge how the *ad populum* argument appeals to the commitment of the audience in the given case. In particular, does the way the argument is put forward in the dialogue of the case allow for the asking of critical questions, or does the argument show evidence of the kind of closed-mindedness that is characteristic of the bad type of dialectical bias? Especially in cases of the common-folks and mob-appeal types of *ad populum*, or any cases where an appeal to some identifiable group is made, one needs to ask whether the proponent is trying to make the group adopt an eristic attitude, or to appeal to the group's eristic attitude, in a way that is antithetical to the kind of open-minded argumentation that is necessary in persuasion dialogue. Of course, there is nothing inherently fallacious about eristic dialogue per se, or of strong-minded group advocacy, or enthusiastic partisanship in argumentation. But if the dialogue is supposed to be an open-minded deliberation or persuasion dialogue, then a shift to the eristic type of dialogue—especially if the shift is illicit or deceptive—is an important red flag that should be raised, indicating that the argument may be defective and misleading.

Chapter Nine

WHEN IS IT A FALLACY?

Chapter 9 is devoted to that particular aspect of evaluating *ad populum* arguments that has to do with judging whether such arguments are fallacious or not, in a given case. The argument of this chapter falls into two parts. The first part considers some particularly significant kinds of cases that have been judged to be fallacious *ad populum* arguments in the past, and it is argued that this blanket evaluation has been too hasty, in several respects. According to the new dialectical method of evaluation, a more cautious and balanced approach needs to be taken in judging the *ad populum* arguments in these cases.

The second part of the chapter then goes ahead to inquire into the general conditions in which an *ad populum* argument can justifiably be judged to be fallacious. The finding is that there are three kinds of faults of this sort: (1) hastily jumping to a conclusion, (2) dialectical irrelevance, and (3) suppressing the asking of critical questions in a dialogue.

1. The Inquisition Case

In many of the cases studied in Chapters 2 and 3, the basis of the *ad populum* was that of a process of intelligent or reasoned deliberation, but this basis was so weak that, in the circumstances, it was overridden by other factors in the case. For example, in the Inquisition case (Case 2.6), the conclusion was that the Inquisition must have been justified and beneficial. This conclusion seems so outrageously false, given what we know, or think we know, about the Inquisition as a historical event, that it is quite easy to dismiss the *ad populum* argument as fallacious. But a more careful analysis should take into account our finding that the *ad populum* argument gives only a small weight of presumption in favor of a conclusion that must be evaluated in relation to the larger body of evidence in the given case.

In the Inquisition case, the *ad populum* argument looks pretty bad, and one can certainly appreciate why Copi (1972) would use this case as an example of the *ad populum* fallacy. But a more balanced evaluation of the *ad populum* argument in this case should take into account the context in which it was used by its proponent, Benedetto Croce, as part of a longer sequence of argumentation in his book, *Philosophy of the Practical* (1913, 69–70). Croce used the argument as part of his analysis of error, wherein he made a distinction between theoretical error and practical error. His use of the *ad populum* argument, as quoted in Case 2.6, was part of a much longer chain of subtle argumentation. Admittedly, it is hard to figure out exactly what he was driving at, without undertaking an exposition of Croce's theory of error, and an extensive exegesis of his text in *Philosophy of the Practical*. However, if one is reasonably sympathetic, or at least fair in interpreting Croce's text, it is possible to see that he was attempting to construct an interesting, if controversial argument to the effect that the Inquisition, though usually thought of as a single, powerful tribunal, whose agents thwarted intellectual freedom in medieval times, is a myth.[1] In fact, according to Croce's argument, there are many inquisitions, and they are a kind of normal and necessary method of social control that are always or generally present in any period, in some form or other. The current climate of "political correctness" in the universities would in fact be an excellent illustration of Croce's thesis.

Looking at a little more of the text of Croce's argument, as quoted from his book, we see that he is discussing what he calls "the principle of justification of the practical repression of error" (1913, 69–70). He seems to mean by this principle that when a group of people adopt a general theory of conduct, like a

---

1. Peters (1988, 3) claims that the Inquisition as a "single all-powerful horrific tribunal, whose agents worked elsewhere to thwart religious truth, intellectual freedom, and political liberty, until it was overthrown sometime in the nineteenth century," is a "myth" of "modern folklore." The Inquisition, according to Peters, is a mythic concept that has been transformed by literature and art into a symbol.

religious dogma or viewpoint, the theory could represent a good intention, but the attempts of the theory advocates to put their theory into practice, and to enforce it as a code of practical conduct, is a sort of "error of the heart" or "bad volition" (68).

Case 2.6a: A consequence of the principle established is the justification of the use of practical measures to induce those who err theoretically to correct themselves, castigating them, when this is of assistance, for admonition and example. It will be replied that these are measures of other times, and that we are now in an epoch of liberty, when their use is no longer permissible, and that we should now employ only the persuasive power of truth. But those who say this are without eyes to look within upon themselves. The Holy Inquisition is truly *holy* and lives for that reason in its *eternal* idea. The Inquisition that is dead was nothing but one of its contingent historical incarnations. And the Inquisition must have been justified and beneficial, if whole peoples invoked and defended it, if men of the loftiest souls founded and created it severely and impartially, and its very adversaries applied it on their own account, pyre answering to pyre. Thus Christian Rome persecuted heretics as Imperial Rome had persecuted Christians, and Protestants burned Catholics as Catholics had burned Protestants. If certain ferocious practices are now abandoned (are they definitely abandoned, or do they not persist in a different form?), we do not for that reason cease from practically oppressing those who promulgate errors. No society can dispense with this discipline, although the mode of its application is subject to practical, utilitarian and moral deliberation.

It is easy to fault Croce with obscurity here, and it is difficult to know what he might really mean to imply by this argument. But it does not seem, in fairness to the text of the argument, that he means to justify the Inquisition in the sense that he sees it as a particular historical event or institution, in the way it is popularly conceived, and an institution that was good or beneficial (as contrasted to periods when it did not exist). Instead, Croce seems to be challenging this conventional view of the Inquisition in a deliberately provocative argument.

What Croce was evidently struggling to say in this passage could even be construed as a point about seeing things from a perspective when trying to do history. He seems to be suggesting that although the Inquisition is a kind of historical myth about "ferocious" practices used by organized groups who advocate a certain ideology to persecute heretics, seeing this myth in a black and white fashion that does not do justice to history. What Croce seems to suggest, like Collingwood after him (Dray 1995, 276), is that a historian always has a certain point of view, relative to the historical period she herself lives in, and that therefore, the task of seeing a historical event from the earlier point of view of the participants, while it is an important task for the historian, is one that is necessarily imperfect. The conclusion indicated is one of relativism about historical interpretations and explanations of past events, meaning that one should be careful about leaping to absolute judgments when condemning or praising some actions that took place in a different era.

Croce suggests that before one leaps to condemning the Inquisition and those who took part in it, one should recognize that similar things still happen today, when believers in various causes advocate all kinds of restrictions on free speech, and institute tribunals to "re-educate" those who are perceived as "heretics" or nonbelievers in the cause, which is taken by popular opinion (though by no means universally) as representing the "correct" or "right" point of view. It would be naive to think that such practices no longer occur, and to look back on events in the past like the Inquisition with a kind of condescension. For it is quite likely that many of those who took part in the Inquisitions saw themselves as doing the right thing, fighting what they regarded as the worst evils of the time, for a holy cause.

This kind of historical relativism that Croce seems to be arguing for can even be seen as a way of making a point about the appeal to popular opinion as a type of argument that rests on popularly accepted viewpoints that change from one historical era to another. For it is no doubt quite reasonable to hypothesize that an appeal to popular-opinion type of argument that might have been quite persuasive at one time, say in the time of the Inquisition, would not, at least in its exact same form, be persuasive today. Whether the hypothesis stands up can only be evaluated by examining case studies of present reactions to past controversies and events—a kind of study that would be best conducted by a historian, or that could be evaluated by looking at a series of such case studies. Such a project will not be attempted here. But still, interpreting what Croce wrote sympathetically, it could well be that it was this sort of hypothesis that he was advocating.

At any rate, whatever should be said about how to interpret Croce's argument as a substantial but controversial historico-philosophical thesis, the basic point needs to be reiterated that just because the conclusion of the argument strongly appears to be false, or is flatly at odds with conventionally accepted views on the Inquisition, it does not necessarily follow that the deliberation-based *ad populum* argument that Croce used to support this conclusion is structurally incorrect or fallacious.

The conclusion that the Inquisition was justified and beneficial carries a high burden of proof, and the deliberation-based type of *ad populum* argument delivers only a low weight of presumption. Thus the argument, certainly the way Copi quotes it (out of context) is a disastrous failure to prove its conclusion. But a weak argument is not necessarily fallacious. An argument that is insufficiently strong to prove a conclusion (especially one that seems to be false) is an argument that ought to be rejected in a critical discussion. But it should not necessarily be rejected on the grounds that it is fallacious.

On the other hand, Croce seems to be his own worst enemy here, even using the word "must" in the conclusion. His argument (especially when taken out of its larger context of use) is eminently susceptible to the charge of fallaciousness it received at the hands of Copi.

But the basic point illustrated by this case is that the standard treatment is misleading, because the examples chosen to illustrate the *ad populum* fallacy are too brief, and have been selectively taken out of a context that, according to the new dialectical theory, should be an important part of the evidence required for evaluation.

2. Public-Opinion Polls and Fallacies

As noted in Chapter 1, much deliberation in business and politics is based on public-opinion polls, and there is a widespread perception that such polls are frequently misleading, or based on dubious assumptions and faulty reasoning, or even that this kind of poll is fallacious.

Despite all the various fallacies and other kinds of errors and shortcomings in public-opinion polls, the thesis that all arguments based on such polls are inherently fallacious is not justified. We have seen that there are certain specific fallacies that are common in the use of public-opinion polls, like the fallacies of hasty generalization involved in using too small a sample, or the fallacy of biased statistics committed when an unrepresentative sample is chosen (Walton 1989, chap. 8; see also Chapter 1). However, these fallacies are generally dealt with by the correct use of mathematical techniques that statisticians have learned to use in their sampling methods.

Scientific polls use sampling procedures where *random samples* are used, that is, where each individual in the group has an equal chance of being selected into the sample, or where some variation on this pattern is used to account for variations in the population that need to be reflected in the sample (Campbell 1974). Scientific popular-opinion polls also compute numerical margins of error indicating the extent to which results can be expected to vary. However, there is a problem here posed by the increasingly common use of unscientific polls, often called "self-selected" opinion polls, or "SLOP" polls (Gooderham 1994). This is the kind of poll the media loves to take to get a gauge of the public pulse, where readers, for example, are asked to tick off a "yes," "no," or "not sure" box in response to a number of questions published in a newspaper or a magazine, and the respondent is then requested to e-mail or fax responses back to the publication. These SLOP polls ignore the probability sampling requirements used in a scientific poll.

From a scientific point of view, the problem with the SLOP poll is that only those interested enough in the issue will spend the time and money to participate in the poll, and therefore, the requirements for the responses to meet the standard of a random sample are not met. So, there is a great likelihood of the results of such a poll being misleading or skewed in a particular direction. As long as one recognizes that a SLOP poll is likely to be biased, and does not meet scientific standards of sampling, there is perhaps no danger in such a poll. However, it may be generally very easy to assume that a SLOP poll either looks like or is a genuine scientific poll—based on correct sampling procedures. Moreover, action taken on the basis of a SLOP poll may be misguided, at best.

According to Gooderham, many people who use SLOP polls defend them on the grounds that no data are better than bad data (D8). This argument is not a good one, however, because bad data can be misleading and deceptive. Also, statisticians object that the public may not be in a good position to tell the difference between a SLOP poll and a scientific poll. This deceptive appearance in a public-opinion poll of being based on scientific evidence when, in fact, the SLOP poll is not, is a good ground for citing cases of SLOP polls as being fallacious instances of the *argumentum ad populum*. However, over and above such particular cases, it would be a mistake to generalize and say that all public-opinion polls are instances of the *ad populum* fallacy. This kind of evaluation would be a mistake. Indeed, it would a kind of hasty generalization itself, because some polls are based on proper use of statistical methods.

There is a subtlety in the way polls are presented that suggests another problem. Even though public-opinion polls conducted by statisticians using proper scientific methods do deal well with criticisms that they commit technical inductive fallacies, like the fallacy of biased statistics or the fallacy of too small a sample, the scientific precision suggested by such polls through their use of numerical margins of error, is misleading. The suggestion conveyed is that, because proper statistical methods of collecting data have been used, that the poll is extremely accurate in measuring public opinion, and that this accuracy can be quantified to a precise numerical degree. However, as we noted in Chapter 1, such polls have to be based on questions that are asked in natural language, using terms that have emotional connotations and colorings that vary from respondent to respondent. The margin of error implicit in this kind of variance would be very difficult or perhaps even impossible to measure using some method of precise scientific calculation. So we could argue that public-opinion polls of the kind that are so familiar, even if they use proper statistical methods, tend to be inherently misleading in suggesting an accuracy that, in many cases, cannot be justified or is even justifiable.

The problems studied in Chapter 1 arose from the fact that political policies, rules and laws are based on popular opinion in a democratic system of government, so that knowing what the popular opinion is, on a particular issue, is an important source of power. But popular opinion, by its very nature, is contradictory, difficult to determine, and can change very rapidly as new information becomes known to the public. But because popular opinion is the source of power for politicians and their advisers, it is very tempting for them to try to manipulate it, by various means. And the mechanisms for doing this have, in recent years, become available, in the form of public-opinion polls. These polls, now widely accepted and trusted by the public, are being exploited by politicians and other ideologues, to promote their own special interests and ideologies. Through the use of push polling techniques, the pollsters are actually using the polls to attempt to persuade the public to accept a particular conclusion, and thereby to encourage the public to take part in the construction of and even to take part in manipulating it in a certain direction.

The deceptiveness in these techniques is accomplished by the appearance of scientific accuracy, while concealing the use of biased questions that contain untested and potentially significant response effects due to question wording. Not only is the premise of supposed public opinion false or unproven, but the inference that the announcement of such a finding suggests, to the effect of implying "This is the way things should be done now" is misleading and manipulative.

Yet, even on these grounds, we should stop somewhere short of declaring that all public-opinion polls are inherently fallacious *ad populum* arguments.

Each case should be looked at on its merits, and an analysis of the case depends not only on the nature of the public-opinion premise, and what claim is made in that premise, but on the methodology used to draw an inference from that premise to a conclusion. Moreover, the evaluation of each case needs to take into account what the particular conclusion is. Clearly, public-opinion polls are used in marketing and in politics, especially in election campaigns, in such a way that they do provide some sort of intelligent basis that the political party or the advertiser can act on, even if the poll is only regarded as giving a result that is highly subject to variance, and that may represent only a snapshot of public opinion at a particular point in time. Such polls are widely used, and do appear to be quite useful for the purposes they are designed to fulfill, and, as long as the conclusions drawn from them are not exaggerated, they can be valuable clues or sources of advice on how to proceed with advertising or election campaigns.

The approach in this book would be to say that the conclusion drawn from such a public-opinion poll should not be regarded as a knowledge-based argument but should only be regarded as a presumptive conclusion that is drawn as a tentative and defeasible basis for action in the course of a sequence of deliberations. So, for example, in an election, if one side, on the basis of a public-opinion poll, appears to be winning at some particular point, even though this finding may not be definitive and may be highly subject to change, nevertheless, it can give the party who conducted the poll some basis for making future strategic decisions on what sort of arguments to put forward to persuade the public or some electorate to move more towards their side of the debate. Here, Yankelovich's notion of seeing the public-opinion poll in a context of practical reasoning used in a deliberation that has a number of points of development in a larger sequence seems to be a very wise approach to getting a perspective on how to deal with the poll-based *ad populum* argument.

In evaluating argumentation based on public-opinion polls, as with all *ad populum* arguments, an important step is to distinguish between the task of evaluating whether the premise has been adequately justified, and the task of determining whether the conclusion indicated follows by inference from that premise or not. With respect to the first task, questions of how the data were collected (if any were collected) and processed, according to statistical methods, are the key to evaluation. Several statistical fallacies, of the kind cited above, are important to consider here. The fallacy of biased question is also an important consideration. But it is with respect to the second task that the method of evaluation of the new dialectical theory can be brought to bear, to assess the argument as having one of the inference structures corresponding to the argumentation schemes for the *argumentum ad populum*.

Often it is not just the poll itself, or its supposed findings that are the most problematic factor. The problem is one of which conclusion has been drawn from the poll, and whether that conclusion can be justified as an *ad populum* inference from the given premise. It is on these questions that the new dialectical theory can be brought to bear, to judge whether the argument based on a supposed finding of public opinion has been correctly used in a type of dialogue like a deliberation or not.

So while public-opinion polls are often associated with manipulative techniques and fallacies—and statistical fallacies, as well as question-asking fallacies, in particular—one must be careful not to leap to the conclusion that public-opinion polls are inherently fallacious, on the grounds that an *ad populum* fallacy has been committed in every case where public opinion has been appealed to. As noted in Chapter 1, there is a real danger that the public loss of trust in the polls may lead to a rejection of the validity of polling altogether, and an increased unwillingness to participate in public-opinion polls.

3. *Ad Populum* Appeals in Commercial Ads

It is naive to judge the *ad populum* arguments used in commercial ads on the grounds that the producers of the ads are "hucksters" and "ballyhoo artists." Supporting an evaluation of these ads as being instances of the *ad populum* by blaming the producers or sponsors of the ads is a simplistic approach. The purpose of the ads is not to present rational arguments, or to convince the viewer that some proposition is true by offering relevant and sufficient evidence to prove it. And the *ad populum* argument used in such an ad should not be evaluated as fallacious or irrelevant, exclusively on the grounds that it fails to fulfill such a burden of proof.

It is important to recognize the *ad populum* arguments used in these ads as distinctive and recognizable and powerful types of arguments that can be, and are commonly used to influence consumers. Although we should be careful about leaping to dismiss these *ad populum* arguments as inherently fallacious, as used in ads, they are well worth studying, identifying, analyzing and evaluating, using dialectical models.

Ideally, in a free market economy, a consumer should engage in informed and intelligent deliberation on which products to buy, evaluating the good and not-so-good features of each competing product in line with the use for that product she has in her personal life. But subjective and emotional factors are inevitably involved in such decisions, because if a product is aesthetically or emotionally appealing or satisfying to a buyer, she may indeed like using that product more, and so for her, it could be a better choice. Even in a rational deliberation on which competing product to buy, there may be subjective and aesthetic factors involved, that should not be dismissed as irrelevant or irrational.

However, those who are in the business of crafting commercial ads can exploit the emotional aspect of these subjective preferences, if viewers of their ads make the mistake of giving an undue weight to the appeals in them, over practical considerations that should properly also play a role in the decision to buy a product, if that decision is to be based on informed and intelligent deliberation. If the viewers can be strongly influenced in favor of a product by appeals to snobbery or vanity that depict a personal fantasy by "glamorizing" the product, then to compete, manufacturers will use such ads, on the grounds that they sell more product.

If consumers become better educated about the merits of the products they buy, or do not buy, and base their decisions more on an intelligent deliberation, and less on *ad populum* appeals to glamorization of the product using "daydreams" and "delusions of grandeur," then the commercials will inevitably reflect this shift. In a free-market economy, a shift to this more practical type of commercial will occur, because the more practical type of commercial that appeals to the kind of considerations useful in a rational deliberation will sell more product to the kind of consumer who makes decisions on this more practical basis. Indeed, from time to time, we see evidence of such a shift in commercials that cite specific practical advantages of their product over those of the competitors.

In evaluating *ad populum* arguments used in commercial ads from a dialectical viewpoint, therefore, we need to look at them in relation to the perspective of the viewer or respondent who may go on to base her decision to buy a product or not on deliberation where the argument in the ad may be one factor in a larger body of evidence used to come to a conclusion. If the viewer goes ahead and buys the product, based exclusively or mostly on the *ad populum* appeal to trendiness, snobbery, or vanity conveyed in an ad for the product, without taking into account available relevant evidence on the various features of the product (compared to alternatives), then that could be a too hasty leap to a conclusion of a kind that could be called faulty, or even fallacious, in the context of a deliberation framework of dialogue.

But here it is not exclusively the "huckster" or "ballyhoo artist" that is at fault. Nor should this blame or condemnation of the advertiser be thought sufficient as a basis to judge a particular case of the use of an *ad populum* as fallacious. Here, both parties have, as it were, in a free-market economy, collaborated in a sequence of moves in argumentation that has not led to a high quality of practical reasoning in a deliberation. The manufacturer or advertiser laid a trap, knowing or thinking the consumer to be vulnerable. And he, instead of deliberating carefully and using practical reasoning to seek out a prudent course of action, fell into the trap (perhaps quite willingly).

In short, whether the *ad populum* appeals to vanity, snobbery, and so forth, used in commercial ads are relevant or not, should be judged, according to the new dialectic, in light of what type of communicative message the ad is supposed to be. Much more thought needs to be put into investigating this difficult and complex question. The task of evaluating argumentation used in commercial speech by normative dialectical models is an important new area of research that has been neglected or ignored for too long.

4. Common-Folks Appeals and Relevance

The common-folks type of *ad populum* appeal could be evaluated as fallacious on the grounds that an emotional appeal to popular sentiments of this kind is an irrelevant substitute for evidence of the kind required to support a conclusion being debated. For example, Schipper and Schuh rule that an argument is said to commit the fallacy of appeal to the crowd when its premises "contain an appeal to popular attitudes or feelings in order to support the truth of some unrelated conclusion" (1959, 34). And of course, it is possible that an *ad populum* argument based on a premise containing a common-folks appeal could be dialectically irrelevant in relation to a dialogue, but used in such a way that its irrelevance is disguised by a shift to a different type of dialogue. In such a case, it would be justified to evaluate the case as one where a common-folks type of *ad populum* has been committed.

But it has proved harder than one might think to find cases where a charge of committing a common-folks *ad populum* fallacy of this kind can be definitely and provably pinned down.[2] Of course, such common-folks appeals are commonly used by politicians in election campaigns and political debates, but care is needed in evaluating such arguments.

2. Hamblin (1970) frequently cites the problem of "pinning down" a claim that an argument in a real case is an instance of the committing of one of the traditional fallacies.

A classic case of the common-folks subtype of *argumentum ad populum*, presented in Walton (1992b, 82–87), arose from the leadership debate televised in Canada in October 1988, just before that federal election. The topic of the debate was the Free Trade Agreement, and the two speakers were Mr. Mulroney, the head of the Conservative Party, and Mr. Turner, the head of the Liberal Party. At one point in his speech, Mr. Mulroney appeared to become somewhat emotional, and said that his father, fifty-five years ago, had gone as a laborer with hundreds of other Canadians, "and with their own hands, in Northwestern Quebec, built a little town, and schools and churches." This powerfully evocative common-folks *ad populum* appeal could not be ignored by Mr. Turner, who subsequently launched into his own version of the common-folks appeal, stating that his mother was a miner's daughter in British Columbia. Neither of these *ad populum* arguments had anything to do with the subject of the debate—that is, the Free Trade Agreement that was currently being negotiated—but as pre-election televised appeals, both were quite popular. No doubt, Mr. Mulroney's common-folks appeal was recommended to him by his media advisers as something that he should include in his speech. Recognizing the rhetorical power of this kind of *ad populum* move, Mr. Turner, who had no doubt also been carefully advised on such matters by his strategists, felt constrained to launch an equally colorful, common-folks appeal to match Mr. Mulroney's.

In this context, should these uses of the common-folks type of appeal be rejected as fallacies of relevance, since, as noted above, neither appeal had much if anything to do with the topic of the debate? It is noted, however, in Walton (1992b, 86) that the context of this dialogue was also that of a leadership debate where each of the participants recognized that part of his rhetorical goal was to demonstrate to the public that he would be a good person to be elected as leader of the government party, who would become Prime Minister. Questions of character and personal values are regarded rightly as relevant to election argumentation in this broader framework of the dialogue. It is inevitably a part of the democratic system that voters will elect candidates at least partly based on their trust and on their evaluation of the character of the candidate as well as on factors related to the issues and questions of where the candidates stand on particular issues. As argued in Walton (1992b, 86), ethics and questions of personal character are therefore, at least to a reasonable degree, relevant in this context of political debate. Moreover, as we have noted earlier, a political speaker will try to establish empathy with the audience he is addressing, and, even more broadly speaking, in any kind of persuasion dialogue, one of the most important sources for an arguer to select adequate premises from is the commitment store of the respondent. Hence, in evaluating common-folks appeal *ad populum* arguments in political debates, care needs to be taken not to rush to judgment in declaring this type of argument fallacious simply on grounds that such a move is irrelevant to the issue that the candidates are supposed to be arguing about.

Of course, as far as having a critical discussion on the Free Trade Agreement was concerned, the little interlude of the common-folks *ad populum* argument exchange between Mr. Turner and Mr. Mulroney could rightly be evaluated as irrelevant. But it is a logical leap from this reasonable evaluation of irrelevance to the conclusion that the *ad populum* argument was fallacious. For there is an extra assumption needed to draw this inference, namely, the proposition that Mr. Mulroney and Mr. Turner were supposed to be engaging in a pure critical discussion of the Free Trade Agreement. Certainly they were supposed to be engaged in a televised political debate on the Free Trade Agreement. But was this debate supposed to be limited purely to a critical discussion of this issue? Is any shift to declarations of personal commitments, deeply held family values, and common-folks sentiments an illicit shift to a different type of dialogue that should be evaluated as irrelevant, and therefore fallacious?

As argued above, this sort of evaluation of televised debate prior to an election is questionable in a democratic political system, even if one can certainly appreciate the reasoning that lies behind it. In fact, political debate is very much a mixed type of dialogue that contains an element of deliberation and negotiation, as well as elements of eristic dialogue and party politics of an adversarial sort. Surely it would be naive, and generally inappropriate, to evaluate political debate purely from the normative standpoint of a critical discussion. To do so would imply that most common political discourse of the kind we are so familiar with in democratic countries falls ludicrously short of our standard of reasoned argumentation.

Once again then, caution is needed in evaluating *ad populum* arguments that have generally been dismissed as fallacious by the standard treatment. Too often these judgments have been based on contextual assumptions that are highly questionable.

5. Two Explanations of the Fallacy

So far then, the dialectical theory has shown that the evaluations of *ad populum* arguments given in the standard treatment accounts are inadequate, and should be taken with a grain of salt. What needs to be done next then is to examine those cases in which the *ad populum* should justifiably be evaluated as fallacious, and inquire into the grounds for such justifications.

Several theories have already been proposed in the literature. One compelling theory is that of Freeman.

> Appeals to popularity are basically hasty conclusion fallacies. The data concerning the popularity of the belief are simply not sufficient to warrant accepting the belief. The logical error in an appeal to popularity lies in its inflating the value of popularity as evidence. (1995, 272)

Freeman's theory is also based on the concept of presumptive reasoning—*ad populum* arguments can be reasonable as presumptive arguments, on this theory. But they can also become fallacious when they are pressed ahead too strongly to bear the weight of presumption that they should properly be judged to have. The *ad populum* fallacy, according to this explanation, is a species of hasty conclusion, or leaping too quickly to a conclusion that is unwarranted.

A different theory of the *ad populum* has been given in Walton (1992b, 102).

> The *argumentum ad populum* is most effective as a technique of argumentation establishing a link—an identification or social alignment—between the commitments of the speaker and the audience. The speaker may not be able to prove all the premises needed to make a case in favor of a proposal put before a particular audience, and such an exhaustive approach to fulfilling the burden of proof may be neither necessary nor effective. If, instead, the speaker can get the audience to go ahead on the presumption that their commitments on the issue are pretty much the same as those of the speaker, he or she can cover a lot of ground in argumentation quickly. The message is "Trust me; I'm one of you." If this message can be effectively put in place by a speaker, it can obviate the need for answering a lot of critical questions that otherwise might be raised by the audience before granting their approval of a proposal.

This theory of the *ad populum* fallacy is even more deeply dialectical in nature. The *ad populum* argument, although it can be reasonable in some cases, becomes fallacious when used to pre-empt or block off the asking of critical questions of a kind that would be appropriate when, say the *ad populum* argument has been used in a case where the participants are supposed to be engaged in an open-minded persuasion dialogue. This fallacious way of using the *ad populum* argument is a device to shield off the need to fulfill a burden of proof—an obligation that is especially important in a persuasion dialogue. According to this theory, the fallacy is explained dialectically as a shift from an open type of persuasion dialogue to a closed type of eristic or advocacy dialogue (negotiation) where burden of proof to support a claim by relevant, objective evidence is of less importance.

By reconsidering some of the previous case studies, it will be shown next that both these theories can be justified. Hence it will be concluded that there is no single *ad populum* fallacy, or at least no single way to evaluate cases where this fallacy has been committed.

Let us start with Freeman's theory, as it is the easier of the two to explain and clarify. Although it is based on the theory of presumptive reasoning, a deeper analysis of how this theory can be built into a usable method of judging allegations of fallaciousness in specific cases requires that the method have a dialectical component as well.

After section 6, the analysis will move toward the other theory, which is explicitly dialectical in nature, and is the more difficult of the two to work into a simple and easy-to-use method of evaluating individual cases. Our study of this theory in sections 7 and 8 takes us into the areas of evaluating arguments for dialectical bias, of assessing styles of rhetoric used in a particular case, and of evaluating cases where there has been a dialectical shift. The evidence required to evaluate such cases is deeply dialectical and contextual in nature.

6. Hastily Jumping to a Conclusion

Generally, the *ad populum* argument is a weak argument, when it is reasonable, as opposed to being fallacious, as noted many times before. In such cases, the function of the ad populum argument is to carry some weight as one consideration with a larger evidential picture. In a balance of considerations situation, the *ad populum* can shift the burden of proof one way or the other, even though it (by itself) is not a very strong argument (Chapter 4, section 7). As one small part of a larger body of considerations in a dialogue, the *ad populum* can be an important argument if used at the opportune moment to shift a weight of presumption from one side to the other in a dialogue. In such cases, the *ad populum* argument can be used in such a way that it is fair to evaluate it as a fallacy, even where it is a relevant argument in the dialogue.

Case 2.1, where the arguer runs out to buy a copy of Gore Vidal's new book, reasoning from the premise that this book has been at the top of the best-seller lists for ten weeks, is a use of the *ad populum* in a deliberation. Presumptive arguments like this one that are weak by themselves, but can have a place in a larger body of relevant evidence on what to do in a given situation, can commonly be used in a deliberation. Such arguments, individually, may only carry a small weight, but when you put them all together in a large body of evidence, each small argument may have a relevant place in the evidence used to arrive at a decision on how to proceed. But no single piece of evidence, by itself, would be sufficient to derive the final conclusion of the deliberation.

The fallacy in Case 2.1 is the arguer's hastily jumping to the conclusion that he ought to go out and buy a copy of Vidal's book, basing this conclusion exclusively on the *ad populum* premise that this book has been at the top of the best-seller lists for ten weeks. This premise certainly implies the conclusion that Vidal's book is popular. But can we get to the conclusion that this particular person ought to, therefore, buy the book? As suggested in Chapter 2, section 4, this argument has some merit, but it is far from conclusive, because it overlooks a host of other relevant considerations that should also be taken into account in this kind of deliberation.

The fallacy in this case then, can be described as an inflation of this weak *ad populum* argument by giving it much more weight than it really should get in a balanced, informed and thoughtful deliberation on whether it is a good idea for this person to buy this book or not. Assuming that many other factors ought to be taken into account in an intelligent deliberation that comes to a prudent and well thought out decision, the argument in this particular case falls short of that standard of use in this type of dialogue. Evaluation of the case in this way, at any rate presumes (as seems appropriate from what Damer tells us about the context of the case), that the arguer went ahead and jumped to the conclusion to buy the book without considering any of the other relevant factors.

The fallacy in this particular case is interesting because (a) it occurs in a deliberation-type of dialogue rather than in a critical discussion or persuasion-type of dialogue, and (b) it is not a failure of relevance. Instead, the fallacy is a relevant *ad populum* argument that is given too much weight in the dialogue. It is more of an error-of-reasoning type of *ad populum* fallacy than a case of the use of this type of argument as a means for one party in a dialogue to deceptively trap or mislead the other party.

An interesting and somewhat comparable kind of case broadcast on the television series, *Marketplace* (CBC television network), March 5, 1996.

Case 9.1: An elderly couple on vacation in Hawaii arrived at a site where you could take a helicopter tour to get an aerial view of the island. They had some doubts about the safety of the tourist helicopter rides, but reasoned, "They must be safe, because everybody's doing it." In the ensuing crash, the wife died and the husband survived.

What was the basis of this *ad populum* inference? Presumably, the couple's conclusion was based on the assumption that there must be safety procedures in place, because the helicopter tours are such a widely established practice. As the *Marketplace* program indicated, it was true that these helicopter tours were popular, and were widely established in many locations other than Hawaii. However, their safety record was, in fact, extremely poor, and there had been many prior accidents with the helicopter tours on these sites.

Of course, in this case, the couple were not aware of the poor safety record of these tours, and it is easy to be wise in hindsight. But even so, where risk to life is involved, prudent deliberation might suggest, in the absence of knowledge, taking a cautious approach sometimes called tutiorism, or erring on the safe side (Walton 1996a, 210).

Here then is a case where appearances were misleading. The observed fact that "everybody's doing it" made the ride appear safe, licensing a plausible but weak shift in support of the *ad populum* argument in favor of taking the ride. In fact, however, the other evidence affecting the balance of considerations, but not known to the tourists, shifted a weight toward the other side of the deliberation. As in the previous case, however, the word "must" in the conclusion "must be safe" suggests an inappropriately strong inference to the conclusion that could be judged fallacious in the context of the deliberation in the case.

7. Evaluating the Golden Rule Case

The problem in Case 2.3, the Golden Rule case, is that from the premise "Everyone accepts the Golden Rule in some form or other," the strong conclusion is drawn "Therefore, it is an undeniably sound moral principle." The basic reason that the *ad populum* argument is judged to be fallacious in this case is the word "undeniably" in the conclusion. This strong form of conclusion is not supported by the inference drawn from a premise based on popular acceptance. The fallacy in this case seems to be an instance of jumping too hastily to a conclusion on the basis of an argument that is too weak to support such a strongly asserted conclusion. However, the fallacy goes a little deeper then this account suggests. From the perspective of the new dialectical theory, one needs to take the context of dialogue into account in evaluating the argument. The problem is that we are not given any information on what the context is.

Since Case 2.3 was meant to be used as an exercise in a college logic course, it might be presumed that the students who have been confronted with this exercise over the years might have in mind the critical discussion of the Golden Rule in an ethics class or seminar, as the context in which one would be expected to judge the argument in this case. In such a context, students are supposed to be learning the ability to critically question conventional views and cultural values they may have previously taken for granted, or not thought very deeply about. The issue in such a critical discussion in an ethics seminar would be whether the Golden Rule, or any other popularly accepted rule of conduct, ought to be accepted as an ethical principle that can be justified by good reasons. In this context of dialogue, how should we judge the *ad populum* argument based on the premise that everyone accepts the Golden Rule in some form or other?

In an ethics seminar discussion, the premise that everyone accepts the Golden Rule in some form or other could be taken as an endoxic premise (see Chapter 5, section 3) that would license the inference in the discussion that the Golden Rule ought to be taken seriously as an ethical principle that may be controversial in some respects, in spite of (and even because of) its widespread acceptance among those who have tried to articulate ethical principles or presumptions that people accept, act on, and recognize. Therefore, to claim that the Golden Rule should have some provisional standing as a presumption, as an endoxic premise on which to base further discussion, in the kind of persuasion dialogue that one would engage in as a participant in an ethics seminar, seems quite reasonable, from a dialectical point of view.

In contrast, however, to claim that the Golden Rule is "undeniably" true, on this *ad populum* basis, suggests an unwillingness to consider critical questions, or discuss the issue any further, that would be grounds for evaluating the argument as inappropriate, or even fallacious in the context sketched out above.

The problem is that in Case 2.3 no context of dialogue based on actual textual evidence is provided to help in evaluating the *ad populum* argument used in the case. So, any evaluations, such as the ones considered above, have to remain hypothetical. But given the use of this case as an exercise in a college logic textbook, a certain context of dialogue, like the one sketched out above, would be very plausible for the intended readers of the book to consider as a natural conversational use of the *ad populum* argument. In this context, the fallacy is not so much that of jumping to a hasty conclusion, as one of using the *ad populum* argument in such a way that it inappropriately closes off the continuing of a persuasion dialogue.

8. Divisive Rhetoric in Mob-Appeal Arguments

As observed many times in commenting on cases, the mob-appeal type of *ad populum* is not easy to evaluate, because it is a composite of several subtypes of *ad populum* argument, and because it is characterized as an argument by a particular rhetorical mode of presentation. Basically, the mob-appeal subtype is a use of argument from commitment, where the speaker targets his argumentation to a bias that the audience has (Chapter 4, section 7). Often this bias represents a commitment that is a bond joining the speaker to the audience as a group, and her speech appeals to the solidarity of the group, and to the enthusiasm evoked by reminding the audience of the shared interests of the group, and their commitment to a common cause.

As observed many times above, and particularly in the analysis of Case 8.1, there need be nothing inherently illogical or fallacious with an arguer's using argument from commitment to appeal to the bias of an audience. Indeed, such a biased or one-sided use of advocacy arguments is quite normal in partisan argumentation, of the kind that would normally be used to try to get an audience to take action for a cause or interest that is being supported. One would expect this kind of rhetoric to be used, for example, by a union leader who is calling for strike action in a speech before a union hall filled with members of a union who have assembled to express their solidarity for the cause.

As explained in the analysis of Case 2.6, there need be nothing fallacious about appealing to the given bias of an audience in this kind of rhetoric, if it is clear at the outset that the purpose of the speech is to rouse the assembled group to action by appealing to their common interests and their solidarity as a group who share certain commitments. However, care must be taken in evaluating such cases, because the mob-appeal type of rhetoric does have certain special characteristics that do make its use tend to be counterproductive in the balanced deliberation or persuasion-types of dialogue. From the viewpoints of either of these types of dialogue, the argumentation in a mob-appeal *ad populum* case would fall short of the conversational requirements set by the maxims appropriate for collaborative dialogues of these types (see Chapter 6).

Another important component of the mob-appeal *ad populum* is the use of the rhetoric of belonging, where a division is postulated between those who belong to the group, and the others—the "opponents" or "outsiders" who are portrayed in confrontational and negative terms. The rhetoric-of-belonging type of *ad populum* argument is used to imply to a member of the audience that if he fails to bond with the group by accepting the argument of the speaker, he will be automatically classed in the outsider group.

The dialectical context frequently associated with the use of the rhetoric-of-belonging type of argument can be described as a divisive rhetoric that divides the world into members of the group and "outsiders," who are defined as those opposed to the aims and interests of the group. This type of rhetoric was evident in Case 2.9, in the speech attributed to Westbook Pegler, in which he portrayed Mayor LaGuardia as a "very noisy member of the crowd known as the labor movement," "racketeers" who are said in the speech to be "parasites," "thieves" and "bread robbers." This use of negative language to characterize a stigmatized, oppressor group is highly characteristic of divisive rhetoric, of a type that can be classified as a species of eristic dialogue. The opposite kind of divisive rhetoric (going from right to left, politically) is evident in Case 3.6, where those who are not in the group at a political rally are described as "outside groups" who are "vested interests" in "big business." Damer (1980), cites the arousing of popular feelings against groups like "labor unions, certain religious or political associations, homosexuals, or even radical college students" as the tools of manipulation of this kind of appeal. What is generally characteristic is the division between the speaker and the audience on one side, and the opposed group, or "outsiders" whose commitments are described in highly negative language.

The implication of this divisive rhetoric, characteristic of cases of the mob-appeal argument is: If you're not for us, you're against us. It is, in fact, the closed, highly adversarial argumentation characteristic of eristic dialogue. The group has a grudge or complaint that it has been "victimized" by those outside the group, who are opposed to the interests and aims of the group, and therefore a "fight" or "crusade" against the actions of the victimizers is being advocated in the speaker's rhetoric.

Once again, it needs to be repeated that the eristic dialogue characteristic of the mob-appeal type of *ad populum* is not inherently fallacious. But divisive rhetoric of this type runs counter to the aims of persuasion dialogue and deliberation. What is important is to recognize this type of rhetoric as a species of eristic dialogue, and to be alert to the possibilities of illicit and deceptive dialectical shifts. If a speaker using an *ad populum* appeal is engaging in this eristic type of dialogue, but purports to be engaged in balanced deliberation, or in an open-minded persuasion dialogue, then the speaker's argument can justifiably be evaluated as a fallacious *ad populum* argument. But even if no fallacy is committed in a given case it is important to be able to recognize and identify this divisive type of rhetoric.

9. Three Types of *Ad Populum* Fallacy

Of the two main kinds of *ad populum* fallacy then, the divisive rhetoric fallacy built into the mob-appeal subtype of *ad populum* fallacy is generally more difficult to analyze and evaluate than the hasty conclusion fallacy. The latter depends on an analysis of a text of discourse in a given case to identify dialectical bias, and to judge whether this bias is of the harmful sort or not. Also, evaluation of this type of case requires the identification of a dialectical shift from one type of dialogue to another. This type of evaluation is deeply dialectical in nature, and requires a comprehensive analysis of the text of discourse and the context of dialogue in a given case.

In short, then, the *ad populum* is not a single fallacy. Two different kinds of pitfalls of argument characteristic of the committing of the ad populum can be found in different cases. We can still argue, and would contend, that *ad populum* should be retained as the name of a type of argument that can be fallacious in some cases. But what has been discovered is that the fallacy has a binary aspect, and that there is not just one single way in which it can be committed.

It should be added that even though the textbooks frequently judge *ad populum* arguments to be fallacious on grounds of irrelevance in cases where such an evaluation is not appropriate, or is fully enough justified, there are cases where the fallacy should be seen as a failure of dialectical relevance. In fact it is just such a failure that is one key aspect of the mob-appeal subtype, when it is fallacious. In such a case, part of the explanation of the fallacy is a dialectical shift. And this kind of case is precisely one where an *ad populum* appeal, although it would be relevant in a group negotiation or eristic dialogue is not dialectically relevant if the context is supposed to be that of a deliberation or persuasion dialogue.

So in all, there can be three different useful explanations or theoretical accounts given of why the *ad populum* argument is fallacious (in those cases where it really is fallacious). All three fallacies have a common root, and in practice they can be intertwined. But each represents a theoretically distinct basis for supporting the evaluation of a case as an instance where the *ad populum* fallacy has been committed.

Section 10 gives a summary of the general method of evaluation based on the new dialectical theory of the *ad populum*, incorporating the judgment of fallaciousness into the process.

10. Evaluation for Fallaciousness

The main goal of the method of evaluation set out in Chapter 8 is to judge in a particular case whether an *ad populum* is weak or strong, as a use of presumptive reasoning for some purpose in a goal-directed type of conversational exchange. Only then, according to the new dialectical theory, should an evaluation go to the next stage of considering whether an *ad populum* argument is so bad, from a dialectical point of view, that it should be concluded that an *ad populum* fallacy has been committed in that case. According to the theory presented in Walton (1995), a fallacy is not just any blunder or error in argument, or any weak argument—one that has been insufficiently supported. A fallacy is a systematic, underlying error of a baptizable type, or deceptive tactic of argumentation to try to illicitly get the best of a speech partner in dialogue that runs counter to the goals of the type of dialogue the argument is supposed to be a part of. Thus the new dialectical theory is definitely at odds with the traditional viewpoint on fallacies reflected in the standard treatment of the textbooks.

In the standard treatment, a given *ad populum* argument is presumed to be fallacious. However, if it is recognized that there could be reasonable (nonfallacious) *ad populum* arguments, then a division would be permitted between the fallacious cases and the nonfallacious cases.

In persuasion dialogue, according to the new dialectical theory, endoxic premises can be used in arguments to draw conclusions on how to proceed, or what to accept, on a presumptive basis. But such a presumptive argument is open to critical questioning, and it is defeasible—meaning that it may need to be given up (retracted) if new evidence comes into the dialogue that goes against it with sufficient strength to justify refutation. Hence, *ad populum* arguments can be justified as reasonable and useful in a persuasion dialogue generally. They are normatively justified by the maxim of nondisputativeness as presumptive arguments that make a critical discussion more realistically interesting, and representative of controversial issues that really matter, by bringing in premises based on views that are popularly accepted.

According to the new dialectic then, evaluating an *ad populum* argument is quite a bit more complex than the traditional viewpoint presumed. According to the new dialectical approach, an *ad populum* argument in a given case needs to be identified, analyzed and evaluated as presumptively weak or strong, depending on how it was used at some particular stage of a dialogue. Only then should the evaluation go to a next stage of assessment to judge whether the argument is so badly off that it can be called fallacious.

Prior to an evaluation of any case, an analysis of the text of discourse is needed, to determine the context of dialogue in which the argument was supposedly used. Also, prior to evaluation, identification of the argument is needed, to define what the premises and the conclusion of the argument are, to see whether, in fact, it fits the definition of an *ad populum* argument. An important part of the identification procedure is to classify the subtype of *ad populum* argument involved, and then look to the form for this type of argument (among the various argumentation schemes) to see what requirements are involved in the sense of what kinds of premises need to be supported to make the argument carry weight or be plausible. Then, finally, one can proceed to the evaluation stage. At this stage, the procedure is to evaluate the argument by asking what critical questions are appropriate for this type of argument and then to look to see whether, in fact, the argument has been expressed in context in such a way that it leaves avenues open for the raising of these critical questions. Moreover, in this phase of evaluation, one should make an assessment of the case to see what evidence (if any) has been put forward by the proponent of the argument, in the prior context of dialogue, that would serve as a basis for answering one or more of these appropriate critical questions.

An *ad populum* argument in a given case can be evaluated as weak or strong, to the degree that it provides evidence that would give some more or less adequate answers to the appropriate critical questions. If it answers all the critical questions and it gives evidence of a kind that is appropriate and also very strong in replying to these critical questions, then the *ad populum* argument should be judged presumptively strong. If it fails to answer any one of these critical questions, it could be judged as weak in that particular respect. If it does not give evidence to answer any of the critical questions, yet meets the requirements for the appropriate form of the *ad populum* argument, it could be judged as a weak subtype of *ad populum* argument that gives some weight in the dialogue to the proponent's argument, in the sense that it shifts over the burden to the respondent to ask the appropriate critical questions, if the respondent wants to be skeptical or raise doubts about the argument. Such an *ad populum* argument should only be judged fallacious if (1) it is too weak to support the given conclusion, and overlooks other relevant evidence that should also be weighed into the balance of considerations, or (2) if it is not dialectically relevant with respect to the type of conversational exchange it is supposed to be part of, yet appears to be relevant, because of an illicit, disguised dialectical shift, or (3) the argument has been put forward in a way that puts too much pressure on the respondent's capability for meaningfully raising appropriate critical questions in the type of dialogue the participants are supposed to be taking part is. With respect to the third kind of *ad populum* fallacy, evidence of an illicit shift from the type of dialogue requiring openness, like a critical discussion, to a closed-minded attitude, as, say in an eristic dialogue, can be an important factor in determining whether the argument is fallacious.

A fallacious *ad populum* of the third type is an argument that has been put forward in such a manner that it is used as a deceptive tactic used to try to pre-empt the asking of appropriate critical questions by the respondent as shown by the evidence in the context of dialogue in the given case. A fallacious *ad populum* argument of this type is more than just a weak or insufficiently supported *ad populum* argument. It is an *ad populum* argument that trades on deception to shift the burden of proof inappropriately or bring in irrelevant considerations that cloud the issue in a way designed to prevent the respondent from replying appropriately by raising the appropriate critical questions or making other kinds of moves that would be reasonable criticisms of the original *ad populum* argument. This fallacious type of *ad populum* argument is a way of trying to get a cheap or quick victory without doing the work of properly supporting the argument and replying to the appropriate critical questions that need to be answered in order to make the argument stronger, or to make it meet reasonable requirements, so that it should be given some plausible weight in a dialogue.

BIBLIOGRAPHY

Aquinas, Thomas. 1970. "Psychology of Human Acts," *Summa Theologiae*, vol. 17, trans. Thomas Gilby. New York: McGraw-Hill. Blackfriars edition.
Aristotle. 1928. *The Works of Aristotle Translated into English*, ed. W. D. Ross. Oxford: Oxford University Press.
———. 1928. *On Sophistical Refutations*, trans. E. S. Forster. Cambridge, Mass.: Harvard University Press. Loeb Library edition.
———. 1937. *The Art of Rhetoric*, trans. John H. Freese. Cambridge, Mass.: Harvard University Press. Loeb Library edition.
Arnauld, Antoine. 1964. *The Art of Thinking* (1662), trans. James Dickoff and Patricia James. New York: Bobbs-Merrill.
Atherton, Catherine. 1993. *The Stoics on Ambiguity*. Cambridge: Cambridge University Press.
Atlas, Jay David, and Stephen C. Levinson. 1981. "It-Clefts, Informativeness, and Logical Form." In *Radical Pragmatics*, ed. Peter Cole, 1–61. New York: Academic Press.
Barnes, Jonathan. 1980. "Aristotle and the Method of Ethics." *Revue Internationale de Philosophie* 34: 490–511.
Beardsley, Monroe C. 1950. *Practical Logic*. New York: Prentice-Hall.
Begley, Sharon, Howard Fineman, and Vernon Church. 1992. "The Science of Polling." *Newsweek*, September 28, pp. 38–39.
Bernard, L. L. 1926. *An Introduction to Social Psychology*. New York: Henry Holt and Co.
Billig, Michael. 1987. *Arguing and Thinking*. New York: Cambridge University Press.
Blair, J. Anthony. 1988. "What Is Bias?" In *Selected Issues in Logic and Communication*, ed. Trudy Govier, 93–103. Belmont, Calif.: Wadsworth.
Blair, J. Anthony, and Ralph H. Johnson. 1987. "Argumentation As Dialectical." *Argumentation* 1: 41–56.
Blyth, John W. 1957. *A Modern Introduction to Logic*. Boston: Houghton Mifflin.

Boethius. 1978. *De Topicis Differentiis* (before 523 A.D.), trans. Eleonore Stump. Ithaca: Cornell University Press.
Byerly, Henry C. 1973. *A Primer of Logic.* New York: Harper and Row.
Byrne, Edward F. 1968. *Probability and Opinion: A Study in the Medieval Presuppositions of Post-Medieval Theories of Probability.* The Hague: Martinus Nijhoff.
CBS News, *60 Minutes.* 1993. "Readin', Writin' and Commercials." Vol. 26, no. 4, October 10, 13–20. Burrelle's Transcript Service, Livingston, N.J.
Campbell, Stephen K. 1974. *Flaws and Fallacies in Statistical Thinking.* Englewood Cliffs, N.J.: Prentice-Hall.
Canadian Press. 1992. "Changed Law Fuels Statistics." *Winnipeg Free Press,* October 10, p. A3.
Castell, Alburey. 1935. *A College Logic.* New York: Macmillan.
Chakrabarti, Kisor Kumar. 1995. *Definition and Induction: A Historical and Comparative Study.* Honolulu: University of Hawaii Press.
Chase, Stuart. 1956. *Guides to Straight Thinking.* New York: Harper and Row.
Childs, H. L. 1965. *Public Opinion: Nature, Formation and Role.* Princeton, N.J.: D. van Nostrand.
Clark, Romane, and Paul Welsh. 1962. *Introduction to Logic.* Princeton, N.J.: D. van Nostrand.
Copi, Irving M. 1972. *Introduction to Logic,* 4th ed. (1st ed., 1953; 7th ed., 1986). New York: Macmillan.
Creighton, James Edwin. 1904. *An Introductory Logic.* New York: Macmillan.
Croce, Benedetto. 1913. *Philosophy of the Practical,* trans. Douglas Ainslie. London: Macmillan.
Crossen, Cynthia. 1994. *Tainted Truth: The Manipulation of Fact in America.* New York: Simon and Schuster.
Crossley, David J., and Peter A. Wilson. 1979. *How to Argue: An Introduction to Logical Thinking.* New York: McGraw-Hill.
Damer, T. Edward. 1980 (2d ed., 1987). *Attacking Faulty Reasoning.* Belmont, Calif.: Wadsworth.
Dauer, Francis Watanabe. 1989. *Critical Thinking.* New York: Oxford University Press.
Davis, Adam, and Aaron Abbott. 1989. "How to Use Expert Public Opinion Testimony." *The Practical Lawyer* 35: 21–32.
Descartes, René. 1960. *Discourse on Method and Meditations,* trans. Laurence La Fleur. Indianapolis: Bobbs-Merrill.
Devereux, Daniel. 1990. "Comments on Robert Bolton's *The Epistemological Basis of Aristotelian Dialectic.*" In *Biologie, Logique et Metaphysique,* ed. Daniel Devereux and Pierre Pellegrin, 263–86. Paris: Editions du Centre National de la Recherche Scientifique.
Dray, William H. 1995. *History as Re-enactment.* Oxford: Clarendon Press.
Duncan, Hugh. 1962. *Communication and Social Order.* London: Oxford University Press.
Edwards, Paul. 1967. "Common Consent Arguments for the Existence of God." In *The Encyclopedia of Philosophy,* ed. Paul Edwards, 2:147–55. New York: Macmillan.
Engel, S. Morris. 1976. *With Good Reason: An Introduction to Informal Fallacies.* New York: St. Martin's Press.
Epstein, Richard L. 1979. "Relatedness and Implication." *Philosophical Studies* 36: 137–73.
———. 1995. *The Semantic Foundations of Logic,* vol. 1 of *Propositional Logic,* 2d ed. New York: Oxford University Press.
Evans, J. D. G. 1977. *Aristotle's Concept of Dialectic.* Cambridge: Cambridge University Press.
Fearnside, W. Ward. 1980. *About Thinking.* Englewood Cliffs, N.J.: Prentice-Hall.
Fearnside, W. Ward, and William B. Holther. 1959. *Fallacy: The Counterfeit of Argument.* Englewood Cliffs, N.J.: Prentice-Hall.
Ficarra, Bernard J. 1968. *Surgical and Allied Malpractice.* Springfield, Ill.: Charles C. Thomas.

Field, Marvin D. 1990. "Public Polls and the Public Interest." In *The Classics of Polling*, ed. Michael L. Young, 389–94. Metuchen, N.J.: The Scarecrow Press.
Fischer, David H. 1970. *Historians' Fallacies*. New York: Harper and Row.
Folsom, Joseph K. 1931. *Social Psychology*. New York: Harper and Bros.
Freeman, James B. 1988. *Thinking Logically*. Englewood Cliffs, N.J.: Prentice-Hall.
———. 1991. "A Dialectical Approach to Statement Acceptability." In *Proceedings of the Second International Conference on Argumentation*, ed. Frans H. van Eemeren, Rob Grootendorst, J. Anthony Blair, and Charles A. Willard, IA: 340–47. Amsterdam: SicSat.
———. 1995. "The Appeal to Popularity and Presumption by Common Knowledge." In *Fallacies: Classical and Contemporary Readings*, ed. Hans V. Hansen and Robert C. Pinto, 263–73. University Park: The Pennsylvania State University Press.
Frye, Albert M., and Albert W. Levi. 1969. *Rational Belief: An Introduction to Logic*. New York: Greenwood Press.
Galt, Virginia. 1996. "Stop Complaining About Cuts, Ontario Universities Advised." *The Globe and Mail*, January 26, p. A6.
Gibson, W. R. Boyce. 1908. *The Problem of Logic*. London: Adam and Charles Black.
Gooderham, Mary. 1994. "When Reading Media Polls, It's *Caveat Emptor* As Usual—And Pass the Salt." *The Globe and Mail*, February 26, p. D8.
Govier, Trudy. 1985. *A Practical Study of Argument*. Belmont, Calif.: Wadsworth.
Grice, H. P. 1975. "Logic and Conversation." In *The Logic of Grammar*, ed. Donald Davidson and Gilbert Harman. Encino, Calif.: Dickenson.
Hamblin, Charles. 1970. *Fallacies*. London: Methuen. Reprinted, Newport News, Va.: Vale Press, 1993.
———. 1971. "Mathematical Models of Dialogue." *Theoria* 37: 130–55.
Hanfstaengl, Ernst. 1957. *Unheard Witness*. Philadelphia: J. B. Lippincott Co.
Herbst, Susan. 1993. *Numbered Voices: How Opinion Polling has Shaped American Politics*. Chicago: University of Chicago Press.
Hibben, John Grier. 1906. *Logic: Deductive and Inductive*. New York: Charles Scribner's Sons.
Hodge, Charles. 1872. *Systematic Theology*, vol. 1. New York: Charles Scribner and Company.
Huppé, Bernard F., and Jack Kaminsky. 1957. *Logic and Language*. New York: Alfred A. Knopf.
Hurley, Patrick J. 1994. *A Concise Introduction to Logic*, 5th ed. Belmont, Calif.: Wadsworth.
Hyslop, James H. 1899. *Logic and Argument*. New York: Charles Scribner's Sons.
Jevons, W. Stanley. 1878. *Elementary Lessons in Logic*, 7th ed. London: Macmillan and Co.
Johnson, Ralph H., and J. Anthony Blair. 1983 (1st ed., 1977). *Logical Self-Defense*, 2d ed. Toronto: McGraw-Hill Ryerson.
Joyce, George Hayward. 1923. *Principles of Natural Theology*. London: Longmans, Green and Co.
Kapp, Ernst. 1942. *Greek Foundations of Traditional Logic*. New York: Columbia University Press.
Kennedy, George A. 1963. *The Art of Persuasion in Greece*. London: Routledge and Kegan Paul.
———. 1980. *Classical Rhetoric and Its Christian and Secular Tradition from Ancient to Modern Times*. Chapel Hill: University of North Carolina Press.
Kerferd, G. B. 1981. *The Sophistic Movement*. Cambridge: Cambridge University Press.
Kesterton, Michael. 1995. "Social Studies." *The Globe and Mail*, June 8, p. A24.
Key, V. O. 1961. *Public Opinion and American Democracy*. New York: Alfred A. Knopf.
Kilgore, William J. 1968. *An Introductory Logic*. New York: Holt, Rinehart and Winston.
Kozy, John, Jr. 1974. *Understanding Natural Deduction*. Encino, Calif.: Dickenson Publishing Co.
Kreyche, Robert J. 1961. *Logic for Undergraduates*. New York: Holt, Rinehart and Winston.

Latta, Robert, and Alexander MacBeath. 1956. *The Elements of Logic*. London: Macmillan.
Levinson, Stephen C. 1987. "Minimization and Conversational Inference." In *The Pragmatic Perspective*, ed. J. Verschueren and J. Bertucelli-Papi, 61–129. Amsterdam: John Benjamins Publishing Co.
Lipset, Seymour Martin. 1990. "The Wavering Polls." In *The Classics of Polling*, ed. Michael L. Young, 272–94. Metuchen, N.J.: The Scarecrow Press.
Locke, John. 1961. *An Essay Concerning Human Understanding* (1690), ed. John W. Yolton, 2 vols. London: Dent.
Loftus, Elizabeth. 1979. *Eyewitness Testimony*. Cambridge, Mass.: Harvard University Press.
Lowell, A. L. 1913. *Public Opinion and Popular Government*. New York: Longmans, Green.
Mackay, Charles. 1980. *Memoirs of Popular Delusions and the Madness of Crowds* (1852). Toronto: Coles Publishing Co.
Mackenzie, J. D. 1980. "Why Do We Number Theorems?" *Australasian Journal of Philosophy* 58: 135–49.
MacKinnon, W. A. 1828. *On the Rise, Progress, and Present State of Public Opinion in Great Britain and Other Parts of the World*. London: n.p.
Makau, Josina M. 1990. *Reasoning and Communication*. Belmont, Calif.: Wadsworth.
McCosh, James. 1879. *The Laws of Discursive Thought: A Text-Book of Formal Logic*. New York: Robert Carter and Brothers.
Michalos, Alex C. 1969. *Principles of Logic*. Englewood Cliffs, N.J.: Prentice-Hall.
Mill, John Stuart. 1874. *Three Essays on Religion*. New York: H. Holt and Co.
Minar, David W. 1960. "Public Opinion in the Perspective of Political Theory." *Western Political Quarterly* 13 (March): 31–44.
Monitor [Anonymous editorial, entitled "The Monitor's View"]. 1996. *Christian Science Monitor*, July 5, p. 20.
Moore, David W. 1992. *The Superpollsters: How They Measure and Manipulate Public Opinion in America*. New York: Four Walls Eight Windows.
Moore, G. E. 1903. *Principia Ethica*. Cambridge: Cambridge University Press.
Mourant, John A. 1963. *Formal Logic*. New York: Macmillan.
Munro, W. B. 1926. *The Government of American Cities*, 4th ed. New York: Macmillan Co.
Nolt, John Eric. 1984. *Informal Logic: Possible Worlds and Imagination*. New York: McGraw-Hill.
Oskamp, Stuart. 1991. *Attitudes and Opinions*, 2d ed. Englewood Cliffs, N.J.:Prentice-Hall.
Pascal, Blaise. 1966. "Reflections on Geometry and the Art of Persuading," trans. Robert W. Gleason. In *The Essential Pascal*, ed. Robert W. Gleason, 297–327. New York: The New American Library.
Perelman, Chaim. 1982. *The Realm of Rhetoric*. Notre Dame: University of Notre Dame Press.
Perelman, Chaim, and Lucie Olbrechts-Tyteca. 1969. *The New Rhetoric*. Notre Dame: University of Notre Dame Press.
Peters, Edward. 1988. *Inquisition*. New York: The Press.
Plato. 1961. *The Collected Dialogues of Plato*, ed. Edith Hamilton and Huntington Cairns. New York: Bollingen Foundation.
Read, Carveth. 1920. *Logic: Deductive and Inductive*, 4th ed. London: Simkin, Marshall, Hamilton, Kent and Co. Ltd.
Rescher, Nicholas. 1964. *Introduction to Logic*. New York: St. Martin's Press.
———. 1977. *Dialectics: A Controversy-Oriented Approach to the Theory of Knowledge*. Albany: State University of New York Press.
Robinson, Richard. 1962. *Plato's Earlier Dialectic*. Oxford: Clarendon Press.

Ruby, Lionel. 1950. *Logic: An Introduction*. Chicago: J. B. Lippincott.
Runkle, Gerald. 1991. *Good Thinking: An Introduction to Logic*, 3d ed. Fort Worth: Holt, Rinehart and Winston.
Salmon, Merrilee H. 1995. *Introduction to Logic and Critical Thinking*. Fort Worth: Harcourt, Brace.
Schipper, Edith Watson, and Edward Schuh. 1959. *A First Course in Modern Logic*. New York: Henry Holt and Co.
Schuman, Howard, and Stanley Presser. 1981. *Questions and Answers in Attitude Surveys*. New York: Academic Press.
Seneca, Lucius Annaeus. 1925. *Ad Lucilium Epistulae Morales* (63–65 A.D.), vol. 3, trans. Richard M. Gummere. Cambridge, Mass.: Harvard University Press. Loeb Library edition.
Soccio, Douglas J., and Vincent E. Barry. 1992. *Practical Logic*. Fort Worth: Harcourt, Brace Jovanovich.
Tindale, Christopher W. 1991. "Audiences and Acceptable Premises." In *Proceedings of the Second International Conference on Argumentation*, ed. Frans H. van Eemeren, Rob Grootendorst, J. Anthony Blair and Charles A. Willard, vol. 1A: 288–95. Amsterdam: SicSat.
Tocqueville, Alexis de. 1966. *Democracy in America* (1835), ed. J. P. Mayer and Max Lerner. New York: Harper and Row.
Toulmin, Stephen, Richard Rieke, and Allan Janik. 1984. *An Introduction to Reasoning*, 2d ed. New York: Macmillan.
van Eemeren, Frans H., and Rob Grootendorst. 1984. *Speech Acts in Argumentative Discussions*. Dordrecht and Cinnaminson: Foris Publications.
———. 1987. "Fallacies in Pragma-Dialectical Perspective." *Argumentation* 1: 283–301.
———. 1992. *Argumentation, Communication and Fallacies*. Hillsdale, N.J.: Lawrence Erlbaum Associates.
Veitch, John. 1885. *Institutes of Logic*. Edinburgh: William Blackwood and Sons.
Vernon, Thomas S., and Lowell A. Nissen. 1968. *Reflective Thinking: The Fundamentals of Logic*. Belmont, Calif.: Wadsworth.
Waller, Bruce N. 1988. *Critical Thinking: Consider the Verdict*. Englewood Cliffs, N.J.: Prentice-Hall.
Walton, Douglas N. 1980. "Why Is the *Ad Populum* a Fallacy?" *Philosophy and Rhetoric* 13: 264–78.
———. 1982. *Topical Relevance in Argumentation*. Amsterdam and Philadelphia: John Benjamins Publishing Co.
———. 1989. *Informal Logic*. Cambridge: Cambridge University Press.
———. 1990. *Practical Reasoning*. Savage, Md.: Rowman and Littlefield.
———. 1991a. Begging the Question: Circular Reasoning as a Tactic of Argumentation. New York: Greenwood.
———. 1991b. "Bias, Critical Doubt and Fallacies." *Argumentation and Advocacy* 28: 1–22.
———. 1992a. *Plausible Argument in Everyday Conversation*. Albany: State University of New York Press.
———. 1992b. *The Place of Emotion in Argument*. University Park: The Pennsylvania State University Press.
———. 1995. *A Pragmatic Theory of Fallacy*. Tuscaloosa: University of Alabama Press.
———. 1996a. *Arguments from Ignorance*. University Park: The Pennsylvania State University Press.
———. 1996b. *Argumentation Schemes for Presumptive Reasoning*. Mahwah, N.J.: Lawrence Erlbaum.

———. 1997. *Appeal to Expert Opinion*. University Park: The Pennsylvania State University Press.

———. 1998. *The New Dialectic: Conversational Contexts of Argument*. Toronto: University of Toronto Press.

———. 1999. *One-Sided Arguments: A Dialectical Analysis of Bias*. Albany: State University of New York Press.

Walton, Douglas N., and Erik C. W. Krabbe. 1995. *Commitment in Dialogue*. Albany: State University of New York Press.

Walton, R. E., and R. B. McKersie. 1965. *A Behavioral Theory of Labor Negotiation*. New York: McGraw-Hill.

Warner, Lucien. 1939. "The Reliability of Public Opinion Surveys." *Public Opinion Quarterly* 3 (July): 377.

Warnick, Barbara, and Edward S. Inch. 1989. *Critical Thinking and Communication*. New York: Macmillan.

Watts, Isaac. 1772. *Logick: Or, the Right Use of Reason in the Inquiry After Truth*, 15th ed. London: J. Buckland.

Weddle, Perry. 1978. *Argument: A Guide to Critical Thinking*. New York: McGraw-Hill.

Werkmeister, William H. 1948. *An Introduction to Critical Thinking*. Lincoln, Nebraska.

Weston, Anthony. 1987. *A Rulebook for Arguments*. Indianapolis: Hackett.

Whately, Richard. 1863. *Elements of Rhetoric*, 7th ed. London: Parker, Son and Bourn.

———. 1870. *Elements of Logic*, 9th ed. London: Longmans, Green.

Wheeler, Michael. 1990. "How to Read the Polls." In *The Classics of Polling*, ed. Michael L. Young, 193–209. Metachun, N.J.: The Scarecrow Press.

Wheelwright, Philip. 1962. *Valid Thinking*. New York: The Odyssey Press.

Wreen, Michael. 1993. "Jump With Common Spirits: Is an *Ad Populum* Argument Fallacious?" *Metaphilosophy* 24: 61–75.

Yanal, Robert J. 1988. *Basic Logic*. St. Paul: West Publishing Co.

Yankelovich, Daniel. 1991. *Coming to Public Judgment*. Syracuse: University of Syracuse Press.

———. 1992. "A Widening Expert/Public Opinion Gap." *Challenge*, May–June, 20–27.

Young, James T. 1923. *The New American Government and Its Work*. New York: The Macmillan Co.

INDEX

Abbott, Aaron, 233
abortion issue, 21, 174–75, 191–92, 239
ad hominem attack, aggressive, 188
ad populum fallacy, 37, 41, 47, 51, 124, 141, 254
  defined, 47–48
ad populum pressure, 37
antiskeptical dilemma, 158, 161–63
aporia, 138
appeal
  ad populum, 49, 52; positive, 42; relevance of, 190
  common-folks, 76, 86, 96, 98, 264
  emotional, 14, 50, 69; emotional appeal to the crowd, 65–66
  ethical, 42
  grandstand, 86
  mob, 65, 70, 72–73, 76, 86, 96; rhetorical, 127
  plain-folks, 214
  to common knowledge; compared to appeal to popularity, 123
  to expert opinion, 102, 118, 128
  to flattery, 82
  to gregariousness, 88
  to group loyalty, 83
  to mass enthusiasms in a crowd setting, 100
  to moral values, 207
  to popular opinions, 110, 128
  to popularity, 123; fallacious, 123
  to prejudices, 86, 88, 126
  to prestige, 72
  to principles, 66
  to public judgement, 124
  to public opinion; three criteria for evaluating, 231
  to shame, 82
  to shared principles, 79
  to snobbery, 73, 91, 214, 262
  to the crowd, 71
  to the gallery, 76, 79, 212
  to the gut emotions, 86
  to the people, 61, 63, 79
  to tradition, 83
  to trendiness, 232, 262
  to vanity, 88, 90, 215, 262
appeal-to-expert-opinion argument, 56–58, 234–35
  critical questions for, 57, 235
  evaluated, 58
appeal-to-popular-sentiments argument, 222
appeal-to-popularity argument, 227, 234
  fallacious instance of, 37
  presumptive variant, 223
  probabilistic variant of, 223
appeal-to-snobbery argument, 214–16, 225, 247
appeal-to-vanity argument, 225, 247
Aquinas, Thomas, 62, 153–54, 167, 184–85

284 INDEX

argument
  cumulative, 176
  evaluation of, 151, 187, 233, 275
  identification of, 232, 249, 275
  linear, 176
  negative, 42
  plausible, 148
  presumptive, 101, 268
  principle weaknesses, 2
  weak, 47, 59, 237, 239, 267
argument from consensus, 93
argument from consequences, 219
argument from expert opinion, 136, 183
argument from plausibility, 150
argument from popular opinion, 75
argument from popularity, 99
argument from position to know, 183
  critical questions, 183
argument from precedent, 39
argument from probability, 148
argumentation from testimony, 203
argumentation scheme, 97, 103–4
argumentum ad hominem (*see also* personal attacks), 64
  relevance of, 188–91
argumentum ad ignorantiam, 63–64, 117
argumentum ad judicium, 63
argumentum ad populum (*see also* bandwagon argument), 34, 36, 64
  defined, 15
  evaluation of, 250–52
  fallacy, 43, 100, 247
  first mentioned as distinct, 156
  group-based analysis, 58
  inherently fallacious, 69
  inherently illogical, 15
  inherently weak, 154
  reasonable, 152
  relevance of, 191, 230
  subtypes of, 196
  as a tactic, 141–42
  validity, 79–80
argumentum ad rem, 64
argumentum ad verecundiam, 58, 63–64, 79, 102
Aristotle, 16, 30, 43–44, 62, 65, 94, 102, 105, 126, 133, 135, 138–43, 149, 184
  contentious arguments, 133–34, 167–68
  demonstrative argument, 176, 184
  dialectic, 30, 62, 128, 166–67
  dialectical arguments, 133–34, 140, 167–68
  didactic arguments, 133–34, 167–68
  examination arguments, 133, 167–68

  On Sophistical Refutations, 133, 140, 142–43
  Physics, 62, 153
  Rhetoric, 133,137
  Topics, 62, 133, 135, 138, 141, 142
Arnauld, Antoine, 62–63, 65, 75, 95
assumptions, 118, 120, 135, 162, 269
  provisional, 116
Atlas, Jay David, 239
attitudinal bargaining, 179
audience, 104, 190, 211, 246, 271
  closed–mindedness, 222
  commitments of, 103
  joined with speaker, 271
  pathos, 190
  prejudices of, 16, 105

bandwagon argument, 63, 65, 95, 102, 118, 136, 144–45, 153, 197–99, 203–4
  advertising industry, 90
  defined, 98–99
  fallacy, 74, 78–79, 83, 87, 89, 212; defined, 75–76; negative variant of, 87
  first articulation of, 147
  identification of, 146
  inherently weak, 119
  mob appeal, 89
  two forms of, 122
  weak, 101, 201
bandwagon effect, 15
Barnes, Jonathan, 138–39, 143
Barry, Vincent, 89–90
Beardsley, Monroe, 13
Begley, Sharon, 3
bias, 2, 81, 106, 242–43, 258
  appeal to, 241, 250
  bad, 242, 251
  consistent and prevalent, 210
  dialectical, 243, 273
  hidden, 55
  of the mass, 246
  new theory of dialectical bias, 242
  normal, 210
  unbiased, 67
Billig, Michael, 16, 102–3
Blair, Anthony J., 92–94, 100, 104–9, 111–12, 121
  fallacy of popularity, 199–200
  position to know, 202
Blyth, John, 70, 95
Boethius, 152
bolster thesis, 223
burden of proof, 41, 47, 267

reversal, 117
shift, 56–57, 113, 267, 276
Byerly, Henry, 79, 96
Byrne, Edward, 152–53

Castell, Alburey, 69
Chase, Stuart, 70
Childs, H. L., 24–25
Church, Vernon, 3
Clark, Romane, 70
closed-mindedness, 221
Cohen, Carl, 73
Collingwood, 256
commercial advertisement, 73–74, 89–90, 247–48, 261–53
  ballyhoo artists, 73, 216, 247, 261, 263
  criticism of, 88
  hucksters, 73, 216, 247, 261, 263
commitment, 23, 107, 117–18, 173, 175, 179
  of the answerer, 130
  conceding, 242
  management of, 238
  retraction, 108, 119, 238
commitment-based argumentation, 109
common-folks appeal argument, 212–13, 222, 226, 263
  politics, 265
common-knowledge argument, 122
condition 3, 118
conformism, 19
consensus, 20–21, 55, 93, 110, 136, 231, 241
consensus gentium argument (common consent argument for the existence of God), 146, 158–61
  antiskeptical dilemma, 158, 161
  biological variant, 158–61
Copi, Irving M., 37–38, 41, 45–47, 51, 73, 75, 95, 195, 216, 247, 254, 258
Creighton, James E., 67–68, 95
critical discussion, 109–11, 170–75
  adversarial, 189, 237
  balanced, 242
  confrontation stage, 173
  cooperative, 237
  goal of, 172, 179
  opposition in, 172
  sources for premises, 175
  as a subspecies, 170
critical questions, 108, 114, 242, 275
  blocking, 267
Croce, Benedetto, 254–57

Crossen, Cynthia, 7
Crossley, David, 85, 96

Damer, T. Edward, 34, 81–85, 96, 192, 268
Dauer, Francis W., 15, 43–44
Davis, Adam, 233
debate, 190
  political, 50, 190, 192, 265
deception, 55
deliberation, 23, 42, 126, 153, 165, 167, 184–88, 192, 206, 231, 268
  argument, 224
  dialectic, 154
  framework for reasoning, 184
  informed, 205–7
  political, 50, 127, 188, 230, 257
  prior, 231
  prudent, 269
  public, 126–28, 231
  solitary, 185
  townhall meeting, 185
Democratic Civilization case (2.4), 41–43, 59, 207–8
demonstration, 133, 155
Descartes, René, 156, 176
Devereux, Daniel, 136
dialectic, 132
  argument, 136, 151
  new, 230, 275
  Plato, 130
  questions, 138
  shift, 187, 263, 273; illicit, 187–88, 223, 243, 252, 276; licit, 187; weak, 269
  subjective, 155
  three uses of, 135
dialectically relevant move, 187
dialogue
  classification of six basic dialogues, 170, 172
  context of, 113
  shift, 181
  ten types of, 170–71
distributive bargaining, 179
Duncan, Hugh, 98

Edwards, Paul, 158–61
eikos, 148–52
elenchus, 130
empathy, 98, 179, 189, 242, 264
emotion, condemnation of, 72
endoxon, 136, 138–39, 142
endoxic argument, 62
Engel, S. Morris, 52, 80–81, 96, 197

Enlightenment, 151, 155–56, 165
epideictic, 218
epistemic component, 110
eristic dialogue, 179–81, 230, 276
　adversarial, 180
Euclidean geometry, 155, 166, 176
Evans, J. D. G., 138–39
evidence, 151
　conflicting, 106
　failure to produce, 216
　objective, 267
　relevant, 248, 262
　scientific, 58
　weight of, 46
expert-consultation dialogue, 182–83
　as a subspecies, 170
expert-opinion arguments, 206, 224

fallacy, 274–75
　abandon ship fallacy, 87, 96, 199
　of abandoning the ship, 96
　appeal-to-common-opinion type of fallacy, 84
　of appeal to popular prejudice, 93
　of appeal to authority, 43, 91
　of appealing to bias, 70
　of appeal to the masses, 85
　of appeal to the people, 89
　of appealing to the gallery, 81–83; four subspecies of, 82
　of biased question, 260
　of biased statistics, 257, 259
　of common practice, 89
　error of reasoning fallacy, 36–37, 268
　of failure of relevance, 95, 264
　of hasty generalization, 257
　identification with the audience, 13
　of irrelevant conclusion (see also *Ignoratio Elenchi*), 65–66, 68
　of irrelevant evidence, 69
　is-ought fallacy, 84, 192
　of jumping too hastily to a conclusion, 123, 251, 262, 266–70
　of mob appeal, 81, 90
　of "popular passions," 49
　of popular sentiments, 77, 96
　of popularity, 89, 92, 199
　of prevalent proof, 78, 96
　of relevance, 35, 43, 68
　of snob appeal, 90
　of too small a sample, 259
Falling Object case (2.5), 43–45, 56
Fearnside, W. Ward, 48–50, 71, 85–86, 96, 190, 211, 221

Field, Marvin, 6
Fineman, Howard, 3
Fisher, David, 78, 96
Freeman, James, 86, 88, 96, 114, 121–24, 199, 266–67
Frye, Albert, 77–78

generalization, 2, 17, 94, 223, 258
Gibson, W. R. Boyce, 68, 95
Golden Rule case (2.3), 37–41, 42, 59, 269–71
Gooderham, Mary, 258
Gore Vidal case (2.1), 34–36, 56, 268
Govier, Trudy, 120–23
Grice, H. P., 187, 229
　maxims, 170, 237–40, 242
Grootendorst, Rob, 107–11, 172–74, 236, 240
Grossman, Larry, 17–18
guilt by association, 82

Hamblin, Charles, 56, 63–64, 103–4, 156 n. 6, 173, 211, 263 n. 2
　commitment, 173
　-type dialogues, 117
Hanfstaengl, Ernst, 213
Hasty Leap, 36
Herbst, Susan, 20–22, 24, 26
herd instinct, 87
Hibben, John G., 67–69, 95
Hitler, Adolph, 213
Hodge, Charles, 159
Holther, William B., 48–50, 71, 190, 221
Huppé, Bernard, 70, 95
Hurley, Patrick, 90–91, 196, 214, 216
Hyslop, James, 67–68, 95

ignoratio elenchi, 94
Inch, Edward, 93
inference, 30, 36, 42, 45, 57, 62, 127, 133–34, 151, 208
　reasonable, 148, 152
　structural requirements of, 103
　warrant, 152
information-seeking dialogue, 134, 170, 182–83, 239
Ingersoll Speech case (2.8), 51–52, 54
inquiry, 133, 175–78
　ad populum arguments in, 230
　characteristics of, 176
　goal of, 175
Inquisition case (2.6), 45–48, 54, 59, 253–57, 271
interlocutors (*see also* audience), 106, 114, 121, 130
　four characteristics, 106
intersubjective testing procedure (ITP), 107–8, 110, 112, 174, 187, 236

Janik, Allan, 89
Jevons, W. Stanley, 65–66, 68–69, 95, 196
Johnson, Ralph, 92–94, 100, 104–9, 111–12, 121
    fallacy of popularity, 199–200
    position to know, 202
Jonsen, Albert R., 156
Joyce, George Hayward, 161–62
Jury Deliberation case (2.2), 36–37, 43, 205
justification, 39, 47

Kaminsky, Jack, 70, 95
Kapp, Ernst, 134
Kennedy, George, 148–49, 156, 190
Kesterton, Michael, 10
Kilgore, William, 75–76, 79, 95–96, 212–13
knowledge-based arguments, 235
Kozy, John, Jr., 77, 79–80, 96
Krabbe, Erik C. W., 104, 117, 170, 173, 238
Kreyche, Robert, 72

language, 95, 102, 210, 213
    expressive function of connotation in, 71
    Hitler's rhetoric, 98
    inflammatory, 27, 50–54, 98
    natural, 2, 4
    negative, 272
    question: biased, 9 ; loaded, 10; statistical jargon, 7; wording, 4–6, 8–9
Latta, Roberta, 70
leaping to a conclusion, 34
legal argumentation, 149
    court witness, 203
    eyewitness testimony, 204
Levi, Albert, 77–78
Levinson, Stephen C., 239–40
Lipset, Seymour M., 7
Locke, John, 63–64, 67, 158–59
logic, 157

Mackay, Charles, 244–45
MacBeath, Alexander, 70
majoritarian opinion, 20, 26
Makau, Josina, 93
Mark Antony case (2.7), 48–51, 54, 69, 71, 73, 77, 80–81, 190
    appeal to the crowd, 221
    dialogue type, 190
Marketplace case (9.1), 269
maxims (*see also* Grice), 239–41, 272, 274
McCosh, James, 66, 68, 94–95
McKersie, R. B., 179
medical ethics, 209
Michalos, Alex, 77–78, 96, 211

Mill, John Stuart, 158
mob-appeal argument, 51, 89, 96, 99, 100, 196–99, 211, 217, 227, 243, 271
    characteristic, 98, 196, 198, 217, 221–22, 272
    classification difficulty, 220
    rhetoric of, 250
mob authority, 133
modus tollens argument, 137
Moore, David, 4, 5, 8
moral-justification argument, 208, 224–25
Mourant, John, 72

Nazi, 98, 196–97, 213
negative prestige, 82
negotiation dialogue, 178–79, 217, 230, 243, 273
    goal of, 179
Nissen, Lowell, 74–76, 79, 91, 95, 199
Nolt, John Eric, 14
Nyaya philosophers, 241

obscenity cases, 234
Olbrechts-Tyteca, Lucie, 114–15, 218
opinion (*see also* popular opinion, public opinion), 12–13
    defined, 26
    degrees of, 26–27
    expert or scientific, 59, 116, 209
    generally accepted, 134
    manipulated, 54
    mass, 124, 231
    popular versus expert, 131
    public versus popular, 27
opinion-based argument, 152
Oskamp, Stuart, 24–25

participant, defined, 186
Pascal, Blaise, 156–57
    wager argument, 163–66
peer pressure argument, 219
Pegler's Speech case (2.9), 52–54, 272
Perelman, Chaim, 114–15, 218
personal attacks, 180
persuasion, 137
persuasion dialogue, 109, 250
    goal, 173
    key defining characteristic, 104
Physician case (7.2), 209
Plato, 27, 123, 126, 129–31, 148–51, 156, 167, 181
politics, 2, 9, 11–12, 15, 19, 26, 53, 87, 100, 129, 166, 255, 258, 260
pop scheme, 200–201, 205, 220, 224–25
Pope Urban's Speech case (8.1), 243–47, 281

Popular Delusions and the Madness of Crowds,
   243–44
popular opinion, 19, 132
   contradictory, 259
   defined, 22
   instrument of destruction, 29
position-to-know argument (PKA), 101, 201–6,
   224
post-Enlightenment, 193
prejudices, 211, 241
premise, 17, 35, 111
   adequacy, 189
   of appeal to expert opinion, 143
   endoxic, 129, 138, 166, 274
   inflation of weak, 35
   irrelevant to conclusion, 48, 53, 140
   as a proposition, 167
Presser, Stanley, 4–5
presumption, 110, 112, 118, 167
   accepted procedure, 116
   balance of, 239
   definition, 113–15
   weight of, 24, 37
probative asymmetries, 113
propaganda, 14, 55
property of evidential priority, 176
proposition, 40, 237
   retraction of, 178
public opinion, 125
   ambiguity of, 19–21
   defined, 20
   four categories of meanings, 20–21
   media reports of, 231
   nine definitions of, 24–25
   politics, 26, 260
   poll, 257; abuse of, 11; biased questions, 259;
      importance of, 261; importance of wording
      (*see also* language), 3–6, 8–9 ; objective
      evidence, 31; scientific, 2, 7, 11

quarrel, 170, 180–82, 221, 230
question-answer exchange, 139
questions, 2, 93
Quintilian, Marcus Fabius, 16

Read, Carveth, 68, 94, 95
reasoning, 135–36, 165
   based on good evidence, 158
   commitment-based, 173
   deductive, 133, 156, 166
   demonstrative, 135–36, 166
   dialectical, 135–38, 140, 156
   dynamic sequence of, 125
   flip-flop, 117
   knowledge-based, 153
   logical, 44
   practical, 153, 155, 184; goal-directed, 184
   presumptive, 117–18, 124, 127, 165, 266–67,
      274
   scientific, 154–55, 177
   syllogistic, 154
reductio ad absurdum argument, 162
refutation, 130, 138, 140, 274
   misconception of, 140
relativism, 105–6, 113, 256
   historical, 256
relevance, 102, 108
   allegation of failure of, 50
   dialectical, 186, 251
   dialectical conception of, 102
   evaluating, 187
   failure of, 15, 47, 69, 213
   fallacy of, 102, 140, 186
   irrelevance, 263, 273
   probative, 174
   problems of, 106
   topical, 174
Rescher, Nicholas, 72–73, 95, 113–15, 215
   differentiate between snob appeal and mob
      appeal, 215
Reuther, Walter, Speech case (7.3), 217
rhetoric
   of belonging, 272
   divisive, 272–73
   goal of, 137
   mob-appeal, 271
   speaker's, 272
rhetoric of belonging, 217–20, 222, 225
rhetoricians, 27, 66, 133, 190, 196, 218
Rieke, Richard, 89
Robinson, Richard, 130–31
Ruby, Lionel, 69
Runkle, Gerald, 87–88, 96

Sailboat Race case (7.1), 206–7
Salmon, Merrilee, 93–94
Schipper, Edith, 71, 95, 263
Schuh, Edward, 71, 95, 263
Schuman, Howard, 4–5
scientific argumentation, 177
Seneca, Lucius Annaeus, 144–48
SLOP poll, 257
Soccio, Douglas, 89–90
Socrates, 130–33, 135, 150–51

sophism, 27, 62, 148–51, 132–33, 181
sophoi, 138, 143
spin doctors, 27
statistics, 8–9
  margin-of-error, 7, 21
Stoics, 144–47
  wisdom, 144, 147
Sunethes, 141–43
syllogism, 133, 154, 157
  statistical, 93–94

tactic, 59, 118, 141
  deceptive, 276
  negative, 217, 221
  political, 50, 213
  rhetorical, 98
  speaker's, 53, 220
  sophistical, 36, 37
  telephone, 10
threat of the demagogue, 214
Tindale, Christopher, 105–6, 108–9, 111–13, 126
To Eiothos, 143
Tocqueville, Alexis de, 11–13, 19, 25–26, 28–29
Toulmin, Stephen, 89, 156
town hall meeting, 192
trade infringement cases, 233–34
Train Station case, 101–2, 202, 205, 230, 234
tutiorism, 269
tyranny of the majority, 11, 28

Van Eemeren, Frans, 107–11, 174, 236, 240
Veitch, John, 66–68, 95
Vernon, Thomas, 74–76, 79, 91, 95, 199

Waller, Bruce, 36–37, 92
Walton, Douglas N., 41, 57, 99, 100, 104, 109, 116–18, 170, 174, 179, 180, 183, 186–87, 202, 235, 238
  concept of position to know, 202
  dialogue on tipping, 191
  indicators of dialectical bias, 243
  leadership debate, 264
Warnick, Barbara, 93
Watts, Isaac, 62–63, 65
Weddle, Perry, 88, 215
Welsh, Paul, 70
Werkmeister, William, 69, 197
Weston, Anthony, 92
Whately, Richard, 64, 114
Wheeler, Michael, 9
Wheelwright, Philip, 72, 82, 95
Wilson, Peter, 85, 96
wisdom, 144–45, 147
  conventional, 43–45, 116, 211–12
Wreen, Michael, 37, 45, 48, 100, 195, 197, 203

Yanal, Robert, 91
Yankelovich, Daniel, 7–8, 23, 124–26, 128, 163, 212, 231, 260
  seven steps of reasoning sequence, 125–26, 18

www.ingramcontent.com/pod-product-compliance
Lightning Source LLC
Chambersburg PA
CBHW031546300426
44111CB00006BA/192